399767

WITHDRAWN
FROM STOCK

D1429283

Seeing Fictions in Film

Seeing Fictions in Film

The Epistemology of Movies

George M. Wilson

OXFORD
UNIVERSITY PRESS

791.
430
1
WIL

ͻ٩٩ ٦٥٦

OXFORD
UNIVERSITY PRESS

Great Clarendon Street, Oxford OX2 6DP

Oxford University Press is a department of the University of Oxford.
It furthers the University's objective of excellence in research, scholarship,
and education by publishing worldwide in

Oxford New York

Auckland Cape Town Dar es Salaam Hong Kong Karachi
Kuala Lumpur Madrid Melbourne Mexico City Nairobi
New Delhi Shanghai Taipei Toronto

With offices in

Argentina Austria Brazil Chile Czech Republic France Greece
Guatemala Hungary Italy Japan Poland Portugal Singapore
South Korea Switzerland Thailand Turkey Ukraine Vietnam

Oxford is a registered trade mark of Oxford University Press
in the UK and in certain other countries

Published in the United States
by Oxford University Press Inc., New York

© in this volume George M. Wilson 2011

The moral rights of the author have been asserted
Database right Oxford University Press (maker)

First published 2011

All rights reserved. No part of this publication may be reproduced,
stored in a retrieval system, or transmitted, in any form or by any means,
without the prior permission in writing of Oxford University Press,
or as expressly permitted by law, or under terms agreed with the appropriate
reprographics rights organization. Enquiries concerning reproduction
outside the scope of the above should be sent to the Rights Department,
Oxford University Press, at the address above

You must not circulate this book in any other binding or cover
and you must impose this same condition on any acquirer

British Library Cataloguing in Publication Data

Data available

Library of Congress Cataloging in Publication Data

Data available

Typeset by SPI Publisher Services, Pondicherry, India
Printed in Great Britain
on acid-free paper by
MPG Books Group, Bodmin and King's Lynn

ISBN 978–0–19–959489–4

10 9 8 7 6 5 4 3 2 1

Contents

List of Figures

Acknowledgments

I have worked on these issues for a very long time, and I have spoken on these topics more often than I can easily enumerate. Several of these chapters are based on essays read at different venues, and I received critical suggestions from various commentators. David Hills was the editor of the special issue in which "*Le Grand Imagier* Steps Out" (Chapter 2) appeared, and I am deeply grateful to David for his marvelously detailed commentary on the essay. A version of what has split and evolved into Chapters 5 and 6 was first presented at the 2005 Oberlin Colloquium, and I would like to thank the participants, especially my commentator, Tom Wartenberg. I also received helpful suggestions and criticisms from Noël Carroll, Amy Mullin, and Katherine Thompson-Jones. "Transparency and Twist" (Chapter 7) was read at the 2004 meetings of the American Society for Aesthetics in Houston and at departmental colloquia at both the University of Southern California and the University of California at Riverside. It was also read at a conference in honor of Kendall Walton that was arranged at the University of Leeds. David Davies was my insightful commentator on that occasion. Among the other people whose comments were especially helpful to me are William Bracken, John Martin Fisher, Janet Levin, Katalin Makkai, Dana Polan, Michael Renov, and Gideon Yaffe.

In addition, I read several different versions of Chapter 8 to a number of audiences: the Conference on Style and Meaning at the University of Reading; the Conference on Film and Cognitive Science, held at the University of Copenhagen in May 2000; the Meetings of the American Society for Aesthetics in October 2000; the Humanities Institute at Northwestern University; Johns Hopkins University; Ohio State University; and the University of Southern California. I thank all of these audiences for their comments and suggestions. I remember with gratitude the sage suggestions from David Bordwell, Marshall Cohen, Karen Hanson, Diana Raffman, William Taschek, and, once again, my USC colleague Gideon Yaffe. Chapter 9, on *The Man Who Wasn't There*, was originally written for a Workshop on Film, Philosophy, and Fiction that was supported by an Achievement Grant from the Mellon Foundation that was awarded to Susan Wolf, and it was Susan who organized the meetings of this group. The paper has also been given as a talk at departmental colloquia at Princeton, UC Santa Barbara, UC Irvine, and the University of Utah. It was given as the Claire Miller Lecture at the Chapel Hill Philosophy colloquium at the University of North Carolina, as an Invited Lecture to the Center for 21st Century Studies at the University of Wisconsin at Milwaukee, as a public lecture at Trinity College in San Antonio, as one of a sequence of lectures at the *Arizona Quarterly* Symposium at the University of Arizona, and as a lecture at a Mini-conference on Film and Philosophy at Stanford University. I deeply appreciate the invitations that gave rise to these talks and lectures, and I thank the various audiences for all the helpful comments that they supplied. The resulting chapters have been hugely improved by these interventions. I was also much helped with support and good advice by Peter Momtchiloff and Eleanor Collins at Oxford University Press.

It has been the greatest pleasure I have had in pursuing these questions, that the pursuit has afforded me the possibility of talking them over with so many good friends and relatives. All of the people I list below have given me advice and suggestions and critical support on numerous occasions. Among these valued friends, I want to mention as especially important, Ed Branigan, Greg Currie, Berys Gaut, Chris Grau, Andrew Kania, Paisley Livingston, Ed McCann, Richard Moran, Victor Perkins, Robert Pippin, Douglas Pye, Sam Shpall, Michael Smith, Murray Smith, Ken Walton, Tom Wartenberg, Susan White, and Susan Wolf. Berys, Chris, and Sam all studied with me at different institutions under different arrangements, but each of them makes me feel that some of my teaching has made a positive contribution, especially when it is reflected in their important work. Victor and Doug contacted me from England a short time after the appearance of my first book on film. Their encouragement was crucial to my continuing in my dogged pursuit of the theory of narration in the cinema even in the face of some initial discouragement. Somewhat later I came to know Gilberto Perez whose friendship has meant a great deal to me.

Finally, my family has been an incredible resource to me—both in scholarly ways and in more basic emotional ways. My daughter Flannery and my son Gareth have grown up to have notable interests in film, and there have been numerous conversations in which they have startled me and thereby aided me with some insightful remark or question about movies. My brother Mark has supported my interest in film from its inception, and that support has continued over the years until the present. I greatly appreciated his energy and interest in helping me find images that could serve as illustrations or as designs for the cover art. Some of his marvelous discoveries were really inspired. But no one has come close to contributing more than my wife, Karen. She has helped me in more different ways than anyone, and in each of the ways that she has helped me she has given me more help than anyone else. She has been my collaborator on this volume and, more importantly, she has collaborated with me on the vagaries of our lives. However, in both instances, I alone am responsible for whatever flaws and errors may remain.

PART I

Introductory Chapters

General Introduction

For a very long time I've pondered the questions, "Do movie viewers see the fictions in the movies they view? And, if they do, what makes it possible for them to do so? How can one see a fictional creation?" For most people, the first of these questions will have an obvious answer in the affirmative. Moreover, if this answer is straightforward and unproblematic, then the interest of the second question is liable to be unclear. I sometimes feel embarrassed to admit how much thought I have given to these seemingly 'trivial' questions, but embarrassment is not really merited. Most people, thinking that one or both of these questions have easy answers, are simply *wrong!* In the first place, the questions raise some issues of great subtlety and difficulty, and I will explain how this is so in the first part of this introduction. Second, getting the right answers to these questions has important consequences for the general theory of fictional narrative, especially as it bears on the nature of the narration of stories in fiction film. I will explain the content and the importance of these more theoretical matters later in this introduction and in the course of the chapter that follows. It is critical at the outset to grasp accurately what the questions are.

If anything seems initially plain about what we see in seeing movies, it is the thought that we thereby 'see' the characters, in their narrative situations, performing the actions that those situations elicit. Still, one may well hesitate a moment over that first certainty when one calls to mind that the characters, and their actions and their circumstances in the diegetic world, are, in the first instance, *fictional*. And since they are all fictional— merely guided constructs of the imagination, so to speak— it seems to follow that really the objects don't exist, really the events and actions don't occur, and the situations and circumstances are not realized anywhere in actuality. But, finally, mustn't we conclude that, however we are naively inclined to think and talk about the matter, we do not— cannot—strictly speaking 'see' these items after all?

This second thought may well cause us to hesitate about the possibility of seeing the various constituents of the fictional world of a movie, but perhaps the doubt will have only a limited impact. The doubt can come to seem too metaphysical—too purely philosophical, as it were—to override a deeply natural way of talking and thinking about our experience of movies. Is it just *false* that I see Ethan Edwards when I screen *The Searchers*? Is it, strictly speaking, *false* that I saw giant ants attacking LA when I watched the sci-fi film, *Them*? Surely not! Even if I am initially daunted by the apparent epistemic implications of the fact that the denizens of movies are fictional,

I am also likely to feel that there must be some reasonable way of blunting the skeptical morals to which those implications seem to point. Skepticism about the existence of an objective world and skepticism about other minds can also seem both tempting and perplexing, but few of us will succumb in the end to the relevant temptations even if we don't know how to resolve the issues. Even in the case of our perception of movie fictions, we can be sure that, seduced into skepticism as we might briefly be, we will backslide when we try the next time to tell a companion at the movie theater what is unfolding in the story on the screen before us.

However, one might hope to save the day by falling back on a weaker, more qualified thought. Perhaps, we don't literally and strictly speaking *see* fictions in films. Rather, strictly speaking, movie goers may *imagine* themselves seeing or, in some fashion, *make-believe* seeing the constructs of fiction film. This is a thought that a number of aestheticians—notably Kendall Walton and Jerry Levinson—have endorsed, and this might be the position that one, on more careful reflection, ought to take. If we did so, we could go on to add that when spectators at the movie claim to 'see' Charles Foster Kane on the screen, then they are thereby speaking a little loosely. They mean to be conveying, roughly, that it is make-believe for them now that they are seeing Charles Foster Kane. Of course, if we choose to adopt this line of thought, then we will incur the obligation of saying something helpful about how the newly favored concept of 'imagined seeing' or 'make-believe seeing' is properly to be construed. After all, there is a sense in which I might imagine (that I am) seeing my Aunt Ruth in a crowd scene in *Easy Rider*. But this phenomenon, if it happened, would simply be the upshot of a certain kind of perceptual mistake. Surely, this sense of the phrase has little or nothing to do with the sense in which viewers commonly imagine looking into the fictional world of a fiction film and seeing what is transpiring there.

Let's grant for a moment—grant for the sake of argument at least—that viewers do 'imagine seeing' the fictional items and events in a movie. So, for instance, I imagine seeing the winged monkeys attack Dorothy in the last third of *The Wizard of Oz* (see figure 1). But then there is a good deal more to say about my perceptual relationship to Dorothy, the Witch, and their interactions with the winged monkeys than simply that. If I imagine seeing these creatures in a static shot, then I imagine seeing them from a fixed and qualitatively determinate perspective, a perspective that arises from within the very fictional space in which they occur. I imagine seeing these creatures and their frenzied behavior at a certain rough distance, and I imagine seeing them from a more or less determinate angle in relation to the surface of the screen. Correlatively, if I see them in a tracking shot, then I imagine seeing them from a series of continuously changing perspectives, where each perspective, at every instant of the shot, is qualitatively determinate in its visual details. I imagine seeing the action from a perspective that moves, as it were, through the segment of space in Oz where fictionally the monkeys are attacking Dorothy. However, the provenance of these visual perspectives is itself perplexing when we think the matter through. If I imagine seeing the scene

Figure 1 The Wicked Witch summons her winged monkeys

from Oz, what is it that I imagine about how I come to see these fictions in these ways—in a perspectival manner whose 'source' is alternatively fixed and mobile? Certainly I don't imagine that I am moving around among the winged monkeys.

In one way, there is no problem whatsoever. Or, at any rate, there is nothing mysterious about what we are seeing. We *know* very well that we are seeing the action from the perspective of a camera—the motion picture camera (or cameras) that shot the scenes in question. We *know* very well how these motion picture shots and sequences came to be formed. And yet, that is not the question. The question is: what is it that movie viewers *imagine* about the mode or manner of the seeing that they purportedly imagine? What is it that they imagine about what makes it broadly possible for them to see these fictional items in this distinctive perspectival way? It is important to keep in mind that it is the question about what we *imagine* that is critical in this context. The explanation in terms of what we know is not in question. In a similar way, there is a contrast about what we are likely to *know* about how the monkeys are (apparently) able to fly toward the ramparts of the witch's castle. We *know* that the actors that portray them have been carried along, e.g. on wires strung through the set that depicts the castle. But, what we *imagine* about this is very different. What we are likely to imagine is that the winged monkeys have magic flying powers bestowed on them by the Wicked Witch. We may imagine further that they are flying for the following reason: because the Wicked Witch has ordered them to go after Dorothy.[1]

Now it is precisely this question about what makes our viewing of the movie fictions possible in the first place that seems so bewildering to answer. Broadly, there seem to be two possible approaches. (A) We imagine that we see the behavior of Dorothy and the winged monkeys *directly*. That is, we imagine that we are present at the Witch's castle and see Dorothy and the monkeys from positions we occupy at that locale. (B) We imagine that we see the behavior of Dorothy and the winged monkeys *only indirectly and in a mediated way*. That is, by seeing them in images like motion picture shots that have been causally derived in some fashion from the actual presence of Dorothy, the monkeys, and the other items in the fictional scene. (Of course, we know that we are watching motion picture images that have been derived photographically, in the first instance, from members of the cast and segments of a set at MGM.) Neither (A) nor (B) seems attractive or even minimally coherent.

Probably, the absurdity of (B) is most obvious. In the present instance, the audience shares visual perspectives on the action that arise from somewhere within the corridors or on the ramparts of a castle in Oz. And yet, it is a fundamental fact about the ongoing fiction in the movie of *The Wizard of Oz* that there *is* nothing like a camera located in the vicinity of the Wicked Witch's castle registering the action. It would be absurd for viewers to worry whether fictionally Dorothy might bump into the moving camera or hope that some of the winged monkeys might injure themselves by flying into it. In the portion of the Oz story in question, there are witches, castles, barking dogs, and winged monkeys, but there definitely is no motion picture camera on the scene. There probably are no motion picture cameras in all of Oz. So, we don't imagine ourselves seeing the narrative action indirectly. Option B is a non-starter.

However, it is equally absurd to suppose that we imagine seeing the action face-to-face. Option A is almost equally implausible. Just to fix our thoughts on an obvious and striking case, consider a tracking shot through a melée of winged monkeys. Surely we don't imagine ourselves as floating around among the swooping and darting monkeys. It is not as if we (the viewers) are seeing the narrative conflict, as if it were before our eyes while we were on the wing. So options (A) and (B) are untenable, it seems. And yet, how can it be that viewers imagine seeing the narrative action, although they imagine their seeing of the fictions as being neither direct nor indirect—neither face-to-face nor mediated? This is a bad result. Maybe the idea that we imagine seeing the narrative action has been misbegotten from the beginning.

---

[1] It is important here to emphasize two related points. There are questions about why it is fictional in a work that so and so may have an answer that is given in terms that are *internal* to the work of fiction and in terms that are *external* to it. This point is a familiar one. But, it is equally important that one and the same question about why something is fictional in a work may have perfectly valid internal and external answers. When this is so, we have to be careful about what kind of question we mean to be posing. This seems to be less well observed.

Bernard Williams, in a famous essay on visualization in the imagination, anticipated many of the hard questions about the neighboring idea of imagined seeing in the movies. In "The Self and the Imagination," Williams pretty effectively introduces some of the key conundrums that continue to haunt this topic.[2] His discussion of our perceptual/imaginative engagement with theater and film is very brief, and he states himself that his remarks constitute " . . . only the crudest gesture towards a complex and fascinating subject."[3] Nevertheless, he says enough to move quickly to the heart of the matter. An overview of his discussion will provide a useful further introduction to some of the central topics that will be investigated in this book.

Williams is prepared to grant that members of an audience, both in the theater and the cinema, normally do (in some sense) 'see' the fictional things and events that are contained in the drama. In watching a stage performance or a film adaptation of the play, the spectator 'sees' Othello and 'sees' Desdemona, and 'sees' Othello strangle Desdemona. However, Williams himself takes the claim to require a significant qualification, and the qualification in question begins to introduce the source of controversy. For it is to be stressed that he also maintains that we do not 'see' Othello and Desdemona *in the same literal sense* that we see the actors who are playing these characters, and we don't 'see' the fictional strangling *in the same literal way* that we see the various enactments of the strangling on the stage. Thus, Williams says, " . . . we as spectators are not in the world of the play itself: we—in a sense—see what is happening in that world. But not in the same sense as that in which we see the actors, nor that in which the characters see one another or events in the play."[4] And yet, this immediately raises the challenge of how this natural but distinctive sense is supposed to be understood.

According to Williams, if X is a something that the audience 'sees' in a play or a movie, then the use of 'to see X' in which this is true is not a sense that carries the normal ontological commitment of the verb. For instance, suppose that a viewer 'sees' X in a movie and suppose further that, in the movie, X is a camel. Suppose finally that, in watching the movie, the viewer 'sees' that this is so. It doesn't follow from all this that there is a camel, presented in the movie, that the viewer literally has seen. Williams says, " . . . if I see Othello and Desdemona, then I see Othello strangle Desdemona; but that will not entail that I, as part of my biography, have ever seen anyone strangle anyone."[5] But once more, what is the sense of 'see' that is supposed to be in question in these instances? What does this kind of 'audience seeing of fictions' amount to?

Williams alludes to the idea that, if a viewer 'sees' X in a movie, then this is because the viewer *imagines seeing* or, in some related way, *thinks of himself (in make-believe) as seeing* the fictional world. Nevertheless, this does not seem to be an idea that he himself accepts. He plainly insists that, when viewers 'see' X in a play or in a movie W, this fact does not imply that they are seeing (or even that they imagine themselves seeing) from

---

[2] Williams (1973).   [3] Ibid., 36.   [4] Ibid.   [5] Ibid.

within the fictional world of W or, more narrowly, from *within* the fictional spaces of (the relevant scene in) W. Hence, Williams grants that the viewers of W don't 'see' and they don't imagine (themselves) 'seeing X,' as it were, from a situation in which they are 'face-to-face' with X. But, further, it is pretty certain that Williams would equally deny that viewers imagine seeing X in some *indirect* or mediated mode or manner. It will not be, on Williams's implicit account, that the viewer imagines seeing X *by* seeing it in a mirror or in a W-internal photographic picture of X or in any other transmitted depiction of X. But, if we combine these two plausible suppositions about Williams's position, then he must hold that, when viewers see a fiction X in a cinematic work W, then they do not imagine seeing X in W either directly or imagine seeing it indirectly either. In other words, Williams repudiates the options (A) and (B) above. This apparent conclusion brushes close to the conclusion that, in seeing X in W, viewers do not *see* and do not *imagine seeing* X in W at all. Thus, Williams is in danger of contradicting the position with which he begins, i.e. that viewers at a movie or a play do, in some sense, 'see' the elements in the fiction.

The situation becomes even more deeply puzzling when Williams discusses movies in particular and affirms bluntly that when a particular viewer 'sees' X in a movie, he 'sees' X, at any given instant in the film, from a concrete visual point of view (visual perspective). He goes on to add that the 'point of view' in question is actually created by the physical vantage point the relevant movie camera occupies. However, he also emphasizes, as I have emphasized above, that, *within the fiction of the film*, this point of view is *not* imagined as the point of view *of a camera*. After all, within the movie story, there is characteristically no movie camera that is present in the scene. This means, in particular, that, in watching the movie, viewers don't imagine seeing X *by* seeing a motion picture shot of it. Their 'seeing' is certainly not an 'indirect' seeing of that sort. Williams also argues further that the point of view (visual perspective) from which the action is presented is characteristically not the point of view of a character in the movie. Moreover, it is not the point of view of the movie's actual audience, and it is not the point of view of the director, nor presumably, of the cinematographer. More broadly, it is not the point of view of any kind of 'witness' that might be implicitly in the scene. Williams allows that there is a sense in which a shot or sequence may manifest, say, the director's 'point of view,' but this is so, he correctly supposes, only in a quite different and derivative sense of 'point of view.' So Williams's contention is that movie viewers not only somehow see the objects and events of the movie drama, but they see them from very definite 'points of view.' It is just that, as he puts it, these are not points of view that are generated by *anything* that figures in the fiction or are embodied in *anyone* that participates in the movie's associated make-believe. But this conclusion leaves one with the daunting task of comprehending the nature of the 'unembodied' points of view from which the fictional items in a movie are supposedly presented. Williams insists that viewers 'see' fictions in movies only by seeing them from such and such a specific visual point of view. If we are unable to understand that basic idea, then the still simpler idea that the audience 'sees' fictions in movies seems threatened as well. To my mind, these are the chief questions that Williams raises about our perceptual/imaginative engagement with plays and movies, and I attempt to address them, as they apply to movies, at considerable length—especially in Chapters 2, 3, and 4.

Gregory Currie (1995), Berys Gaut (2004, 2010), and Andrew Kania (2005, forthcoming) have all explicitly affirmed this striking and implausible result: spectators at the movies don't literally see and don't imagine seeing the fictions the movie incorporates. Williams, as I say, seems to be committed to it. Whatever reflections might give the impression of supporting it, however, such skepticism leaves one with nothing that explains the thought that almost everyone (including Williams) pre-theoretically accepts—that the audience can be said, in some appropriate sense, 'to see' the fictions that they view on the stage or in the movies. As I have indicated several times, it is doubtful that Williams takes 'audience seeing' of fictions to be construed in terms of some version of 'imagined seeing' or 'make-believe seeing' at all. And yet, this refusal leaves what seems to be a major lacuna in his position. What, according to Williams, can 'the audience's seeing of fictions' in the dramatic theater and in the cinema conceivably amount to?

In later chapters, I will defend a heavily qualified version of the position that, in watching fiction films, viewers do (normally) imagine seeing the characters, seeing the events, and seeing the circumstances that are depicted in the film.[6] (These same viewers concurrently imagine hearing the sounds and noises that are produced from within the movie's diegesis.) Indeed, I maintain that it is the standard *function* of the image-track to prescribe what the movie viewers are to imagine seeing in individual shots and collections of them. Similarly, the sound-track prescribes what the viewer is to imagine hearing from within the world of the story. I will argue that it is because the sound-track and the image-track have these complementary functions in a fiction film, that we are justified in thinking of them constituting an 'audio-visual narration' of the cinematic narrative.

Compare the conceptual situation in the movie case with the situation in the case of works of literary fiction. In producing a work of fiction in literature—let *Moby Dick* serve as our example—the actual author, Herman Melville, 'tells the story' by making it sequentially fictional that certain things have transpired in Ahab's demented search for the great white whale. But, as a part of the work itself, it is the character Ishmael who, in a different and more familiar sense, 'tells us the story' of the *Pequod*'s voyage. It is the intended function of Melville's words in the text to prompt us to imagine Ishmael's recounting of the ship's adventures and his commentary on their resonance and (sometimes veiled) significance. I hold that 'narration' in works of literary fiction and 'narration' in cinematic fictions are similar in the following regard. As a rule, movies mandate for their viewers at least roughly what they are to imagine seeing and

---

[6] This formulation needs to be restricted to apply to objective shots, but subjective shots can be captured within a more elaborate formulation.

hearing in the fictional world, and this is the basis of the distinctive way in which stories are presented on film.

However, these remarks are barely adequate as even a first formulation of the issues about cinematic narration, and these issues quickly require a lot of elaboration and a range of qualifications. Hence, in the chapter that follows, I will make a start on this by offering a short overview of certain key aspects of narratological theory. The overview is meant to provide an adequate background of knowledge in the general theory of narrative to frame and motivate the later discussions in this book. In particular, I will try, in this setting, to explain more fully why I claim that 'imagined seeing' lies at the foundation of the distinctive mode of narration in narrative fiction films. Systematic defense of this contention takes up most of the remainder of this book. The defense occurs in Chapters 2, 3, and 4 especially. These chapters constitute the rather labyrinthine core of the present book.

If movies employ audio-visual 'narration' in the telling of their stories, it is possible to wonder whether they sometimes or always involve audio-visual 'narrators.' Although questions about the existence of audio-visual narrators have been extensively scrutinized in narratological writings on film, I think that the interest of these investigations has been exaggerated. I give my reasons for my current assessment in Chapters 5 and 6, and I attempt to sort out the genuine problems in this domain from the bogus ones. If movies have cinematic narrators, then these narrators will have to be, in general, 'effaced.' They will function quite recessively in the audio-visual telling of the story. This simple point has led a number of authors to reconsider the case for 'effaced narrators' in literature, and Chapter 5 addresses various key points in this longstanding debate. The conclusions reached in this chapter make it possible, in Chapter 6, to deal with narrators in film more briefly and efficiently. Finally, in Chapters 7, 8 and 9, I scrutinize the narrative strategies in three films. The first of these, David Fincher's *Fight Club* (1999), is a striking and original example of unreliable narration in the movies. The second film, Josef von Sternberg's *The Scarlet Empress* (1934), provides a subtle instance of self-conscious, reflexive film narration. Finally, the Coen brothers' 2001 movie, *The Man Who Wasn't There*, seems to be a perfect paradigm of the postmodern narrative *pastiche*. It may, in fact, be an instance of *pastiche*, but I argue that it systematically exemplifies a kind of serious, thematic unity that is not characteristic of the mode. Moreover, the structures of narrative and narration by means of which this unity is achieved define a possibility of point of view that is of interest on its own. Each chapter takes up broader problems about how these more complicated modes of cinematic narration should be conceived. In short, readers will travel from some intensely limited but foundational questions about how movie viewers characteristically experience fictions in film to some relatively more specific questions about the workings of certain sophisticated strategies of narration in the movies.

I hope that this introduction serves to provide a helpful overview of the problems discussed in this book, but I should add a brief disclaimer to the preceding remarks. In fact, there are lots of interesting questions about what viewers, or a limited group of viewers, do when they see and comprehend a traditional movie. For instance, it is widely recognized that movie stars often carry with them a 'screen persona' that they have acquired from earlier roles that they have played, and that this familiar 'persona' normally has a considerable impact on how viewers imagine seeing the character that they portray in a given film. I certainly agree that this is an important phenomenon, and one would like to understand it better. However, I have not pursued the matter in this book, and there is a host of similar issues that I have also not managed to investigate. In writing this book, I made the decision to work through certain problems rigorously and in a fair amount of detail, hoping thereby to avoid confusing these problems with others—even when some of the other neglected problems are significantly related. The phrase 'the phenomenology of film' is often used to designate this large, complex network of issues about the perception of film, and, for better or worse, this book is not, in any general way, a contribution to the phenomenology of film. Of course, I hope that the problems I do discuss will cast light on some of these adjacent domains, but my ambitions for this volume have been more circumscribed and narrowly focused.

1

Narrative and Narration: Some Rudiments

In *The Art of Fiction*, Henry James asserts: "The story and the novel, the idea and the form, are the needle and thread, and I never heard of a guild of tailors who recommended the use of the thread without the needle, or the needle without the thread" (James 1986: 178).[1] Although James is here granting the existence of a distinction between the *story*, on the one hand, and the novel (as *text*), on the other, he insists, in the larger context of his remarks, on the ambiguity and elusiveness of the concept of 'story.' After James, a guild of narratologists has arisen to explicate the ambiguities and mitigate the elusiveness of the concept. For instance, a story is undoubtedly a *narrative*, but the term 'narrative,' like the term 'statement,' is 'act-object' ambiguous. Thus, compare

(a)   There are often both film and literary versions of the same narrative

with

(b)   Flannery was interrupted several times in the course of her narrative by bouts of weeping.

In the 'object' sense, featured in (a), the word also refers to a series of represented events, processes, and states, together with the temporal and causal relations in which those occurrences are represented as standing. This is narrative as *'fabula'* or 'narrative product,' and it is probably the favored conception of 'story.' However, the term 'narrative' may also refer to the extended representational activity in virtue of which the events and their temporal/causal relations come to be articulated. In other words, it may mean 'narration,' as it does in (b). The more technical phrase 'narrative discourse' bears this sense as well, although it is further employed to denote the concrete text in which the narrational activity is embodied. In the statement

(c)   The narrative of the accident had been erased from the report,

---

[1] Since this chapter surveys a range of works in narratology, I have employed the practice, not used in other chapters, of inserting a parenthetical citation for most of the works mentioned in the text. These works are listed in the bibliography included at the end of this volume.

'narrative' occurs also in this third use. Gerard Genette drew a famous distinction between '*histoire*,' 'narration,' and '*recit*' (Genette 1982), and his terms correspond at least roughly to the use of 'story,' 'narration,' and 'text' outlined above. It will emerge in the course of the present discussion that each concept in the trio generates significant problems.

Narratology (the term comes from Tzetvan Todorov) is the general theory of narratives and the structures they exemplify. The classical structuralist narratology of Todorov, C. Bremond, A. Greimas, and early Roland Barthes was concerned primarily with narrative as narrative product. In selecting that emphasis and in other methodological matters, these authors were influenced by their proto-structuralist predecessors, Russian formalists such as V. Shklovsky and V. Propp. Theorists in the linked traditions highlighted the fact that stories, both fictional and non-fictional, can be represented in very different narrative discourses. Indeed, the same story can be rendered in discourses that have been constructed within different media, such as literature, film, or theater. A key analytical task of structuralist narratology has been to delineate the features of stories that are invariant across the fiction/non-fiction division and across the variety of their more specific realizations in different discourses and media. Hence, given any narrative discourse, it should be possible to distinguish, without major equivocation, a text, a narration, and a story that is told. However, this assumption of classical narratology is a substantive one, and it deserves to be investigated. As we will see at some length in this and later chapters, even the narrower idea that literature and film are structurally isomorphic in this way is extremely dubious. A number of important theoretical issues are involved in the very idea of cross media isomorphism, and the difficulty of the issues warrants a careful investigation of the idea.[2]

Many theorists of narrative have defended proposals concerning the essential nature of narratives, and it has been widely agreed that a genuine narrative requires the representation of a minimum of two events and some indication of the ordering in time of the events depicted. It is often claimed, in addition, that the domain of narrative events has to exhibit at least some sort of fragmentary causal structure, although even this weak and apparently plausible claim has been disputed. In fact, various modes of causal relation can be distinguished, and among these their represented instances in a particular discourse will comprise the 'narrative connections' that help to constitute it as the presentation of a narrative. The whole enterprise of trying to give necessary and/or sufficient conditions for being a narrative seems misguided. Modernist and postmodernist experiments in literary fiction, not to mention much earlier works like Sterne's *Tristram Shandy* and Diderot's *Jacques le fataliste*, have experimented with 'stories' that abrogate nearly every familiar convention and schema of narrative construction. In an early essay, Genette declared: "We know how, in various and sometimes contradictory ways, modern literature . . . has striven and succeeded, in its very foundations, to be a

---

[2] As I indicated in the introduction, it will be one of the main goals of this volume to carry out such an investigation with some care.

questioning, a disturbance, a contestation of the notion of narrative" (Genette 1982: 127). It is fruitless, in the aftershock of that disturbance, to argue too sharply about the boundary at which genuine story-making has come to be replaced by something else. Nevertheless, the careful delineation of a range of prototypical narrative connections can illustrate the diverse intuitive bases of our judgments concerning narrativity (Carroll, 2009).

In any case, such questions of definition or essence easily distract from other issues of at least as great an interest. For instance, it is obviously not essential to a plot-like structure of events that its sequential representation tends to awaken curiosity, personal identification, and suspense in potential audiences. Nevertheless, it is an important fact about certain events in many stories that they have the specific narrative function of defining the predicaments the characters face and of thereby eliciting suitable responses from a concerned audience. Similarly, it is not essential that a narration eventually provide additional depicted materials whose function is to satisfy the audience's engagement with the characters by showing how the predicaments come to be resolved. And yet, of course, most popular narratives have been designed with the aim of achieving both of these objectives. Such general considerations about the audience's attention and imaginative involvement presumably help to explain why audiences value storytelling so much and why they repeat the stories they learn, with variations, in many settings and contexts. What is more, a wide range of the strategic features of particular narratives are most naturally explained in terms of the storyteller's intentions of arousing and gratifying an audience's expectations of dramatic closure. Classical narratology was inclined to abstract from the strategic objectives of storytellers and the anticipatory interest of their audiences, and because it conceptualized 'narrative' primarily in terms of structure, it paid scant attention to the dilemma-driven forces that animate the more familiar narrative forms for their readers and spectators.

Some recent theorists of narrative have sought to rectify this omission. They have rightly emphasized that narratives are structures of events that are themselves 'meaningful,' although the meaning of a narrative episode is of an altogether different nature from the meaning of a linguistic construction or act. Narratives assign meaning or significance to the events they incorporate by situating them within an explanatory pattern that typically delineates both their causal roles and their teleological contributions to the needs and goals of the characters. They provide a global account of dramatically highlighted behavior by specifying salient causes of the agents' actions, charting some of the consequences that those actions engender. In constructing a story, narrators typically seek to provide a surveyable pattern of explanatory connections that opens up its component occurrences to plausible perspectives of evaluation, where these perspectives may invoke prudential, moral, political, and other frameworks of assessment. The meaning of a designated episode is determined by its place in an explanatory pattern of this kind, and it is constituted by whatever that *position* reveals to an audience from the evaluative perspectives they deploy (Wilson 1997). Confusion about the concept of 'meaning,' as the notion applies to the events of a narrative, has badly distorted many accounts of what it is to interpret by assimilating narrative meaning to one or another of the types of meaning that are expressed in language use.[3]

Wayne Booth, in *The Company We Keep* (1988), and Martha Nussbaum, in *Love's Knowledge* (1990), have made extended attempts to recover these vital aspects of narrative for contemporary theory and criticism. They have defended at length a number of bold claims about the distinctive character of the moral and psychological knowledge that complex narratives, including fictional narratives, can supply. Nussbaum maintains that "certain truths about human life can *only* be fittingly and accurately stated in the language and forms characteristic of the narrative artist" (Nussbaum 1990: 4; my emphasis). More specifically, she holds that these are principally truths concerning 'the projected morality' (in Henry James's phrase) that are implicitly exemplified in suitable configurations of narrative events. Moreover, she maintains that 'the language and forms of narrative,' in their most subtle and incisive instances, teach us the fine discrimination of ethically relevant attributes in agents, actions, and the circumstances of significant moral choice. These reflections explain one main aspect of the kind of interest and importance that narratives may have—an important topic that is little discussed in the chapters that follow.

In a related but contrasting vein, critics like Frank Kermode (2000) and Peter Brooks (1984) have explored the powerful but often-suppressed agendas that partially govern the idiosyncratic trajectories of plot construction. Most narratives are devised from the outset to reach an ending that will realize the audience's desire for the dramatic development to culminate in an apt and satisfying conclusion. But Brooks, in particular, stresses that the reader's sense of a proper ending is highly variable and has a complicated range of determinants. Moreover, these determinants will probably include the reader's self-censored wishes concerning the fictional action, wishes that may be perverse or otherwise threatening to awareness. Hence a form of narrative closure that readers find 'apt and satisfying' may, at the same time, disturb them and even represent an unconscious source of revulsion or horror. These are important topics about the interpretation of narratives—especially fictional narratives—but they also will not be featured extensively in the present volume.

It is frequently claimed that the recounting of narratives is a human universal. However, given that any telling or showing of something that purportedly took place is already the production of a narrative, it is hard to see how narrativity could fail to be ubiquitous among cultures where a system of representation that registers causation is in use. Early narratologists characteristically maintained that the types of story within a culture (or even across cultures) were strikingly similar in terms of their basic narrative constituents and the underlying configurations of their plots. These similarities, it was argued, are such that the stories from an appropriately large and significant corpus can often be 'generated' by suitably general rules of combination

---

[3] Interested readers should consult the interesting and complex discussion in Chapter 10 ("Making Sense") in Williams (2002).

and transformation. Vladimir Propp's *Morphology of the Russian Folktale* (1968) attempted to establish that the 'wonder tales' he studied could be represented as the product of certain generative rules, where those rules operate on a restricted base of narrative 'functions,' i.e. roughly, types of fictional action, situation, and effect. Many of the theorists who followed Propp and were influenced by him thus thought of themselves as developing a grammar of narrative. Unfortunately, the import of the analogy with linguistic grammar is generally murky in these writings. Some of their authors describe themselves as analyzing a basic conceptual competence that shapes, more or less *a priori*, the creation and the comprehension of stories that humans tell, whether the stories are make-believe or not.

It is difficult to evaluate either the correctness or the interest of proposals elaborated along these lines. First, the fundamental categories in terms of which the story-generating rules get formulated are extremely general and correspondingly vague. Second, it is usually unclear just what domain of actual and possible stories is covered by the generative rules in question; hence even the descriptive adequacy of the theories is hard to assess effectively. Third, even if the descriptive adequacy of a given theory were conceded, it remains uncertain what explanatory force the 'grammatical' model in narrative theory is supposed to have. Structuralist narratology has espoused the etiological priority of schematic narrative structures over their more concrete manifestations in storytelling discourse. It is maintained that storytellers are guided in their construction of a concrete narration by grasping, in the first instance, a relatively abstract narrative structure which then governs the elaboration, within a chosen medium, of the more concrete and accessible particulars of 'shallow' narrative discourse. This may be so, but the evidence in its favor is slim and equivocal at best.

A number of critics and theorists, less influenced by semiotics and structuralism, have devoted considerable attention to some of the more systematic ways in which the activity of narration and the flow of narrative information gets regulated in narrative discourse. An early instance of such a study is Percy Lubbock's *The Craft of Fiction* (1921), and Wayne Booth's *The Rhetoric of Fiction* (1983) is a classic of this alternative tradition. Both books elaborate and extend the topic of (narrational) 'point of view,' and subsequent narratologists have taken up this subject and the investigation of other intrinsic parameters that are implicated in the normal telling of a tale. For example, Genette (1980) observed that talk of 'point of view' was liable to run together questions of narrational *voice* and questions of narrational *focalization* (or *mood*). In literary narrative fiction, it is one thing to ask who or what it is that is fictionally producing the words of the narration. The fictional or fictionalized being who does the narrating (the *narrator*) may be a person who is portrayed as belonging to the narrative action (*homodiegetic*); or the narrator may be a fictive creation of the work who is not a character within the story at all (*heterodiegetic*). This is the question of who 'speaks' the narration—the question of 'voice.' On the other hand, it is possible that the fictional information that the narrator conveys may be restricted to the information available only to a certain character, but the focalizing character in question need not be the narrator. Henry James's novel *What Maisie Knew* (1897) is famous for rendering the events of the story as they are seen and imperfectly understood by a young girl, Maisie. The words of the narration, however, are not her own; they are the product of a highly articulate Jamesian 'voice' who has unlimited knowledge of her thoughts and feelings about the action. In many mystery novels, it is not the detective who relates the progress of his or her investigation, although the narration is focalized from the detective's perspective. Alternatively, the narrator may dispense information that is methodically constrained in any one of several other general ways. For example, it may be a tacit condition upon the narration that the narrator has no direct access to the inner life of other characters. And, of course, the narration may operate without any significant epistemic constraints at all and hence be 'omniscient' in that sense. These matters all fall under the broad conception of 'focalization.'

Genette and his intellectual descendants also explored other types of systematic interrelation between narrative texts, on the one hand, and the stories they narrate on the other. In his book, *Narrative Discourse*, Genette (1980) scrutinized the connections that hold between the implicitly represented *time* of the narrational activity and the temporal framework in which the narrated events are embedded. Thus, the *order* in which the occurrences are introduced and described in the narration may be different from the order these events are supposed to have exemplified in narrative time. The *duration* of a depicted episode may or may not correspond to the relative length at which it is elaborated in the narrative discourse, and the *frequency* with which a type of event occurs in the story, or the *frequency* with which a single event is mentioned in the text, may vary significantly from instance to instance. Many of these distinctions will prove useful as we proceed.

Gerald Prince (1982) has underscored the importance of the fact that many fictional narrations are represented as being addressed to an internal audience, a *narratee*, whose implied characteristics influence the nature of the narrator's performance in notable ways. Mieke Bal (1985), Meir Steinberg (1978), and Thomas Pavel (1986) are other important practitioners of approaches to narrative construction that are more flexible, more nuanced, and more broadly conceived than the standard analyses of early structuralist narratology. While the earlier works were likely to treat 'narrative discourse' as a vehicle from which the narratologist abstracts suitable structural generalities of story content, the more recent tradition has given closer consideration to the variety and complexity of the ways in which the activity of narration is goal-directed and internally monitored to meet those goals. Like Booth and Lubbock before them, these theorists are concerned with the ways in which narrational strategies complicate an audience's epistemic and empathetic access to the narrative occurrences. It is very important, in the debates that follow, that one have a fairly lively sense of the varied possibilities of point of view and temporal structures in narratives, or various oversimple theories of narration—of film narration, in particular—will take on a spurious plausibility.

Although a lot of studies of narrative and narrative discourse are subtle and complex, the basic concept of 'narration' has been and continues to be a source of foundational puzzlement. In narratology, the paradigm of narration has been literary narration, despite the fact that it has attributes that do not generalize easily to other narrational modes. We will shortly examine some of the ways in which this is so. In a literary work of non-fiction narrative, the narration consists of the various kinds of *speech acts* (illocutionary acts) performed by *the author* in the construction of the story. That is, the actual author, in the course of composing the linguistic text, asserts propositions, introduces suppositions, raises questions, etc., and it is this linear network of linked linguistic acts that tells the purported history. The reader is meant to grasp both the 'propositional' contents expressed and the illocutionary force of the linguistic acts the author has performed. However, when works of narrative fiction are in question—in novels for instance—the concept of 'narration' exhibits a widely recognized ambiguity.

The novelist Anna Sewell told a story about a horse, Black Beauty, when she wrote her novel of that name; but in the novel it is Black Beauty, the horse himself, who tells his own story. So there are two activities of 'telling a story' connected with the very same literary text, and there is a difference in agency, ontology, and illocutionary kind between them. One distinguishes between the 'storytelling' activity of actual authors who, sentence by sentence, *make it fictional* in their stories that certain happenings and circumstances took place, and the counterpart *fictional* activity of recounting or reporting those occurrences as real. It is customary, in discussions of literary narrative fiction, to reserve 'narrating' for the fictional recounting of narrative events, and I will use 'fiction-making' to designate the activity of telling that it is the business of the author to conduct. Narration (narrating), so understood, is an internal component of the total work of fiction, although it is generally no part of the story that is being narrated. It is an implicitly indicated activity that is, so to speak, 'scripted' for the reader in the words of the text. As I suggested earlier, the narrator of a fictional story is the agent who narrates the story, the person who fictionally asserts that certain events took place and who, in many cases, comments fictionally on aspects of the evolving plot. The narrators of fictional stories are themselves fictive (fictional or fictionalized) constructs of the works that incorporate them. By contrast, the author, in writing the text, creates both the fictional history of narrative action and the wider fiction that an actual record of that history has come to be transcribed in the text. It is through the mediation of the facts about the fictional telling that the fictional facts of the narrative product are generated, either directly or by implication. Later we will consider the question of what 'machinery of generation' might be in operation here.

There has been a weak consensus among theorists that the fictional activity of narrating a literary story conceptually *presupposes* the existence of a fictional or fictionalized narrator who carries out that task, although the conceptual character of the presupposition is certainly open to question. Our intuitions about the issue are less than decisive. Nevertheless, it is usual for narrators to be created in narrative fictions, and the existence in literature of a rich variety of fictional narrators is a familiar and important part of our experience in reading novels and short stories. The reader's imagined relations with narrators, complicated or otherwise, can be one of the chief pleasures in reading a complex story. Many studies of literary point of view, like Booth's *The Rhetoric of Fiction* (1983), are concerned with potentially central features of fictional narrators and with their possible relations to the characters and circumstances within the story.

I have already noted that narrators may themselves be characters that figure in their own stories or, at least, within some broader fictional history that explains how they have come to have their knowledge of the story they relate. Alternatively, the way in which a narrator knows of the events recounted may not be specified, and hence he or she may stand in no determinate epistemic relation to the world of the story at all. These questions pertain to the type of *authority* with which the narrator speaks. What is more, in either of these cases, the psychological properties and moral attributes of the narrator may be, in varying degrees, delineated, either because the narrator simply *self-ascribes* them, or because they are implicitly *dramatized* in the manner of the telling or both. At one extreme within this range, the narrator may remain *effaced*—a relatively neutral voice who simply tells the story. At another extreme are *self-conscious* narrators who comment on their own performances as narrators and on the nature of the reflexive narration they are fashioning. In addition, it is possible for a dramatized narrator to be represented as a type of person who is, relative to the norms endorsed by the work, wholly admirable, totally unsympathetic, or, more often, somewhere in between. Finally, the narration may reveal that the narrator is *unreliable* in the rendering of at least certain key aspects of his or her recounting. These and other systematic considerations have formed the basis for an elaborate and still evolving taxonomy of fictional narrators. The notion of an 'effaced narrator' will play a large role in the disputes of the later chapters, but it will only be in the last three chapters, Chapters 7, 8 and 9, that some of the more complex distinctions of 'point of view' will play a sizeable role in our analyses.

In the context of his discussion of narrators, Booth also introduced the further concept of *the implied author*. The experience of readers in reading the total work of fiction, including their imaginative relations with the work's narrator, will very often present them with a lively, well-grounded impression of the personality, sensibility, and intelligence of the person who actually crafted the work, i.e. the real author. And this impression may be a critically and aesthetically important part of the reader's reaction to the work, whether or not the impression accurately reflects true facts about the historical author. Thus, in characterizing their perception of what the work as a multifaceted artifact conveys, readers may well want to incorporate an account of the way in which the fiction-making activity that produced it serves as an apparent expression of the author's psychology and outlook on the world. If so, then the reader is thereby describing the properties of the work's 'implied author'—or, better, is describing a version of the author that the work apparently implies.

The basic concepts of narratology have often purported to apply univocally to different instances of particular narratives, including narratives represented in different media. This is the broad assumption of 'structural isomorphism' that I mentioned earlier. Given this assumption, one might therefore expect to find that different modes of narration stand at the foundations of each of the different kinds of storytelling. One might expect, in other words, that, whenever a narrative has somehow been presented, there must be some kind of 'narration' that has presented it. Therefore, one large question that will be systematically explored in the following chapters is the question of the extent to which analogues of this structured set of distinctions can and should be extended to the storytelling medium of fiction film. This is the important question of the generality, over art forms, of the fundamental tenets of classical narratology. It has been common to complain that narratology has simply assumed that literary narratives constitute the paradigm of the narrative 'structure,' a structure that also gets exemplified in movies and other kindred texts. At any rate, this question of the generality of the key concepts of narratology in relation to literature and movies is perhaps the chief theoretical topic about narratives and narration that this volume addresses.

The thesis of generality can sound trivial, but the thesis quickly gives rise to problems of real substance. Consider, first, the case of stories that have been staged and enacted, say in a theater, for an audience that is present at the staging. Many theorists, following Aristotle, maintain that theatrical performances of stories do not as such involve narration, contrasting stories that are conveyed by *telling* or *recounting* of the fictional action with the stories that are transmitted by *mimesis*, or by histrionic imitation. On this conception, genuine narration requires an articulated, perspectival telling of the story, a situated recounting of the relevant events. This conception does allow that the telling in the narration need not be linguistic, although it is not always clear just what the range of non-linguistic tellings might be. Of course, the intermittent use of voice-over narration, as part of a play or a film, is relatively unproblematic, and that device is not in question here.

The case of fiction film is particularly interesting in this regard. It is *prima facie* plausible that the edited image track of a film involves a genuine pictorial telling, i.e. a showing or visual displaying of fictional events that is both perspectival, because of the nature of cinematic photography, and articulated, principally because of the editing. If this is so, then the pictorial telling characteristic of films supplements the purely mimetic dimension of staging and dramatic performance in the cinema. However, even if it is granted that a sort of pictorial telling is intrinsic to narrative film, it is still not obvious, in the first place, whether its presence presupposes the existence of a cinematic narrator who does the telling. Could there not be an activity of visual telling that, like the activity of showing, is not itself the action of an agent? In an extensive debate among film theorists, affirmative and negative answers to this second question have been endorsed with equal conviction. Seymour Chatman has vigorously pursued these issues over several works, accepting the highly controversial view that film and literature are isomorphic in terms of narrative and narration (see especially Chatman 1990). I will explore both his position and those of others in the next chapter.

But let it be allowed provisionally that every fiction film involves, in the sense adumbrated above, a visual telling of its story. Nevertheless, it is not obvious, in the second place, that this mode of visual telling constitutes a true analogue to narration in literary fiction. I have emphasized, in discussing fictional narratives in literature, that the preferred referent of 'narrator' is, by stipulation, the fictional or fictionalized agent who reports them. If there is to be an analogous activity of audio-visual narration in movies, then some argument is needed to establish that a movie's image-track implicitly adumbrates a fictional activity of visual telling, i.e. an activity of showing (displaying to vision), the objects and events that are represented therein. In the absence of such an argument, there is no reason to accept the thesis that the articulated, perspectival pictorial telling in fiction films is anything more than a matter of an articulated, perspectival fiction-making by means of motion picture images—the undoubted activity that the actual film-makers have carried out. The expressive characteristics of visual and, for that matter, audio-visual fiction-making, whether they are global or strictly local, may provide grounds for analyzing the apparent psychology of the implied (albeit collective) film-maker, but they do not, as such, comprise evidence for the existence of a distinctively cinematic narrator.

The needed argument will not be easy to make persuasively. Relatively simple forms of visual narrative construction, like hand-shadowed shows and simple comic strips, normally do not depict or otherwise evoke a work-internal activity of visually exhibiting the narrative action to an implicit audience. Of course, the creators of these rudimentary forms of visual narrative mean to be showing a story to prospective viewers, and they present the constituent fictional states-of-affairs by fashioning images that depict them. This, of course, is just the pictorial fiction-making they perform. However, in the absence of any special strategy of reflexive self-representation, the pictures do not further depict an activity of someone or something showing a viewer the narrative events. They do not portray, for instance, a fictional activity of setting the events of the story before the viewer's eyes.

It is not surprising that there should be strongly conflicting intuitions about these questions when the topic of narration in film is investigated. Insofar as a movie narrative has been created by means of staging and acting, it should fall with theater among the mimetic, non-narrational forms of storytelling. And yet, the fact that these dramatic materials are displayed to spectators through a mediating chain of edited photographic shots gives film an additional discursive character, a character that potentially suffices to establish a dimension of fictive pictorial narration. Whether or not this is so depends, as we have seen, on further hard questions about the nature of photographic representation in the cinema and our imaginative involvement with it, and these are questions to which many of the ensuing chapters have, in various degrees, been devoted. As I indicated in the introduction, I believe that we 'imagine seeing' into the fictional world of a traditional film and that we standardly are meant to be engaged with the movie fiction in just that way. For purposes of starting out, however, I have merely wanted to draw attention to the ways in which the general concept of 'narration' in works of fiction is conceptually underspecified and exhibits conceptual tensions that have remained quite seriously unresolved in earlier discussions of audio-visual narration in film. In the next chapter, I will begin to address these issues head-on and at length.

There is a further problem area that is a critical part of narrative theory. This is the problem of how readers and viewers determine, when they can, what fictional truths obtain, explicitly or implicitly, in a given work of fiction. An adequate theory of narration in fiction needs to offer some account of the ways in which the narration establishes a corresponding narrative, and a view about the determinacy of the story contents that get established in those ways. A theory of narrative fiction needs a plausible account of 'truth in fiction' for the form of narrative art in question. (This is not at all to say that an account of 'truth in fiction' suffices for an account of 'interpretative correctness'. It does not.[4]) Issues concerning truth in fiction are themselves delicate and difficult. However, as we will see in later chapters, otherwise attractive proposals concerning the epistemology of narration are demolished by inadequate reflection on how the facts of narrative get generated. Noël Carroll, in particular, offers a suggestion about what viewers rightly imagine in seeing shots or sequences in fiction films. It is a suggestion whose specious plausibility, it seems to me, depends almost wholly on oversimplifying the ways that fictional truths get generated by a suitable text (Carroll 2006).

If it is assumed, as I have assumed here, that narration in literary fiction is to be identified with the series of story-generating fictional speech acts that are directly represented in the text, then literary narration, so constructed, significantly under-determines the constituents of the corresponding narrative. The event-describing propositions that the narrator overtly affirms fall far short of encompassing everything that a minimally competent reader grasps as part of the story being told. It is evident to able readers that the narrator fictionally presupposes that various other story-relevant propositions are true and, moreover, that the narrator is fictionally implying more than he or she overtly says about what is happening in the story. The salient presuppositions and implications will usually count as part of the contents of the narrative, and the phrase '*syuzhet*' (standardly used to contrast with '*fabula*') might be valuably adapted to cover this wider domain of explicit and implicit narrational statement.

Nevertheless, even the wider domain of narrative information is not sufficient to establish the whole of the story (the *fabula*) that the work conveys. In reading a piece of narrative fiction, the audience is expected to bring a vast range of background assumptions that will be utilized in working out the detailed development of the story, and the background will not, in general, coincide with the class of propositions

---

[4] See Lamarque (2004) on this and Currie's (2010) discussion of his views.

that fictionally the narrator presupposes. What is more, the portion of the reader's background information that bears upon the unfolding of the story will normally alter over time. As the narration progresses, readers will discover that some of their heretofore pertinent background beliefs should now be dropped or held in abeyance; furthermore, the narration, at that stage, may well dictate new information that the audience is supposed to assimilate into their subsequent construction of the story. Readers' comprehension of narratives would be sketchy and riddled with gaps if their readings were not regularly supplemented by the reasonable inferences they draw on the basis of the overt text and the shifting set of background assumptions that they progressively assemble. These considerations show that an adequate theoretical grasp of the determination of narrative content requires an adequate account of the dynamics of narration—an account of the changing suppositions that readers are *entitled* to exploit in their reading. And it concomitantly requires an account of the *legitimate* forms of supplementary inference that mediate their indirect comprehension of the plot.

Readers recognize that even the most definite and unambiguous claims within a fictional narration cannot automatically be accepted at face value. On the one hand, it is probably the case that the explicit statements and evident suggestions in a standard narration are treated as *defeasibly* correct. That is, readers are licensed to add to the story any proposition that the narrator either asserts or distinctly implies unless there are clear-cut and specific grounds, internal to the work, for declining to do so. On the other hand, narrative works certainly exist in which an unreliable narrator asserts or suggests incorrect claims about the fictional world, doing so with or without an intention to deceive. In these cases, the standard mechanism for fixing the facts of the narrative fiction is overridden by forces internal to the mechanism that fixes the facts concerning the narration. Ford Madox Ford's *The Good Soldier* is regularly cited as a novel in which the text supplies ample evidence for distrusting the first-person narrator of the work.

Suppose, however, that there is some more extensive framework of fictional truths that are more or less directly established by the text. There is, as mentioned above, a further question about the modes of inference that the readers may correctly adopt in 'generating' all the rest. In *Mimesis as Make-Believe*, Kendall Walton (1990) discusses this problem of 'the mechanics of generation,' and he specifically explores at some length two conceptions of legitimate narrative inference. One conception embraces the so-called 'Reality Principle,' and is grounded upon the reader's convictions about what facts really hold in the actual world. The other conception is based upon the 'Mutual Belief Principle,' and is governed by the reader's convictions about the beliefs that audiences contemporary with the work would have shared. The first approach corresponds to readings that extrapolate to the implied aspects of the story on the basis of the reader's judgments about what actually would follow if certain states of affairs are already established as part of the story. The second approach extrapolates on the basis of the reader's sense of how the readership envisaged by the author would have filled the story out.

According to the Reality Principle, if readers accept P1 to Pn as fictional in the story S, and if they also accept the truth of 'the generating conditional,' i.e.

If P1, P2, . . . , and Pn then Q

then they are authorized to accept Q as fictional in S as well. The Mutual Belief Principle, by contrast, says that, if readers accept P1 to Pn as fictional in S and also accept that the original audiences for the work mutually believed 'the generating conditional,' then Q is authorized for these readers as fictional in S. Walton holds that we regularly make piecemeal use of one or both of these principles and, no doubt, of still other principles besides. He denies that any single type of inferential strategy provides adequate, fully general coverage of the ways that readers (or, for that matter, viewers) add to their legitimate beliefs about the constituents of narrative. In fact, towards the end of the discussion, he concludes that the inferences we rightly make are too 'unruly' to be readily codified by an orderly and uncluttered account. As he colorfully puts the point, "The machinery of generalization is devised of rubber bands and paper clips and powered by everything from unicorns in traces to baking soda mixed with vinegar" (Walton 1990: 183). Whether these reservations about the possibility of systematic theory in this matter are justified, and, if they are, what their consequences for the interpretation of works of narrative fiction might be, continue to be important components of a lively controversy.

There is one other debate about narrative that I want to introduce very briefly and only as a conclusion to this chapter. It concerns an easy and, as I see it, a pernicious kind of skepticism about narrative and narration that deserves much more critical attention than it has tended to receive. Jonathan Culler claims that ". . . the basic question for theory in the domain of narrative is this: is narrative a fundamental form of knowledge (giving knowledge of the world through its sense-making) or is it a rhetorical structure that distorts as much as it reveals? Is narrative a source of knowledge or of delusion?" (Culler 1997: 94). Culler is certainly right that skeptical questions of this ilk have figured prominently in recent discussions of narrative, but it is hard to make out just what the import of these questions is supposed to be. The skepticism about narratives that is characteristically on offer strikes me as a vulgar brand.

In the first place, fictional narratives do not, at the first level of endeavor, purport to offer us knowledge: they primarily prescribe imaginings and not beliefs. Second, it is plain that most non-fiction narratives present a certain amount of genuine knowledge about the events they portray, but they may also convey falsehoods, distortions, and, less frequently, out-and-out absurdities, and may do so with a certain amount of rhetorical flourish. On the other hand, narrations in works of both fiction and non-fiction are frequently significantly infused with rhetoric. Nevertheless, rhetorical persuasion is not, as such, incompatible with knowledge. Rhetoric may very well convince an audience of something true. In fact, one would expect the mix of truth and error in narratives to vary substantially from one instance to another. After all, narrative is a loosely defined form or collection of forms that easily accommodates both knowledge and false opinion, and no overall question about the epistemic integrity of the narrative mode makes obvious good sense.

As a rule, narratives are thick with causal claims, and, of course, it is possible to entertain some kind of global skepticism about causation. However, skeptical discussions of narrative do not mount systematic challenges against the very idea of cause and effect, and it would be hard to do so successfully in any case. Hence it is unlikely that universal doubts about causality, or other types of explanatory connection, form the basis of general anti-narrative concerns. Yet, a narrative is necessarily selective in the events it picks out to explain, and it is selective, for a given phenomenon, in the accounting of causal factors it draws up. Some of the selectivity is orchestrated by the global aim of constructing an illuminating pattern of explanation and evaluation for the episodes under examination, and both the principles that guide the selection and the guiding objective of evaluative intelligibility are potential sources of critical suspicion in connection with the explanatory dimension of narrative.

For instance, when a 'correct' judgment has been made that an event E caused another event F, the correctness of the claim is normally grounded in the narrower fact that E was among the causal factors that helped give rise to F. The explanatory judgment identifies E from out of all the events, circumstances, and conditions that also played a productive or facilitating role for F. For instance, it may be true enough that certain of an agent's desires and beliefs were causes of her action; but the psychological explanation may leave out larger social and economic forces that equally shaped her behavior in the context. And the exclusion of social determinants from the explanation may serve a questionable ideological agenda or promote other ends that deserve self-conscious scrutiny themselves. Here the objection to such a narrative will not be that it is predominantly false. It will be that the narrative paints a limited and severely distorted picture of the confluence of causal factors that produced the targeted narrative actions. What is more, the repeated exclusion of perfectly legitimate causes— political causes, for example—may yield grounds for misgivings about the world-view that governed the choice of admissible explanations. Nevertheless, doubts of these types need to be dealt with in terms appropriate to each individual case. Selection in narrative is unavoidable, and the selective discriminations in a particular history, fictional or non-fictional, may be altogether sound and proper in the epistemic setting that gave rise to them. None of the considerations just rehearsed supports a general skepticism about 'narrative' as such.

As discussed earlier, story audiences are inclined to want their narratives to have 'apt and satisfying' conclusions, or at least to fall into other large-scale configurations of explanatory significance. It is this hungering after 'narrative meaning' that prompts some of the most persistent skeptical reservations about familiar strategies of plot construction. Audiences are likely to accept one narrative account over an alternative, because the former seems to cast the depicted actions in an especially intelligible light— a light that promotes an apparently convincing assessment of them. However, many theorists of narrative suppose that intelligibility and evaluability are largely conventional attributes that have simply been 'projected upon' the relevant actions without having any justifying basis in the facts. In the passage by Culler quoted above, he may be presupposing that these and similar normative attributes are merely 'rhetorical' considerations that move readers to adopt some preferred story even in the absence of genuine 'evidential' considerations in its favor.

Now, claims of this sort could turn out to be right, but once again, we are being offered a sweeping brand of skepticism that questions the objectivity and rational grounding of our ordinary frameworks of explanation and evaluation. It would require a very general argument, framed in detail and attentive to key distinctions, to render any of these fashionable skepticisms particularly plausible. Recent theory of narrative has elaborated at great length its qualms about the structures and functions of storytelling, but in my opinion the underlying issues have not been substantially advanced. This is not to deny that there are important questions about the epistemology of narrative, but it is to express a hope for more nuanced and more judicious investigations of them in the future.

In any case, with this short survey of narratology as a backdrop, we will turn back in the next chapter to more specific questions about the nature of audio-visual narration in movies. It will be questions about narration that will chiefly concern me here, but I will also discuss briefly the murkier topic of whether audio-visual 'narration' presupposes, sometimes or always, the existence of a fictive audio-visual 'narrator'—a constructed someone who fictionally is telling the story in audio-visual terms.

PART II

Narratives and Narration

2

Le Grand Imagier Steps Out: On the Primitive Basis of Film Narration

It was Christian Metz who first introduced me to *le grand imagier*, or at least Metz first introduced him to me under that elegant description. Here is the famous passage in which Metz evokes the mysterious figure in question:

The spectator [of a narrative film] perceives images which have been obviously selected (they could have been other images) and arranged (their order could have been different). In a sense, he is leafing through an album of predetermined pictures, and it is not he who is turning the pages but some 'master of ceremonies,' some 'grand image-maker' ... situated somewhere behind the film, and representing the basis that makes the film possible.[1]

Metz is endorsing the view that narrative films routinely have 'filmic narrators,' the counterparts, in cinema, of the more familiar 'verbal' narrators in works of literature. The filmic narrators, he tells us, conduct their business by selecting and arranging film images instead of sentences in a linguistic text.[2]

However, this apparently appealing idea has set off an explosion of controversy and debate in film studies. A number of distinguished writers have worked out elaborate theories about the nature of cinematic narrators and their proper job description.[3] Despite the energetic theorizing, it seems fair to say that there is precious little agreement among the different theories and a plethora of confusion on the subject. Indeed, some authors have maintained that cinematic narrators do not exist, at least in

---

[1] Metz (1974), 20–21. In fact, Metz credits the concept and the phrase to the French phenomenologist Albert Laffay.

[2] In this passage, Metz makes reference only to the image track and not to the soundtrack. Many other writers on film narration speak only of the visual aspects of 'the primitive basis' of film narration. For simplicity, the hypotheses I formulate and my discussion of them will largely conform to this practice. However, I assume in these discussions that the chief views under scrutiny can readily be reformulated as counterpart hypotheses about *diegetic* sound.

[3] The literature on this subject is immense. For a useful survey, see part 3, 'Film-narratology' in Stam, *et al.* (1992), 95–117. This section was written by Burgoyne. Of course, movies have 'narrators' in a number of more restricted senses of the term. The voice-over narrator is probably the most familiar of these. I will not be discussing these more restricted concepts of 'narrator' and 'narration' in this chapter, but the omission is not meant to suggest that questions about the nature and roles of the more specialized narrators are unimportant. Their importance and interest are amply documented in Fleishman (1991).

standard movies.[4] And these debates have sputtered on for a long time and over many pages.

It is not my ambition in this chapter to side with friends of the grand image-maker or with his enemies. In fact, I think that the literature on this topic has tended to mix together different issues that ought to be kept distinct. In what follows, I will try to do some disentangling—to set out certain questions that need to be settled first before we speculate (or refuse to speculate) about the leading attributes a cinematic narrator might have. By the end of the discussion, I will identify a simple conception of what narration in film might be which has attracted little notice despite the fact that it has merits which should be explored further.

I. The ontological status of film narration

In his book *Coming to Terms*, Seymour Chatman has argued that fairly minimal considerations establish that all fictional stories, whether they are told, shown, or enacted, imply the occurrence of a 'narration' of the relevant fictional events, and, correlatively, imply the existence of a narrator—the agent of narration.[5] Chatman allows that, if the terms 'narration' and 'narrator' carry too strongly the connotation of *verbal* tellings and tellers of fictional tales, then in cases where the fictional story has been shown, we can speak instead of a 'show-er' or '(visual) presenter' of the fictional narrative. Nevertheless, it is his position that the show-er of a fictional story plays the same functional role within a primarily visual work as verbal tellers play in literary works of fiction. Therefore, both are properly subsumed under a general category of 'narrator.' For instance, Chatman states, "It stands to reason that if shown stories are to be considered narratives, they must be 'narrated,' and only an overly restrictive definition of 'to narrate'—identifying it solely with telling—keeps that observation from being self-evident. To 'show' a narrative, I maintain, no less than to 'tell' it, is to 'present it narratively' or to 'narrate' it."[6] Subsequently, he adds, "I would argue that every narrative is by definition narrated—that is, narratively presented—and that narration, narrative presentation, entails an agent even when the agent bears no sign of human personality."[7] The argumentation in these and surrounding passages is not entirely clear (as we will see), but the following is a plausible reconstruction of Chatman's line of thought. If an audience is presented with a 'text' which visually or verbally conveys a series of fictional occurrences, then the text serves as a medium or instrument by means of which the events and situations of the story are progressively shown or told. Thus, the text is understood to be the product of an *activity* of either showing or telling the events that constitute the story, an activity

---

[4] Bordwell (1985), 61–66, and my *Narration in Light: Studies in Cinematic Point of View* (1986), 132–137. My views on this topic have changed, as the present chapter will reveal.
[5] Chatman (1990).   [6] Ibid., 113.   [7] Ibid., 115.

that proceeds in a certain temporal order. Moreover, given that such a narrating activity is presupposed, there must be an *agent*, also presupposed, who performs the relevant activity of showing and telling. Chatman is at pains to insist that the narrating agency need not be human or humanlike, but that claim is not one that will concern us in the present discussion.

What needs to be investigated, from the very outset, is the notion that a narrative text is to be conceived as the product and instrument of a narrating activity. In the case of literary works of fiction, the claim is ambiguous in a familiar way, and the ambiguity is important when one turns, as Chatman does, to the narration of fiction films. The text of the novel *David Copperfield* conveys the fictional story of David's early adventures. But, in writing the novel, Charles Dickens *told* (verbally constructed) the story of David's adventures, and the text is the actual product of his writing. But, in the novel itself, it is fictional that David *tells* (recounts) the story of his own adventures, and it is fictional for the reader that the text is the product of his activity of telling. This distinction between the *actual* telling of the Copperfield story by Dickens and the *fictional* telling of that story by the narrator, David, is, as noted, well established.

However, this distinction does not simply concern, as it were, actual and fictional instances of the same kind of activity. We should observe that the type or force of an actual telling of a fictional tale is typically different from the type or force of the fictional telling that supervenes upon it. Characteristically, in the work *David Copperfield*, it is fictional that the narrator asserts that such and such events (actually) took place, while, in writing the relevant parts of the text, Dickens does not, actually or fictionally, assert these same propositions. Indeed, very often, he is not asserting any propositions at all. If Dickens is directly performing any type of 'illocutionary act,' it is this: he is using his words to make it fictional in the novel both that David asserted the propositions and, in most instances, that those very propositions are true. On the other hand, if the narrator is a storytelling narrator, then it is fictional that the narrator is using the words to make it fictional in his/her story that certain things took place.[8] By contrast, the author of *The Exhaustive Cliff Notes for David Copperfield* also tells in full detail the story of David's adventures, but his telling consists of actual assertions about what is fictional in the Dickens novel.[9] Clearly, we have to be careful about what sort of activity any particular 'telling' of a fictional story specifically amounts to.

In the case of fictional tellings, the text both represents the narrative events and is itself implicitly represented in a certain way. Very roughly, the sentences of the text, in virtue of their semantic properties, represent types of situations or events. But those same sentences are implicitly represented—are correctly imagined by the reader—as utterances or inscriptions of someone who thereby asserts that an event or situation of the designated type actually took place. Hence, the text makes it fictional that the

[8] For the concept of a 'storytelling narrator,' see Walton (1990), 368–371.
[9] This is not one of the more popular or helpful works in the Cliff Notes series.

utterer or inscriber asserted that thus-and-so, and typically, either by convention or reasonable inference, it also makes it fictional 'in the story' that thus-and-so obtains. In the standard case, the text fictionally describes the narrative events, while, 'in the same breath,' it 'scripts' the narrator's fictional speech-act performance. It will emerge shortly that similar discriminations have to be made in connection with fictional showings.

It has become normal practice, when we speak of 'the narration' and/or 'the narrator' of a work of literary fiction, to be referring to the fictional telling of the story and to the fictional or fictionalized agent of that telling. Thus, one assumes that Chatman intends to be maintaining that a text which shows a fictional story gives rise, as a part of the total work, to a *fictional* activity of showing that depicts narrative events, and that the existence of such a fictional showing implies that there is a *fictional* or *fictionalized* show-er of the story. At the conclusion of his positive arguments, he affirms that he has been concerned with "the someone or something *in the text* [my emphasis] who or which is conceived as presenting (or transmitting) the set of signs that constitute it."[10] However, it is hard to see how the considerations he adduces support his stated conclusion. On the face of things, the most that Chatman's considerations show is that there cannot be an actual activity of showing the events of a fictional story in the absence of an actual agent who performed the activity. This claim can also be questioned, but let it stand. It still does not follow from this thesis that the showing of a fictional narrative invokes a fictional activity of showing (in any sense) the relevant series of narrative events. In the remainder of this chapter, I will be primarily concerned with the thesis that fiction films presuppose the existence of some narrative-establishing activity of fictional showing. The problems that this claim engenders are surprisingly delicate. Therefore, I will largely leave aside the question that most vexes Chatman and many other writers, i.e., given the assumption that there *is* a presupposed activity of fictional showing, does that imply that there is also a fictional or fictionalized cinematic narrator? I will explore the more restricted topic: is there even a primitive basis for a fictional activity of cinematic narration?

II. Fictional showing and showing the fictional

I believe that Chatman does not see how there can be an issue about the existence of fictional showings. He thinks, in effect, that the concept of 'a fictional story that is shown' somehow implies the concept of 'a fictional showing of the story.' Nevertheless, it is doubtful that any such relatively direct connection exists. Grounds for doubt are illustrated by the following rudimentary form of visual representation. Nixon presents, by means of the production of certain hand shadows, a fictional story in which a certain hawk attacks and kills a hapless mole. The hand shadows, occurring in a

---

[10] Chatman (1990), 116.

field of light, depict the hawk, the mole, and their respective actions, and Nixon is the agent who actually produces the shadow 'text.' However, there is no obvious reason to postulate that the hand shadows are themselves the fictional product of some fictional activity of 'showing-as-actual' the elements of the depicted tale. Indeed, the very idea that this might be so appears to lack a determinate sense, and, at a minimum, one would want some explanation of and justification for this claim. It is wholly unclear what type of 'showing' could be fictionally instantiated in such a case. The only showing that appears to be involved in "The Hawk and Mole Story" is the actual showing by Nixon of the pertinent fictional events. In this example at least, the 'text' does not instantiate the crucial property of representing and being represented at one and the same time. And yet, it is just this status of the text as both means and object of representation that is basic to the creation of fictional tellings in literary fiction.

The hand shadow example illustrates an important point about the showing of fictional events. If I want to show you what *actually* happened in certain historical circumstances, then I might do so in at least one of two ways. If we are appropriately present at the circumstances in question, I can direct your perceptual attention to the events themselves as they take place. But, alternatively, I might show you the events by displaying to you a picture or series of pictures that visually record, accurately and in enough detail, the historical episode of interest. Similarly, if I want to show you a fictional episode, I can show you a series of fictional events by exhibiting to you a suitable series of pictures in which it is fictional that events of the envisaged kinds take place. My showing you those pictures is sufficient to present the story, and there need not be facts about the pictures, and about the context of their imaginative reception, that make it fictional or make-believe for the viewer that the pictures are the products of some additional 'fictional showing.'[11] It is for that reason that a special argument needs to be given to justify an inference from 'T depicts the fictional incidents in a narrative N' to the conclusion 'T involves a fictional showing of the incidents in N.'

Similar thoughts apply to the visual presentation of a fictional story in a standard comic strip or comic book, although this case illustrates an additional complication. The story is primarily transmitted by presenting to the reader a sequence of cartoon drawings, each of which depicts a fictional event or situation in the unfolding narrative.[12] Here, as before, it seems that the frames that make up the strip are not imagined to be the upshot of some kind of fictional showing. As in the hand shadow example, it is doubtful that there are any general grounds for positing such a fictional showing and obscure what sort of activity one could be positing. However, we should not state the conclusion too broadly. It is easy to think of possible comic strips in which a fictional

---

[11] In this chapter, I understand the concept of 'being fictional (in a work or in a game of make-believe)' and the concept of 'being make-believe (for a viewer or reader)' along the general lines that are set out in Walton (1990).

[12] Of course, even the case of comic strips is more complicated than this. Usually, they will include some verbal narration in their frame inserts. And this is not to mention the representation of the characters' speech in 'word balloons.'

showing would be implicated. The frames of the comic strip could be rendered in such a fashion that they are themselves represented as being, say, photographs taken by a witness to the events depicted. Going a step further, one can conceive of ways in which the represented character of the frames and the nature of their selection could convey fictional facts about the personality and sensibility of the 'implied' photographer. In this example, there plainly is a fictional activity of showing the story that the viewer is to imagine, i.e., the fictional activity of taking and assembling the photographs. And here there *is* a fictional agent of that activity, i.e., the fictional eyewitness and photographer. Various other more subtle and sophisticated strategies would give rise to analogous fictional results.

The example of comic strips suggests a couple of cautionary morals. First, we should not ask, in the absence of further qualification, whether showings of fictional stories do or do not engender fictional showings or (visual) presentations. The answer is: some do and some do not. Moreover, the same mixed answer generally holds for narrower categories of texts, e.g., the comic strip. Second, when a text that shows its fictional story does involve a fictional showing, it does so in virtue of some relatively clear-cut representational strategy implicit in and appropriate to the imaginative context of the text's reception. Detailed facts about the particular nature of the text and facts about the proper mode of apprehending that text serve to prompt us to imagine about the text that it is the product of an appropriate kind of fictional showing. Naturally, in the case of writing and reading works of literary fiction, the basic components of the implicit representational strategies are highly familiar, ubiquitously deployed, and almost automatically invoked for the reader on the basis of pretty minimal cues. But in other cases—the comic strip is a good example of this—rather special strategies of implicit representation of the text have to be more distinctly set in place.

These conclusions would not be accepted by Chatman, and there is a line of argument against them which is hinted at in some of his discussions. Consider, for example, these remarks: "[W]e must avoid the metaphor that the camera 'sees' *the events and existents in the story world* [my emphasis] at such and such a distance, from such and such an angle. Rather it *presents* them at those distances and angles." Or a bit later: "The convention [in fiction films] is that the particular rectangle of visible material constitutes a 'favored view,' a selection of the implied author which the cinematic narrator is delegated to present."[13] The import of these and related passages is murky, but I believe that we can articulate the basic idea behind them in the following fashion.

First, we are concerned with cases in which a fictional story has been shown by means of a text which either is a single picture or consists of a series of pictures. Let us suppose, in addition, that we are dealing with visual representations that determine an implied vantage point upon the scene. That is, we suppose that these are visual representations each of which determines a position in the implied space of the picture,

---

[13] Chatman (1990), 155–156.

a position such that the scene depicted is represented as if viewed from that fictional location. This added supposition will cover all of the cases which we will henceforth be investigating. When we are looking at 'perspectival' representations of this sort, viewers normally imagine and are intended to imagine seeing the objects and events depicted in the image, and, moreover, they imagine seeing these contents from a reasonably distinctive visual perspective.

Second, from these suppositions we can construct the relevant argument as follows. In imagining that they actually see the depicted scene, a part of what viewers thereby imagine is that the contents of the scene are being displayed or exhibited to their perception. In the case of fiction film, they imagine the movie shots before them as offering a perspectival view of those contents, and it is the function of the shots to prescribe an imagining of this kind. So, it is in this sense that the shots of a film *present* a view of or perspective on some spatio-temporal slice of the 'story world' and *show* us what that view contains. Of course, it is only a fiction that 'the events and existents' in that world have been presented and shown in this manner. Both the constituents of the story and the visual exhibition of them are fictional constructions of the work, although the items thus presented belong to the world of the narrative while the 'presentings' of them belong to the 'world' of the narration. Still, these considerations should be enough to convince us that fiction films *do* incorporate a series of 'fictional showings' in their narration, i.e., the fictional presentation of views of characters, actions, and circumstances which are themselves merely fictional. This argument, if correct, would demonstrate that any or almost any showing of a fictional scene or story involves a fictional showing (to the viewer) of the represented elements. Moreover, given the generality of the considerations deployed in the argument, it should work for comic strips as well and would undercut the remarks I made earlier.

A similar argument is developed in Jerrold Levinson's article "Film Music and Narrative Agency."[14] Levinson affirms there his broad agreement with the claims of Chatman sketched above. But Levinson is more careful and explicit than Chatman is about the distinction between fictional showings of fictional events in movies, on the one hand, and actual showings of the movie images, on the other. Having correctly highlighted the distinction, he maintains that there *is* a coherent conception of what *fictional* showings in standard movies consist of. He says, for example:

The presenter [show-er] in a film presents, or gives perceptual access to, the story's sights and sounds; the presenter in film is thus, in part, a sort of *perceptual enabler*. Such perceptual enabling is what we must implicitly posit to explain how it is we are, even imaginarily, perceiving what we are perceiving of the story, in the manner and order in which we are perceiving it. The notion of a presenter, whose main charge is the providing of perceptual access on the fictional world, is simply the best default assumption available for how we make sense of narrative fiction film.[15]

[14] See Levinson's fine essay, Levinson (1996), 248–282.
[15] Ibid., 252.

Notice that Levinson asserts that a fictional activity of giving the viewer 'perceptual access to the story's sights and sounds' is needed to explain the viewer's fictional activity of perceiving the sights and sounds in question. There is some vagueness in Levinson's description of what the presenter does by way of enabling the viewer's perception of narrative events, but this quotation and other remarks in his article certainly suggest something like the reasoning delineated above. Let us call this proposal 'the Fictional Showing Hypothesis.'

However, Levinson's statement of the hypothesis seems crucially schematic at a certain point, as does my earlier extrapolation from the Chatman quotations. What is the activity of the presenter by means of which the audience is given perceptual access to portions of a fictional world? What kind of displaying or exhibiting of fictional constituents is supposed to be in play? I mentioned earlier that there are different ways in which I can provide you with perceptual access to a certain range of actual sights and sounds. If the sights and sounds are in our immediate vicinity, I may be able to single them out ostensively. Otherwise, I may be able to supply you with adequate recordings of them. Levinson simply does not specify which of these means of affording perceptual access (or others) are constitutive of the fictional showings of stories on film that he is prepared to postulate. Nevertheless, it seems unlikely that his visual 'presenter' shows us recorded images of the story world. The actual film-makers have already pre-empted that task.[16] The most natural interpretation of Levinson's proposals takes him to be arguing that the movie's image-track leads viewers to imagine that they are seeing the events of the narrative, as we may put it, 'face-to-face.'

After all, if it is fictional for the viewer that she is seeing a scene in the story, then, apparently, it should be correlatively fictional for her that the items in the scene are located, at a viewable distance and a suitable angle, before her gaze. This means, in other words, that it is fictional in her perceptual game of make-believe that she has somehow been situated in the picture's implied space and has had her visual attention directed from that vantage point to the objects and events that it encompasses. On this interpretation, the work of the film narration (in its visual dimension) is to effect a fictional placing of the scene in front of the viewer's receptive and attentive eyes so that she may see it from just that place. Naturally, it is not fictional *in the work* that the viewer occupies such a position and is present as an observer on the scene. It is fictional only in the viewer's imaginative perceptual engagement with the film that this is so. I will call this interpretation 'the Face-to-Face Version' of the Fictional Showing Hypothesis and assume, at least tentatively, that it is the position that Levinson has in mind. Similarly, I will take him to be urging that the movie's sound-track prompts viewers to imagine being 'within earshot' of the characters and their circumstances and hearing the diegetic speech and other sounds in that direct fashion. Certainly, whether either Levinson or Chatman would endorse this version of the Fictional Showing

---

[16] However, we will have reason to reconsider this assumption later.

Hypothesis, it can seem, as explained above, the almost inevitable elaboration of their explicit claims.[17]

III. Fictional seeing from a perspective

Late in *The Spirit of the Beehive* (Victor Erdice, 1973), the young protagonist is sitting at night beside a river, and, bending slightly forward, she sees her own reflection in the waters. She sees herself transparently imaged in the gentle river, until the image of her is rumpled by the water's slight current. Eventually she comes to see her face replaced by the troubled visage of Frankenstein's monster. (She has seen the movie *Frankenstein* at the beginning of the film, and the monster, or at least his spirit, has haunted her from that time forward.) Or, in any case she now sees or, more probably, she imagines seeing this familiar fiction before her here, presented in the medium of the river (see figure 2). For me this crucial moment in the movie is emblematic of the special kind of perceptual engagement that I take to be at the primitive heart of the way in which we relate to movie imagery. I hope that these remarks combined with the wonderful sequence of transmuting imagery will go a certain way toward communicating my thought. But, if it doesn't, let it pass for now. I will take up the project of further explication as we go along.

So, as I have been arguing, the Face-to-Face Version is implausible. It is true that when people actually see a scene from a certain visual perspective, they are, in fact, located in a position which, given the circumstances, offers them that perspective. But it does not follow that if a person *imagines* seeing a scene from a certain perspective, then he thereby also imagines being at a place which offers him that view. Similarly,

Figure 2 Ana's reflection in the river changes into an image of the monster

[17] Chatman, in particular, makes several remarks that can be interpreted as repudiating the Face- to-Face Version. For example, he says, "The cinema frame, too, presents events and characters from a post this side of the story world; there is never any question about what is included and what excluded from our perception" (Chatman 1990: 156). If these and similar comments are directed against the Face-to-Face Version, then it continues to remain quite unclear what his fictional showings amount to. On the other hand, he may be insisting that (as I would put it) it is fictional only in the viewer's game of make-believe that she sees the objects and events in the story and it is not fictional in either the narration (discourse) or the narrative that she sees these items. The second point is correct, but it is not incompatible with the position of the Face-to-Face Version.

when, in viewing a perspectival visual representation, a person imagines seeing a scene from the visual perspective established by the pictorial field,[18] he usually does not imagine himself occupying a point in the picture's implied space that would yield this visual perspective and seeing the scene from that place. As a rule, I think that it is false that we ordinarily imagine ourselves being anywhere in the depicted or implied space of the image. Speaking specifically of movie imagies, Gregory Currie has registered the intuitive objection forcefully:

> For me the most striking thing about the view . . . is that it seems to me to misdescribe the *experience* of movie watching. Do I really identify my visual system, in imagination, with the camera, and imagine myself to be placed where the camera is? Do I imagine myself on the battlefield, mysteriously immune to the violence around me, lying next to the lovers, somehow invisible to them, viewing Earth from deep space one minute, watching the dinner guests from the ceiling the next? None of this corresponds to my own experience of movie watching.[19]

Despite lapses on this question in an earlier work of mine, I think that Currie is right about this.[20] In general, when one views a movie, one does not imagine oneself to be present within the depicted and/or off-screen space of the story.

Our ordinary ways of describing our perceptual connections to story space provoke confusion on this topic. Often we do say things like "In viewing that shot from *Rear Window*, I saw Thorwald's threatening gesture from Jeff's apartment window in the building across the court." But we need to distinguish two distinct claims that can be naturally conveyed by formulations of the form,

(1)   In viewing picture A, I imagine seeing X from position P,

where P is a place in the space depicted or implied by the picture. One claim we could be making is the following:

(1a)   In viewing A, I imagine being situated at P and seeing X from that position.

But, the same words could also be used to say,

(1b)   In viewing A, I imagine seeing X from the visual perspective one would have if one were situated at P.

When we make statements like the one about the shot from *Rear Window*, we are likely to intend the (1b) version of our utterance and not, it seems to me, the version in (1a). This is a case in which the face-value proposition expressed by the words is not the

---

[18]   I take this use of 'pictorial field' from Budd (1995), 64. Briefly, he states that the pictorial field is "the visible nature of a picture's surface."

[19]   Currie (1995), 171.

[20]   See my *Narration in Light*, (Wilson, 1995) 55. Currie is here responding to this passage in my book. The passage he quotes was intended as metaphorical, but he is right in judging that it is best taken as a metaphor for what he calls the 'Imagined Observer thesis.'

message we normally aim to convey. Understood in the manner of (1b), such statements often report our experience correctly. Movie advertisements sometimes promise to place us "in the middle of the [depicted] action," but we recognize that this is simply hyperbole and hype. Currie correctly insists that reading of instances of (1) along the lines of (1a) would usually misdescribe what we imagine in seeing films and other perspectival visual representations.

However, Currie also wants to draw a further, much stronger conclusion, and his conclusion depends upon denying, in effect, that there is a substantive distinction between (1b) and (1a). Currie contends, plausibly enough, that

(2)   If in viewing a picture A, I imagine seeing X, then I thereby imagine seeing X from the visual perspective established by the pictorial field of A.

But, as before, let P be the depicted or implied position in the fictional space of A which a person would have to fictionally occupy in order to see X from the visual perspective in question. Call this "the [fictional] vantage point in [the implied space of] A."[21] Currie maintains that if, in viewing picture A, I imagine seeing X from the visual perspective established by A, then I thereby imagine being at P and seeing X from that vantage point. In other words, Currie holds that

(3)   If (1b) is the case, then (1a) also obtains.

Since he holds, as the previous quotation indicates, that viewers never (or very rarely) imagine being at the vantage point in the picture and seeing from there, he infers from this in combination with thesis (3) that

(4)   There is never (or almost never) a visual perspective from which viewers imagine seeing the depicted contents of a picture.

Then, from this step, in conjunction with (2), he goes on to conclude that we never (or almost never) *imagine seeing* the depicted contents of the picture at all. Naturally, if Currie's line of argument is sound, then *no* version of the Fictional Showing Hypothesis could succeed. There cannot be a fictional process or activity of giving perceptual access to viewers of the picture if it is generally not fictional for viewers that they perceive the depicted scenes in the first place.

Here is Currie's own formulation of the point: "To see *is* to see from a point of view: there is no such thing as nonperspectival seeing. You cannot imagine, of a certain scene represented to you on screen, that you are seeing it, but not that you are seeing it from any point of view. To imagine seeing it is to imagine seeing it from the point of

---

[21]   Very often, we are able to specify the vantage point only in pretty rough terms. We can do no better than, e.g., "I see the contents of the picture from such-and-such a distance and from so-and-so an angle," where 'such-and-such' and 'so-and-so' are vague. Especially in paintings, it is only sometimes that anything substantial is suggested about the specific character of the 'place' in question. In films, where earlier or later shots may have established the spatial layout of the scene in considerable detail, we typically can describe our 'vantage point' in a more determinate way.

view defined by the perspectival structure of the picture."[22] Currie has made precisely the mistake that the conflation of (1a) and (1b) so readily encourages. Not only is it possible for a viewer of a picture to imagine seeing the pictured prospect from a certain visual perspective without, at the same time, imagining being at the vantage point in the picture, but normally this is just what viewers do. They imagine having perspectival visual perceptions of the contents of the picture from, as we might say for brevity, an unoccupied perspective.

In looking at a picture, the viewer imagines having a veridical visual experience of the items in a certain scene, and those elements, as the viewer imagines seeing them, have what Currie here calls "a perspectival structure." That is, various of the items are presented as foreshortened, as overlapping one another, and as having appropriate relative occlusion sizes.[23] Thus, the viewer imagines seeing the scene from the visual perspective defined by the network of properties and relations. The visual perspective may well be the one a viewer would or might have if he were located at a certain site in relation to that scene, but the identity of a perspectival view is not constituted by its relation to a vantage point from which it could have been secured. Hence, the question is: Is it possible to imagine seeing the scene from a specified perspective without imagining being at the vantage point and obtaining one's visual perspective from that position? In the final sentence of the quotation above, Currie illegitimately forecloses the pertinent option by running the two concepts together under the dangerous rubric of "point of view." The question here is a complex one and deserves more space than I can give it, but the following reflections provide grounds for answering it in the affirmative.

Just as I can imagine romping in the buff on Neptune without imagining anything about how I came to do so or about what makes it possible for me to be dancing on that distant planet, so also I can imagine having a (veridical) visual experience of a scene without imagining anything about how I came to have the experience or about what enables me to have it. In particular, I may imagine nothing about whether I am having that experience *because* I am situated face-to-face with what I see. These further matters, normally essential either to visiting other planets or to seeing a scene, are simply left *indeterminate* in my imagining.[24]

Perhaps the following thought experiment will help to establish that the concept of 'visual experience from an unoccupied perspective' is at least minimally coherent. We seek to conceive of *one* way in which I might imagine seeing a scene from a certain visual perspective without imagining, as part of this, that I am seeing from the implied vantage point. (1) I can imagine in detail the qualitative and perspectival character of the kind of visual experience I would (or might) have if I were to look at a scene S from

---

[22] Currie (1995), 178.

[23] For a helpful summary account of perspective in painting and of some notions upon which depicted perspective depends, see the entry on "Perspective" by Hyman (1992), 323–327.

[24] Walton offers much the same response to Currie; see Walton (1997) 68–70.

a 'face-to-face' position P. (2) I can imagine having a visual experience of just that character while imagining that I am *not*, as I have the experience, situated at the vantage point P. Maybe, in the broader context of my imagining, I imagine that a devious neurophysiologist is causing me to have that very visual experience while I am sitting in his laboratory. (3) Finally, I can imagine having this same experience while, nevertheless, imagining of the experience that it constitutes an instance of my *seeing* S. Thus, it may be a part of the broader context of my imagining, that the processes whereby the neurophysiologist induces this visual experience (and others) in me are such that my having the visual experiences he produces count as a kind of 'prosthetic' seeing of S and other scenes. Here, then, is a case in which I imagine myself seeing a scene from an unoccupied visual perspective.

I hasten to add that in ordinary cases when we imagine having a visual experience from an unoccupied perspective, our imaginings are *not* contextualized in this manner. First, I do not imagine that I am *not* at P—imaginatively, it is indeterminate where, if anywhere, I am. And, second, I do not imagine anything about the causes and conditions of my having the relevant visual experience—it is imaginatively indeterminate how this came about. Still, the fact that all these important matters are left indeterminate in what I imagine does not preclude me from imagining seeing S from a P-like perspective while I am not at P. The content of such an imagining has the same kind of minimal coherence as the content 'running naked on the surface of Neptune,' and each content specifies something I can imagine.

Similarly, when looking at a representational picture, we usually imagine having a (veridical) visual experience of the scene depicted, where the qualitative and perspectival character of the experience corresponds in detail to the pictorial field of the picture we are viewing. And we do this without imagining that we are somehow present at the vantage point in the picture. As before, we can imagine this perception from an unoccupied perspective because we imagine nothing about the potential fictional circumstances that would have enabled us to have the visual experience we imagine. Of course, we know a great deal about what it is before our eyes which is actually cueing our experience. The pictorial field prompts and guides our imagining of the visual experience (e.g., determines a certain perspectival structure for it) without establishing much of anything about the causal conditions of the imagined experience. This, I believe, is the standard case when we view perspectival visual representations.

It is the *standard* case, but not the only one possible. For it *is* possible for a perspectival image (a painting, say) to lead the viewer to imagine himself being at the vantage point in the picture and seeing from that place. The artistic strategies that are meant to elicit such an imagining are not frequently deployed, but when they are, they represent an important aspect of how we comprehend the visual significance that the painting offers us. Richard Wollheim, in *Painting as an Art*, describes a class of paintings that involve what he calls "internal spectators," and it partially defines the class that these paintings are visually and dramatically so constituted that they are intended to induce the spectator into imagining himself at the vantage point in the picture.[25] Wollheim carefully delineates the different ways that various fully classic paintings rely upon the imaginative endeavor in question. For example, he argues that Manet's *Le Bar aux Folies-Bergère* is a striking instance of the category.[26] A viewer of the painting is encouraged by a panoply of its key features to imagine himself as standing before the bar and as seeing the barmaid with her eyes averted from him. However, one can also conceive of a painting, broadly similar to the Manet both in subject matter and angle of depiction, in which we imagine seeing the barmaid standing behind the bar with her averted eyes, but one for which we have no inclination and are not meant to have any inclination to imagine *ourselves* standing in front of the bar. This example and others like it underscore the point that, in looking at the perspectival representation, imagining seeing a scene from a visual perspective is one kind of imaginative achievement, while imagining seeing from the picture's vantage point is of a different and somewhat more complicated kind. If so, it is a mistake to identify, as Currie does, the state of affairs described by (1a) with the one described in (1b).

Confusion about (3) is endemic in these debates. I have just argued that Currie's acceptance of (3) leads him to argue wrongly against the existence, or at least the prevalence, of imagined seeing in our viewing of images. But, if we look back to my reconstruction of the background considerations for the Face-to-Face Version of the Fictional Showing Hypothesis, we observe that the acceptance of (3) plays a crucial role in that argument as well. As Levinson correctly points out, in viewing perspectival pictures, we imagine seeing the scene from a certain visual perspective, and it seems to follow by way of (3) that we thereby imagine ourselves having been placed at a vantage point in the picture space and seeing the prospect from that site. But both parties to the disagreement are mistaken. It is (3) itself that should be rejected. It is hard to keep in focus that (3) is false, because, given our understandable temptation to waver between (1a) and (1b) interpretations of (1), the equivocal character of (3) lends it the deceptive guise of a tautology.

IV. The incoherence of some founding fictions

It is natural, especially for philosophers, to feel discomfort with the position outlined above. Let Q be a possible condition whose realization is obviously essential for it to be the case that P. I have claimed that it is possible for it to be fictional, in a work or game of make-believe, that P, despite the fact that it is not fictional in either the work or the game that Q. Worse yet, it can be fictional that P even though, if we were to take the first steps toward imagining how P could have come out, then the supplemented

---

[25] Wollheim (1987), ch. 3. There are some nice questions about how precisely Wollheim's position is best formulated, and he might object to aspects of my (very brief) statement of his views. However, I believe that nothing relevant to present concerns turns on any possible divergences.

[26] For his discussion of Manet's use of 'the spectator-in-the-picture,' see Wollheim (1987), 141–183.

fiction would be paradoxical or otherwise incoherent. Troubling as these claims may be, I think that we will have to learn to live with the discomfort. Kendall Walton has done a lot to support this somewhat severe prescription.[27]

It is not at all uncommon for it to be fictional for a reader or viewer that she is Φing and not fictional for her that she is in condition G, even though being in G is obviously required as a means to make it possible for her to Φ. In other words, what she imagines is *merely* minimally coherent. In many "Old Dark House" movies, it is fictional that the ghosts are completely invisible to human eyes, but audience members imagine seeing them as glowing, diaphanous creatures gliding among the furniture. Still, it is no part of the viewers' imaginings that they have special powers that permit them, unlike other human beings, to see ghosts. There are numerous similar examples, but I suspect that the threat of imminent paradox looms as most threatening when the coherence of the foundations of representational and/or narrational practices appear to be at risk—as in the domain of perspectival pictures discussed before. However, the tensions which exist in that case are hardly unique.

When a person reads the text of a work of literary fiction, she imagines herself to be reading the very words (word types) that fictionally were produced by the narrator of the tale. But paradox or incoherence easily impinges in this case also. To illustrate, we begin with what is admittedly a special kind of example, i.e., cases in which the reader imagines herself reading the narrator's own words despite the fact that there are propositions fictional in the work which imply that this should be fictionally impossible for her to do. Thus, it might be fictional for the reader that she is reading the narrator's diary even though it is clearly indicated, at the end of the work, that this diary must have been consumed in a story-culminating fire. When a reader steps back from the fiction and focuses upon the relevant facts, the situation will strike her as paradoxical. But in the course of reading the work, this same reader is likely to ignore or discount the conflict, and she surely will not stop imagining that what she is reading are the words of the diarist/narrator.

A more common and more subtle conflict of narrational background assumptions is the following. Again, it is usually fictional for the reader that the words she is reading were produced by the narrator, but it is often fictionally indeterminate how those words were initially produced by that narrator. That is, it is indeterminate whether fictionally the narrator originally uttered them out loud or only in his mind, or alternatively, set them down in writing. Moreover, in these same cases, it will also be fictionally indeterminate for the reader how those words came to be *transmitted* to her or to a readership in general. Nothing will fictionally connect an original production by the narrator of the words (whatever mode of production may have been involved) with the appearance 'in print' of the text of which the narrator's activity is fictionally the source. The reader will imagine nothing whatsoever about how the words came to

---

[27] See especially the section on "Silly Questions" in Walton (1990), 174–183.

be transcribed into a publicly distributed version.[28] Thus, the reader imagines reading a transcription of the narrator's own utterances or inscriptions, but her imagination does not specify anything about what makes it possible for her to do this. Fictionally, it is indeterminate how the reader can be acquainted, as she is, with the product of the narrator's storytelling performance.

Such indeterminacies at the core of the fictions that ground some types of literary narration open up the possibility that a related indeterminacy underlies our fictional perception of narrative events in film and that it does so deeply and extensively. This possibility suggests in turn a serious challenge to the *overall* approach of the Fictional Showing Hypothesis. Chatman and Levinson hold, and I have agreed with this, that it is fictional for movie viewers that they imagine seeing (on screen) the fictional activities of the characters portrayed. This fundamental fact, they conclude, implies that it is fictional for the viewer that the movie's image-track is the product of an 'activity' that somehow enables the viewer to see the narrative fictions. I have rejected the Face-to-Face Version of the Fictional Showing Hypothesis which says that the fictional activity of perceptual enabling is achieved by situating the viewer face-to-face with the story scenes. But now, our recent discussion demonstrates that it could be altogether fictionally indeterminate for movie viewers what, if anything, permits them to see episodes in cinematic worlds. There needs to be an argument to establish that such a fictional enabling activity is to be recognized as part of the work, an argument to rule out the hypothesis that audiences imagine seeing movie fictions without being expected to imagine a means by which such seeing would be achieved. Neither Chatman nor Levinson supplies the missing argument.

So far, then, we have no plausible reason for supposing that the showing of a fictional film story involves the fictional showing of the events related in the film. However, we have, in this discussion, bypassed an obvious dimension of fiction film which is potentially crucial to the topic. We have concentrated on the fact that cinematic images in fiction films depict fictional characters and situations, but we have ignored the fact that they do this by showing us actors and actresses in real places—cast members who play the characters and places that represent the narrative locales. If we factor in this extra dimension, an alternative conception emerges of what narration in fiction films might be.

Our discourse about movies wavers between reference to shots that are 'of' the cast and their performances and reference to shots said to be 'of' the characters and the fictional actions they perform. Normally, these vacillating forms of description cause no confusion, but plainly there is an ambiguity in our talk about the 'content' of shots in fictional film. Let us signal the rough distinction by saying that a shot is a *motion*

---

[28] David Hills, in correspondence, offers the following beautiful example of the point. He says, "*The Adventures of Huckleberry Finn* . . . represents itself as a carefully crafted 300 page memoir by its title character, a barely literate young man getting ready to light out for the territories because the prospect of any work that requires him to sit still terrifies him."

picture shot of the actual objects and events before the camera and that the same shot is a *movie story shot* of the fictional characters and their fictional behavior. Naturally, any movie story shot (in a given film) is also a motion picture shot, but not conversely. In fact, let X be a shot in movie M, a shot in which it is fictional that a certain character C performs an action A. Shot X, in M, is also a motion picture shot of the actor who portrays C making the movements that represent the action A. But, if X were edited into a documentary, *The Making of Movie M*, then, in the altered context, it would not be a movie story shot in which C does A. It would merely be a motion picture shot of the actor in the course of playing C. It is not a simple task to give an adequate positive account of the further conditions required for such a motion picture shot to be, in the full sense, a movie story shot, and I will not try to construct one here. Intuitively, a movie story shot is one which has as a primary function, in its filmic context, the role of making it fictional in the movie that P, where the fact that it is fictional that P sustains or elaborates the movie's narrative progress.

In any case, we start with the following proposal. If X is a movie story shot in M of a fictional scene S, then *it is fictional for the viewer of M* that X is a motion picture shot of that same scene S. In other words, fictionally for the viewer, it is as if the scene S actually took place, there exist motion picture shots of S, and X, as it occurs in M, is one of these. Viewers imagine that the events of the fictional narrative have been registered directly, without dramatic mediation, and that these events are exhibited to us 'on screen' in the projection of the film.

There are many potential questions about how exactly this proposal is to be construed, but let us set them aside for now. We have here the basis for an alternative account of the type of narrational activity which movies might implicitly invoke. That is, the fictional showing involved in a fiction film would be the fictional exhibition and sequential arrangement, by means of editing, of *motion picture shots* of the occurrences that constitute the story. On this view, although an image-track actually consists, as we well know, of a selection of motion picture shots of actors and actresses acting, we imagine and are intended to imagine that we are shown a selection of motion picture shots of fictional characters and their deeds. If one hears an echo of Metz in all of this, the fact is not surprising. Our new alternative sounds like a description of the business his great image-maker regularly conducts.

If one further aesthetic component were added to the proposal, the result would be, so to speak, a "Mediated Version" of the Fictional Showing Hypothesis. Suppose that we accept the thesis, developed and defended by Kendall Walton, that still photographs and motion picture shots are *transparent*.[29] Walton argues that, in seeing, e.g., a motion picture shot of a real scene S, viewers actually *see* the photographed scene, although, naturally, they see S in a rather special, mediated way; they see S *through* or *by means of* the motion picture photographs. Just as an observer can see a scene by means of

---

[29] Walton (1984), 801–806, and Walton (1997).

mirrors or through a telescope or on live TV, so, in the same natural sense of the word, viewers see photographed objects and events through or by means of photographs. If the transparency of photography is genuine, then our new account of the nature of film narration entails that when a viewer sees a movie story shot of a (fictional) scene S, then it is thereby fictional for her that she is actually seeing S by means of a motion picture shot. Thus, the presentation and ordering of actual motion picture shots in a fiction film have the function of fictionally enabling the viewer to see the progression of the fictional narrative, albeit to see this 'photographically.'

Gregory Currie gives glancing notice to the Mediated Version of the Fictional Showing Hypothesis, although he states it in a misleading manner. He says, "[T]he only candidate [for an alternative to the Face-to-Face Version] seems to be this: that we imagine someone to be filming the action as a documentary, and that we are seeing the visually restricted result." Currie, however, thinks that the supposed alternative can be dismissed quickly. He goes on to object that "[b]ut to imagine this (something I have never been aware of imagining) would be to imagine that the fiction contains as a part of the assumption that the action is being filmed by a camera crew and that we are watching the result. Occasionally, as with *Culloden* (Peter Weir, 1964) this would be an appropriate piece of imagining, but it certainly would not be for most fiction films."[30] In other words, it cannot be that, in watching a fiction film, the viewer imagines seeing a motion picture shot of the portrayed events, because imagining this would entail imagining that it is fictional, in the movie or for the viewer, that a motion picture camera was present in the fictional circumstances and that it photographed the events before its lens. But, in the standard case, it is not fictional, in the movie or for the viewer that a camera was at the scene. In fact, if anything, it is fictional that no camera was there at all.

This objection can seem devastating, but it is really just another instance of a philosophical outlook we have had ample reason to repudiate. It is true that if an actual scene is filmed, then a motion picture camera must be present to do the filming. It is the operation of the camera that enables that scene to be photographed and incorporated into a motion picture. However, we should not conclude from this unquestioned fact that if spectators imagine that a motion picture shot of a scene exists and has been displayed to them, they must also be imagining that the real world means for producing that type of state of affairs are realized as well. For all that has been said thus far, it should be an open question whether or not it is wholly indeterminate for a movie viewer how it is that S came to exist and to be selected for the film. I have already pointed out that narration in works of literary fiction may rest on indeterminacy about how the narrator's words became available for us to read. The reply to Currie's objection is that a related truth applies to movie story shots construed as

---

[30] Currie (1995), 173.

fictional motion picture shots. It is fictional that they were not taken by a camera at the fictional scene, and it is otherwise indeterminate how fictionally they came to be.

And yet, is this even minimally coherent? Isn't what we are supposed to imagine, on this proposal, a blatant contradiction? For what can it mean to imagine, of the film shots, that they are motion picture shots, without thinking of them as images formed by a motion picture camera? Are we supposed to imagine that the shots were produced, in some indeterminate fashion, by a motion picture camera which was nowhere in the vicinity of the fictionally photographed scene? Are we supposed to imagine motion picture shots that were *magically* created?

The last two rhetorical questions miss the point. It is not that it is fictional that motion picture shots of fictions are imagined to have bizarre or supernatural enabling conditions. As I have stressed throughout this section, we do not imagine anything in particular about what makes their existence possible. For the rest, the problem posed here is at least partly terminological. *If* 'being a motion picture shot' were to be taken to entail 'photographed by a motion picture camera,' then perhaps we should say something like this: viewers imagine the motion picture shots in fiction films 'as naturally iconic images,' where this new concept is explained in terms of aesthetically salient attributes of motion picture shots that do not directly implicate the property of being made by a particular kind of picture-generating device.

Thus, an actual motion picture shot exhibits several fundamental and characteristic features. One of these, discussed by both Walton and Currie, is that motion picture shots have a kind of *natural counterfactual dependence* on the rich collection of elements and their properties found within the photographed situation.[31] To call this kind of counterfactual dependence 'natural' is, at least in part, to say that it does not itself depend upon an intervening counterfactual dependence between the array of items and features in the image, on the one hand, and the beliefs, desires, and intentions of the human image-maker, on the other. In reality, this natural counterfactual dependence arises in virtue of the mechanical operations of the motion picture camera, the film stock, the projection, and so on, but the same kind of dependence could have been achieved in some different way.

So this is one basic characteristic of motion picture images, and here is another. Because motion picture images are formed on a fixed screen by means of the projection of light, they, unlike paintings, do not exhibit the sort of worked surface produced, for example, by strokes of paint on a canvas. As a consequence, film images do not have the same potential for eliciting the experience of seeing the drawn or painted scene *as arising out of* the fine-grained configurations of material on the displayed surface— an aspect of our total experience of painting whose aesthetic importance Richard Wollheim has done so much to elucidate.[32] The absence in film images of this

---

[31] See Walton (1984) and Currie (1995), 182–183.

[32] See his "Reflections on Art and Illusion" and "On Drawing an Object" in Wollheim (1974), and Wollheim (1987), esp. 46–47 and 72–75.

property, foundational for representational painting, both enhances our impression of the 'immediacy' of their depictive power and denies to them the special artistic possibilities of well-created facture.

Now we can simply stipulate that we will say that a visual representation is a *naturally iconic representation (or image)* just in case: (1) It is one whose production depends essentially on a process involving the kind of natural counterfactual dependence just mentioned. (2) The process in question is of a type which has been designed to store and/or transmit the visual information in the resulting images. And (3), the image lacks the sort of worked surface that characteristically supports the impression of the pictorial field as supervening upon it. No doubt the envisaged definition could be, in various ways, expanded and emended. But, for present purposes, it is the strategy of introducing such a concept which is important and not the details. However any possible revisions might go, we are in a position to state the Mediated Version with much less conceptual stress and strain. What we rightly imagine of the shots, when we watch a movie, is that they are naturally iconic shots of the fictional events in question. And it is fictionally indeterminate for us what specific sort of mechanism caused those naturally iconic shots to be produced and assembled as they are. It may be that what we are thereby intended to imagine is only minimally coherent, but this does nothing to establish that we do not imagine these things as we view fiction films. This is just the way, it seems to me, that Ana imagines seeing the fictional monster reflected for her in the river's current.[33]

David Hills has reminded me that it is not uncommon for us to be asked to imagine, as a part of particular fictional worlds, the transmission of such naturally iconic images whose mode of operation is largely indeterminate. He observes, "Consider the view-screens that were standard equipment in the old *Flash Gordon* serials. Here, perspectival visual access to a distant scene is afforded by means of an image whose structure is somewhat photograph-like, but the process giving rise to these images is not imagined to involve, and in some instances may be actively imagined not to involve, the processing of causal inputs collected at the point in space on which the image is centered"[34] (see figures 3 and 4). Similarly, in the later Oz books, Ozma has a 'Magic Picture' which can show her contemporaneous happenings anywhere in Oz, although, presumably, there is no device at the site of happenings that sends signals back to Ozma's wonderful screen.[35] If we are ordinarily untroubled by imagining these and similar contraptions as the *subject* of fiction, it seems likely that we may well

---

[33] The Mediated Version of the Fictional Showing Hypothesis is the conjunction of the thesis that viewers imagine movie image-tracks as selections of motion picture (naturally iconic) shots of fictional events *and* the thesis that photographs are transparent. The first thesis is of interest even if it were to be divorced from the second, so it deserves a name of its own. Call it, then, "The *Grand Imagier* Hypothesis."

[34] Quoted from private correspondence.

[35] See, for example, L. Frank Baum, *The Emerald City of Oz* (New York: William Morrow and Company, 1993), 192–196. However, the *Flash Gordon* example is better because, in Oz, the mediation of magic is naturally to be suspected.

Figure 3 Ming's minion looks on the Space-o-scope

Figure 4 He sees strange goings-on at the pagan statue

cheerfully imagine motion picture image-tracks as naturally iconic but causally un-grounded in a similar manner.

It should be clear what is so misleading about Currie's statement of the proposal under scrutiny. On the most natural way of understanding the phrase, to imagine a film as being a *documentary* is to imagine that its shots are motion picture shots of fictional events, shots which were made by a camera present at the fictional scenes. And, of course, there are movies in which this fiction is adopted. In *This Is Spinal Tap* (Rob Reiner, 1984), and, apparently, in *Culloden*, it is a part of the total fiction that a camera was present to shoot the narrative situations and that (most of) the shots in these movies were fictionally created by that camera. As Currie remarks, these are exceptional cases, but it is also not the type of case which the Mediated Version describes. That account, properly understood, is not subject to such easy refutation.

V. Conclusion

The Mediated Version of the Fictional Showing Hypothesis offers a novel account of the primitive basis of cinematic narration, and it deserves to be investigated thoroughly. It will be hard to make a serious assessment of the position unless and until it is more fully stated and embedded in a larger, multifaceted theory of how movies present fictional narratives. As it has been stated above, this version only tells us something about how we imaginatively construe motion picture images in movies. That hardly counts as an explication of the purported activity of visual presentation of film stories.

A more or less random series of events does not constitute a narrative, and a series of movie shots depicting a mélange of unconnected events does not constitute a narra-tion. But the Mediated Version focuses on individual shots and does not address the question of how they come to show an articulated story. The little that has been said in this connection about, for instance, film editing is extremely general and relatively insubstantial. According to the Mediated Version, editing in fiction films is construed by the viewer as a selection and arrangement of motion picture shots of fictional scenes. However, there are several kinds of editing transitions (straight cut, fade, dissolve, etc.), and there are many distinctive structures of editing employed in whole sequences and larger units. It needs to be shown that the Mediated Version allows us to make good sense of how viewers imagine the storytelling patterns that these devices help establish for them. For that matter, something would have to be said about the imaginative effects of camera movement within a single shot. Moreover, even if we assume that the Mediated Version adapts successfully to the presentation of diegetic sound, that adapted account will have to be extended, in some form, to fit sound-track music and voice-over narration.[36] In fact, the use of intertitles and other written documents

---

[36] Levinson (1996) discusses this question extensively. His remarks suggest that the best case for recogniz-ing 'cinematic narrators' may rest upon the viewer's proclivity to imagine an agent who coordinates all of the different dimensions of film to serve a unifying, e.g., narrative-constructing, function.

in film would need to be considered here as well. A genuine analysis of cinematic narration based on the Mediated Version calls for careful elaboration and defense.

Nevertheless, even the limited proposal we have before us has significant attractions. We have seen that it avoids the implausibilies of the Face-to-Face Version without denying that movie audiences imagine seeing the fictional action on screen. It does not ask us to believe that we *actually* see the movie fictions (just as we see the actual motion picture shots), through a kind of magical window that opens, from the theater, onto the fictional prospects of the story. Film theorists have been tempted by all these options and by others, but each of them has led pretty directly to conceptual disaster. The Mediated Version promises, at a minimum, to hold the more familiar disasters at bay.

In trying to work out a full-scale theory of cinematic narration, various authors have embraced various theses about how we imagine motion picture shots in fiction films. According to the Face-to-Face Version, we imagine movie images as objective views of fictional situations perceived from an internal vantage point. Semioticians have tended to treat movie shots as statements which are iconically encoded. Others have favored the idea that the image-track implicitly represents the visual experience of a camera observer. And, finally, in recent theory, the shot is often described as if it were a kind of subjectless apparition—a mirage-like visual field—with which the spectator 'identifies' in fantasy-driven perception. Compared with any of these, the Mediated Version gives a rather deflationary account. "No," it replies, "we imagine motion picture shots as motion picture shots [or as naturally iconic images], but as motion picture shots for which the fictions they construct are real."

But what is the force and content of imagining the image-track in this way? An answer to this question will not be trivial, and, indeed, it will not be easy to supply. For it simply refers us back to other questions and puzzles concerning the epistemics and aesthestics of (non-fiction) photography and film-making. These, of course, are major topics in their own right. However, if the Mediated Version is correct, much of what we know or will come to learn about these topics will bear critically upon the nature of our special imaginative relations to visual narration in fictional films.

3

The Imagined Seeing Thesis

I. Introduction

In his essay, "Theater and Cinema—Part II," André Bazin makes the following remark about watching movies: "Alone, hidden in a dark room, we watch through half-open blinds a spectacle that is unaware of our existence and is part of the universe. There is nothing to prevent us from identifying ourselves in imagination with the moving world before us, which becomes *the* world."[1] Although this statement formulates a significant aspect of Bazin's thinking, the thought it expresses is not especially distinctive to him. It is a view that Bazin shares with many other film theorists. He is attempting briefly to characterize the perceptual/imaginative relation that viewers have to the world of the movie that is depicted before them on the screen. It is a familiar suggestion in this connection that viewers imagine themselves looking into the cinematic world and seeing its characters, seeing their actions, and seeing their dramatic circumstances, and this is the suggestion that Bazin apparently endorses here. Indeed, the thesis may strike some as almost a truism, hardly meriting the standing of 'theoretical' claim. In any case, the passage from Bazin is a somewhat metaphorical expression of what I will refer to hereafter as 'the Imagined Seeing Thesis.' In the Introduction, I have already broached the idea that this thesis more formally encapsulates, and I explained at some length how the intuitive idea is puzzling. I will shortly offer a more careful formulation of what this Thesis amounts to, and a little later I will discuss its more than intimate relationship to what in Chapter 2 I called "the Fictional Showing Hypothesis." In the quoted passage, Bazin goes a bit further and implies that viewers imagine the screen as a kind of window that opens onto the world of the narrative. That proposal is also familiar from earlier and later literature on film, but it is a debatable add-on to the broader claims of the Imagined Seeing Thesis.

In Chapters 1 and 2, I have implicitly endorsed a version of this thesis, and, in fact, a great deal of Chapter 2 is taken up with defending it against an objection raised originally by Gregory Currie, but seconded since then by many others. In this and in later chapters, I endorse the Imagined Seeing Thesis once again and now I endorse it by name. However, I have come to realize rather keenly that the Imagined Seeing Thesis deserves more direct and systematic attention than I have given it in any of these earlier

---

[1] Bazin (2004), 102.

discussions. First, there are a number of delicate and fundamental issues about how it ought to be formulated more accurately. Second, there are issues about the considerations, intuitive and theoretical, that might lend it credence. So far I have said very little, either implicitly or explicitly, about either of these matters—questions of motivation and questions of evidence. Third, there are also questions about its scope. The Imagined Seeing Thesis makes clearest sense when it is applied to non-subjective shots and sequences. But, naturally there are various kinds of 'subjective shots,' and it is not obvious just what, if anything, the Imagined Seeing Thesis might be understood to say about these variously 'subjectivized' cases. This last set of questions is addressed in Chapter 6. Fourth, there are questions about how the Imagined Seeing Thesis might underwrite a correlative conception of audio-visual narration in fiction film.

The present chapter is primarily directed at problems and puzzles that belong to the first two categories listed above. Chapter 5 goes on to discuss questions from the fourth category about 'narration' and about some related topics. Since some of the matters investigated in the present chapter and the one that follows have already come up in Chapters 1 and 2, what I say here will overlap to some extent with things I have said earlier. Nevertheless, I hope to present here a reasonably methodical overview of the Imagined Seeing Thesis and an improved account of its content, its plausibility, and aspects of its aesthetic significance.

However, to avoid expositional confusion, there is one topic, belonging more to the fourth category of questions, that calls for some preliminary clarification. The Imagined Seeing Thesis is tightly connected with a corresponding claim about the nature of the audio-visual narration of fiction films. This is the claim that, in "*Le Grand Imagier* Steps Out" (Chapter 2), I began dubbing "the Fictional Showing Hypothesis." Here is the formulation that I gave there:

It is fictional in the cinematic work that (as a rule) the shots of the film show or visually register segments of the film's narrative world.

Of course, one really needs to add to this a corresponding thesis concerning film sound. That is, it is also fictional in the cinematic work that the sound-track of a movie predominantly registers the speech and other sounds from the narrative world of the movie.[2] In the remainder of this chapter, I will take it that the Fictional Showing Thesis subsumes both of these claims, although I will principally consider the narrower formulation given above, hoping to clarify its somewhat elusive content and to add some qualifications to it. Much of what I say in this regard will apply under certain modifications to the counterpart thesis about the dimension of film sound as well. In

---

[2] Of course, a major exception to this formulation is the non-diegetic (sound-track) music that occurs in many fiction films. I will discuss the distinction between diegetic and non-diegetic elements in sound- and image-tracks in Chapter 4.

the remarks that follow, I am chiefly concerned with the way in which 'fictional showing' and 'imagined seeing' are related.

One preliminary point of elucidation: the verb 'show,' in its varied ordinary usage, is too vague to capture the sense of the Fictional Showing Hypothesis that I have in mind. In one use of the word, I can 'show' you Smith's murderer by showing you a reasonably detailed sketch of him. However, from the fact that you were shown Smith's murderer in this way, it does not follow that you have literally seen the murderer. The sketch is intended to help someone spot the murderer, but it may be that no one, including the artist, has seen him yet. On the other hand, if I show you Smith's murderer by pointing him out in a line-up, or by showing you his reflection in a mirror, or, perhaps, by showing him to you in a security video, then my showing you Smith's murderer in these and related ways does seem to entail that you have seen the murderer, either face-to-face or indirectly, e.g., with the assistance of the mirror or some other device of visual enhancement.

The verb 'show' in the construction 'X showed an F to Y' seems to have two distinguishable uses here. In its 'transparent' use, the construction entails that there exists an F that X showed to Y. In its 'opaque' sense, the entailment does not hold. After all, X could show a unicorn to an audience by showing them a suitable drawing, and it would not follow that there exists a unicorn that X showed to Y. It also would not follow that there exists a unicorn that Y has thereby seen. In all that follows, I will be employing 'show' in its transparent use, and it is of some importance to keep this modest restriction in mind.

Especially in Chapter 2, I contended that the Fictional Showing Hypothesis is a *necessary* condition for the existence of audio-visual narrators in movies. If there is nothing to be recognized as the *fictional* showing of the narrative action (and the *fictional* recording of narrative sound), then there is nothing that constitutes the *fictional* recounting of the film narrative.[3] Thus, movies will fail to include anything that corresponds, even in the broadest terms, to the 'narration' (the fictional telling) of a story in a work of literary fiction. And, naturally, if there is no audio-visual narration in fiction film, there can be no question of there being audio-visual narrators who purportedly engage in it. For this reason, the Fictional Showing Hypothesis occupies a central position in the tangle of confused debates about whether narrative fiction in movies presupposes the existence of intrinsic cinematic narrators, narrators who fictionally present the dramatic developments on the screen. In fact, I am convinced that there *is* a strong *prima facie* case in favor of the Fictional Showing Hypothesis—a case that is not defeated by any of the objections with which I am familiar. This is what I maintained at the end of Chapter 2,

---

[3] As I will discuss late in Chapter 4, fictional recounting in a movie involves more than the fictional showing of narrative sights and the fictional recording of narrative sounds. Notably, if shot A fictionally shows X and shot B fictionally shows Y, then editing A and B together in a certain way may fictionally *indicate* that X bears relation R to Y.

and much later in the present chapter I attempt to explicate the claim further and to justify it more securely.

But, let's examine first things first. How exactly is the Fictional Showing Hypothesis related to the Imagined Seeing Thesis? The latter, after all, is a claim about the nature of our imaginative engagement with movies. The former concerns the narration of the movie and the question of the intrinsic fictionality of the facts that constitute the narration. The Imagined Seeing Thesis states (at least as a first approximation) that

In viewing classical narrative films under standard conditions of movie spectatorship, viewers normally do imagine seeing (in the image-track) and hearing (in the sound-track) the objects and events depicted in the movie. Further, in normal cases they are justified in so imagining.

As we'll see in a moment, the case for the Fictional Showing Hypothesis arises rather directly from the Imagined Seeing Thesis. Many commentators have criticized and rejected 'Imagined Seeing' and have taken their objections to constitute the basis for skepticism about 'Fictional Showing.' Certainly, this much is right. The Imagined Seeing Thesis and the Fictional Showing Hypothesis *are* intimately bound together. One is, as it were, the conceptual flipside of the other.

Here is why the correctness of 'Fictional Showing' derives almost exclusively from the correctness of 'Imagined Seeing.' If, in watching a movie, viewers imagine seeing the narrative action on screen, then presumably they thereby imagine that the pro-jected motion picture images they are watching are, in some way, 'showing' the narrative action to them. To state the matter in this schematic way leaves the relevant meanings of 'see' and 'show' significantly underspecified, but the idea that there is a fairly simple and direct conceptual connection between 'seeing something,' when one's attention has been directed to the pertinent sight, and 'being shown the thing that is in sight' seems pretty trivial. What is more, *it is a standard function* of a cinematic work of fiction to prompt viewers to *imagine*—to make believe—themselves being shown the narrative events and circumstances in the successive shots. Moreover as I am using the phrase, *it is fictional* in the movie that its shots have 'shown' them those narrative constituents.[4] *Modulo* these two assumptions, the two theses in question are effectively equivalent. Since 'fictional showing' is putatively what the movie's images are meant to achieve, and 'imagined seeing' is putatively what movie viewers do in response to those images, it is often easier to formulate certain points in terms of one thesis rather than the other. But, to repeat, the two theses are utterly interdependent, although, of the two, the Imagined Seeing Thesis is probably the more fundamental.

---

[4] Here I am, in effect, adapting Kendall Walton's notion of its being 'fictional in a work.' See Walton (1990), 58–61. I am tempted to say that it is fictional in work W that P just in case it is an *intended function* of some part or aspects of W to prompt audiences of W to imagine that P. However, the formulation in the text in terms of 'its being a standard function' is more vague and is probably weaker, and the formulation leaves some reasonable alternatives open. Also, this formulation is, I believe, more in alignment with Walton's approach.

Movies tell their stories in audio-visual terms. They present audiences with narratives, and so, presumably, there is an audio-visual way in which the narratives have been told. In this sense, films necessarily involve a 'narration' of their narratives. It is trivial that there is some way in which the film-makers have presented the story in the film. Still, as I have insisted in Chapters 1 and 2 and earlier in the present section, this trivial sense is not the sense of 'narration' that normally applies to works of literary narrative fiction. In the case of literature, the concept of 'narration' refers to the *fictional* recounting of the story, typically performed by the fictional or fictionalized narrator implicit in the work. Therefore, if movies involve a mode of audio-visual 'narration' that is seriously analogous to narration in literary fiction, there must be some kindred sense in which fiction films also involve a *fictional* recounting of the story—a work-internal recounting that presumably is performed in the relevant audio-visual terms. But what can this mean? I will argue that it implies that the image-track in movies fictionally purports to show us the objects and events in the story it elaborates, and the sound-track fictionally registers the associated diegetic sounds. In other words, if the parallel between movies and literary fiction is to hold, then a suitable version of the Fictional Showing Hypothesis (for movie images and for sound) must be true. Moreover, I will explain in the last section of the following chapter why the fictional recounting of a story in a movie involves *more* than just fictional showing and fictional audio recording of the narrative's sights and sounds. This brief elaboration of fictional recounting in the cinema will serve to underscore, I believe, the significant structural parallel between storytelling in literary fiction and in fiction film and to solidify the grounds for speaking univocally of 'narration' in both cases.

In Chapter 5, I will return to the question of whether movies have audio-visual *narrators*. Once the question of whether movies normally involve audio-visual *narration* has been settled, I think that it is hard to be sure what further question the debate about cinematic narrators is intended to address. It is unclear, in the first place, whether something more than the mere presence of intrinsic narration in a film is supposed to be required for there to be audio-visual narrators (who would be normally effaced) in movies. Moreover, if the satisfaction of additional conditions *is* called for to underwrite serious talk about 'cinematic narrators,' it is also murky what such additional conditions might be. Finally, the question of whether movies sometimes or always have audio-visual narrators, as it is usually understood, tends to presuppose at least two assumptions that are highly dubious. I will state those assumptions in the later discussion of the topic. In short, the conceptual underpinnings of the question are a mess! In arguing these points, I try to diagnose why the extensive literature on the topic of 'cinematic narrators' has been so confusing and inconclusive. One should not expect that a simple answer, either affirmative or negative, is to be had.

In my judgment, the fundamental issues about the Imagined Seeing Thesis have themselves been widely misunderstood. This was one of the central contentions that I advanced in Chapter 2, but various strands in the topic deserve the expanded elaboration I provide in the present chapter. Although many of these misconceptions are quite seductive, they *are* misconceptions nevertheless, and, because the misconceptions are so frequently repeated in the literature, the resulting confusions really do need to be set straight. At the same time, I will emphasize in the course of the discussion how difficult some of the chief subsidiary issues turn out to be. Thus, the main purpose of the present chapter is to motivate, explicate, and defend the Imagined Seeing Thesis in a reasonable amount of detail. However, I don't suppose that the discussion comes close to providing a conclusive defense of 'imagined seeing.' In fact, the conceptual and other questions that arise in this connection are so fundamental to our thinking about movies that the very notion of a 'conclusive' defense or objection is probably illusory.

II. A positive case for imagined seeing

Let me begin by outlining what I regard as the basic considerations in favor of the Imagined Seeing Thesis. These considerations are based on a puzzle about what it is to 'see' fictions in movies. Perhaps it seems initially surprising that there even should be a puzzle about such a familiar idea, but there *is* a puzzle, and it is a difficult one. I have sketched the puzzle in the Introduction, but it merits a considerable stretch of exposition just to state the problem in reasonably adequate and qualified terms.

Certainly, we regularly think and speak of ourselves as if we 'see' the fictional objects, events, and situations that movie shots and sequences depict. We say, for instance, "In this shot, you can see the werewolf creeping through the maze to attack the heroine, although you can't see the heroine at the moment because she is hidden by the garden shed." These judgments about what we do and do not 'see' among the depicted fictions in a movie are not only ubiquitous, but they correspond to the fundamental distinction between those narrative items and occurrences that are presented on screen in a given stretch of the movie and those that aren't. Thus, for example, it is fictionally true in the movie *M* (Fritz Lang, 1930) that a certain child murderer, Hans Beckert, famously played by Peter Lorre, meets a little girl, Elsie Beckmann (Inge Landgut), on a Berlin street, buys her a balloon, and subsequently murders her. However, although viewers of *M* arguably 'see' the meeting with the murderer,[5] Beckert, on the street and certainly 'see' the purchase of the balloon, they notoriously do not 'see' the murder of young Elsie. The latter is a fictional episode in the story, but its occurrence is merely (although quite distinctly) implied in the narration (see figures 5, 6, and 7). One would be hard pressed to make even the most rudimentary distinctions about how a movie gives rise directly or indirectly to the range of fictional

---

[5] The short interlude in which the murderer meets the little girl is something of an intermediate case. We know that the little girl is present because we hear her voice and see her ball bouncing off a kiosk. We know that the murderer arrives on the scene because his shadow is reflected on the kiosk, and we hear him greet the little girl. So do we 'see' them meeting? I'm tempted to give an affirmative answer here, but clearly we have a borderline case.

Figure 5 The murderer meets Elsie Bechmann by a kiosk

Figure 6 He buys her a balloon as a present

truths that it involves without adverting to the fictional objects, events, and situations that viewers do or do not 'see' on screen.

The division between the fictions that are 'seen' and 'unseen' in a given movie may suggest a simple, indirect account of what might be meant by saying that the viewer

Figure 7 The balloon is tangled in telephone wires

sees a fiction F in movie N. That is, it might be proposed that statements of this and variant forms are simply to be construed as idiomatic shorthand for counterpart instances of the following propositional schema:

The viewer sees a cinematic image or a constellation of cinematic images, contained in N, that depict the fiction F.

After all, viewers don't see the girl's murder in *M* because there are no shots in *M* that depict her murder, although there are shots that indicate that such a murder has occurred. However, this simple proposal cannot possibly get off the ground. Every movie shot or portion of a shot depicts an immense range of fictional items and incidents, and it is inevitable that any given viewer during any given viewing will fail to 'see' some of the things that have been depicted for her on the screen. If the creeping werewolf is only barely visible in the dark shadows of the maze, then many viewers may fail to 'see' the creature altogether, despite the fact that he has unquestionably, although dimly, been depicted in the shot. Or, if the viewer of a particular scene allows her attention to wander from the movie to an absorbing problem of philosophy that obsesses her, then she may just sit there staring at the shots on screen and fail to see much of anything that those shots depict. It is one thing to ask for an account of what it is for fictions to be depicted in the movies, but that is not the question that concerns us now. What we presently want to understand is what is communicated by intuitively correct claims about a viewer's 'seeing' fictions in narrative fiction films. Surely the viewer who says or thinks, "I saw Charles Foster Kane pacing through the halls of Xanadu," is not simply *wrong*, even if it turns out that her words, parsed literally, express something false. Surely, she is correctly reporting something about what she visually experiences in seeing the film. No doubt there is some strong connection between the question about the nature of cinematic depiction and the question about what it is to 'see' fictions in a movie, although it is only the second question that is under scrutiny at present.

Unfortunately, the idea that movie viewers actually 'see' movie fictions when they see a movie story is surprisingly opaque. As I have stressed above, judgments of this sort are often explicitly affirmed and often accepted in ordinary conversation as being correct. And yet, if the linguistic expressions of these judgments are taken strictly and literally, it is difficult to grasp how the propositions expressed in such judgments can possibly be simply *true*. Seeing an object, like kicking one, generally involves a causal interaction between an agent and the object acted upon. No one supposes that a movie viewer can kick a fictional character. Why should it be so much easier for a viewer to 'see' one?[6] In the sense in which we 'see' actual objects or events in our environment, we have to be 'looking at' the object or event we see. When I say that I see the character in a film and the action he is doing, then I have to be looking at the actor who is playing the character's role, but it is dubious that I am thereby looking at the role or, for that matter, looking at the character herself. After all, where is she? On screen? Fictionally in Paris? One's first reaction is that an answer to these questions should be easy to concoct, but it is surprisingly hard to give a coherent and satisfying response. Here is a striking instance of the oddness of some of our first linguistic intuitions on the question.

Many speakers will affirm, without having any second thoughts, that they have seen Charles Foster Kane, George Bailey, and Francis, the Talking Mule in certain movies, because they remember seeing *Citizen Kane* (Orson Welles, 1941), *It's a Wonderful Life* (Frank Capra, 1946) and the 'Francis' movies (from the early 1950s). But many of these same speakers will hesitate to affirm that they have seen Napoleon in a film just on the grounds that they went to *War and Peace* (King Vidor, 1956) or that they have seen William Jennings Bryant on film because they watched *Inherit the Wind* (Stanley Kramer, 1960). They will similarly deny that they have seen the streets of nineteenth-century London because they screened *Oliver Twist* (David Lean, 1948). Now, it is clear where these intuitions are coming from. You haven't seen the 'real' X in a movie simply because you have seen a fictionalized version of X depicted in some film. But, if X is something depicted in a movie that is *not* a depiction of some actual person or thing, then you are likely to be more comfortable in reporting flatly that you have actually seen that character X on screen.

In point of fact, most recent philosophers who have explicitly discussed the question have denied that viewers do, strictly speaking, see or otherwise literally experience

---

[6] Despite Colin McGinn's odd suggestion that characters in the movies are, like Cartesian egos, massless and invisible. See McGinn (2005), 91–94.

fictional characters, objects, and events in movies. Here is a rather straightforward formulation of that negative thesis by Colin McGinn:

Nor, I think, is [the fictional character, Charles Foster Kane] the thing we are looking at, for we are not *seeing* him. It is not Kane who stands before the camera, causing the image that confronts us on the screen; it is [Orson] Welles. Kane is an *imaginary* character. Our relation to Kane is mediated by our imagination, not the mere act of seeing. We *see* the image of Welles and we *imagine* Kane . . . You can't photograph fictional characters, only the real people who play them. Nor can fictional characters be literally looked at . . .

So the right description of this complex visual relationship is as follows: the image on the screen is seen but not looked at; the actor is seen and looked at; the fictional character is neither seen nor looked at, but imagined.[7]

Thus, McGinn's position is that movie viewers literally see the images projected on the screen, and he also affirms that in general they also literally see the actors, sets, and other photographed material that have been recorded by the camera for the film. But he holds that viewers don't literally 'see' the constituents of the fictional world depicted in the movies. These fictional objects, events, and situations are items that, prompted by what they genuinely do see on screen, the movie's viewers merely 'imagine.'

It is not obvious how 'imagine' should be construed in the setting of such a proposal. When we read a work of literary fiction, we see and grasp the words upon the page and this activity *sometimes* prompts us to visualize internally certain constituents of the story. That is, we 'imagine seeing these constituents *in our mind's eye*,' although we certainly don't imagine seeing them before the eyes in our faces. In this special sense, we, as readers, may thereby 'imagine' them inwardly. But, surely, in seeing the film's images and in seeing the filmed material, viewers are not characteristically induced to visualize the movie's fiction in their minds' eyes. There is patently no need to 'imagine' the characters etc. in this 'inner theater' sense. In some sense (that needs further clarification), the fictive elements are already present to the audience 'on screen,' i.e., on the screen of the quite public theater in which the audience is seated. If, in these passages, 'imagine' in the McGinn quote were to mean 'imagine seeing (before one's eyes)' then McGinn would be an exponent of the Imagined Seeing Thesis. Later in the chapter, I will examine this view of McGinn's more carefully and offer some more developed reasons for rejecting it. For now, however, the passage is merely meant to illustrate the rather surprising philosophical contortions that the question of what we 'see' in movies can provoke.

The consideration that seems most often to motivate the thesis that viewers do not really see the fictions in fiction film is the following. In general, statements of the form

(a)   X sees Y

---

[7] Ibid., 41.

imply or presuppose the proposition that 'Y exists,' and similarly statements of the form

(β)   X sees Y Φ

imply or presuppose the proposition that 'Y actually did Φ' or that 'Y's Φing actually did occur.' I will say that tokened instances of (α) and (β) that carry the indicated implications are 'environment involving' uses of the form in question. However, when 'Y' refers to a fictional entity or when 'Y's Φing' refers to a fictional event or situation in a movie, then these presuppositions are apparently not satisfied. We have at least some inclination to agree that fictional objects do not exist and that fictional events do not genuinely occur. For instance, if someone judges that, in watching a certain horror movie,

(1)   Flannery sees the werewolf of London,

or, more specifically, that

(2)   Flannery sees the werewolf creeping through the castle maze,

then, because there really are no werewolves, and, by the same token, because there really are no creepings performed by werewolves, the propositions strictly and literally expressed in (1) and (2) ought to be untrue, given the 'environment involving' conditions that generally govern the forms (α) and (β). I suspect that these are the considerations that have moved most philosophers of film to agree that, speaking precisely, we don't really 'see' the fictional denizens of movies (in the same sense that we 'see' the things that portray them in the film).

At the same time, it is surely the case that the words in (1) and (2) can somehow assert perfectly correct judgments about what Flannery's experiences of the horror film in question have been. But how are these reflections to be reconciled? What *are* the true thoughts that (1) and (2) are somehow used to express? And *how* do the true propositional contents in question come to get contextually asserted when, as we are assuming, the propositions that have been literally expressed in the very making of the assertions are always false? After all, the verb 'to see,' as it occurs in (1) and (2) is not obviously used to express some non-standard sense in relation to visual depictions in films, and it doesn't appear to be used figuratively in such cases either.

It may be tempting to suppose that the difficulty arises from accepting too readily the doctrine that fictional items are, so to speak, shrouded in non-existence. It is natural to protest, in response to that view, that fictional characters, their actions and circumstances, are somehow created by—*come into being* with—the construction of the work in which they occur. Hence, in some important sense, fictional objects and events really do appear to have some kind of respectable existence. I myself am inclined to think that this conception has a notable plausibility. Perhaps then, movie characters and their fictional events and circumstances do exist in a manner that may be compatible with the notion that they are literally seen by spectators at the movie. I don't want to get into all of the daunting complexity and nuance that has been involved in traditional debates about the ontology of fictional objects.[8] This is just one of the relatively intractable philosophical topics that make the present questions so hard to navigate. However, the following remarks may be enough to indicate why I do not think that this kind of proposal can provide any easy escape from doubts about whether movie fictions are among the things that we, when we are speaking univocally, literally see and hear.

There *is* a range of theories that grant that fictional items do, in some substantial fashion, exist. Nevertheless, according to the most plausible of such theories, fictional characters and events, *qua* existing things, are construed as abstract or quasi-abstract objects—abstract *artifacts* that have been engendered by the works in which they figure.[9] But, abstract objects (artifactual or not), since they fail to have a concrete occurrence in space and time, are not, or so it seems, among the things that people can, strictly speaking, see. When you and I have established a binding contract between ourselves, the contract[10] is not something we can strictly see, and when you come to occupy a new, higher position in the company, your higher position is not something that people photograph and see.

Some of the relevant complexity is illustrated by the following case. Consider the correct statement that

Dick Powell played Philip Marlowe in *Murder My Sweet.*

Now Philip Marlowe is surely a fictional character, but the reference to 'Philip Marlowe' in the highlighted sentence appears to make reference to something like a certain dramatic *role*—the role originally created by the author, Raymond Chandler, developed by the pertinent screenwriters, and embodied by the actors, including Powell, who performed the role. Moreover, the 'role' of Marlowe surely qualifies as a kind of abstract entity. After all, 'Philip Marlowe,' i.e., the character *qua* dramatic role, was played by several different actors in different 'Philip Marlowe' movies, and hence the character has an existence that has been instantiated in all of the distinct performances of the part.

It is true that we may cheerfully assert that we have 'seen' Philip Marlowe in several movies, but this is not to be understood on a par with the claim that we have seen Herbert Hoover in many newsreels. In the latter case, we have seen the same (actual)

---

[8] For a good overview of the problems and a striking and nuanced positive approach to solving them, see Salmon (2005), 55–91. A number of the key points in his discussion are influenced, as Salmon notes, by Saul Kripke's unpublished John Locke Lectures given in 1973–74. Also, see Thomasson (1999) for a defense of a version of the view that fictional objects are 'abstract artifacts.' In these and most similar discussions, it is literary fictional characters that are under discussion. The added complexities about the creation of characters that are engendered when fictional characters from movies are considered are rarely, if ever, investigated.

[9] It is my view that the view that takes characters to be abstract objects that are artifacts created by human agents is the most attractive of the 'realist' possibilities. In the formulations that follow, I will assume the correctness of the view but not defend it.

[10] Of course, if we establish the contract by signing the paper, we can see the paper we have signed but not the contract that we thereby establish.

man, Hoover, in each of the different films, but we haven't, in a comparable way, seen the same man (actual or non-actual) in each of the Philip Marlowe movies. If there is a single man Philip Marlowe in all the movies, then what in the world does he look like? Besides Dick Powell, Marlowe was played by, e.g., Robert Montgomery, Humphrey Bogart, and Robert Mitchum, and none of these actors looks very much like any of the others (see figures 8, 9, and 10). Clearly, our difficulties about the character's appearance do not arise from changes over time. The question about what the character Philip Marlowe 'really' looks like is patently a silly one. In fact, it is doubtful that we can say, without explanation, what Marlowe looks like in a particular work like *The Big Sleep*. After all, Marlowe was played by Bogart in the 1946 version, and, in the 1978 adaptation, he was played by Robert Mitchum. What is more, we also have not seen several possible but 'non-actual' detectives who bear the name of 'Philip Marlowe' either. Rather we have seen several movies in which the 'Philip Marlowe' role (character) has been played by a number of different actors. We have seen the dramatic role performed in each of the movies, but the dramatic role itself is not among the things that have appeared to us visually in one or several of the pertinent films. Alternatively, should we concede that there is a different 'Phillip Marlowe' character corresponding, say, to each of the actors who played Phillip Marlowe in the different movies? If so, could there be a sequel to the series in which all the particular 'Phillip Marlowe' characters appear and collaborate with one another to solve a crime together? If such a movie could have been devised, it would only work as an amusing kind of

Figure 8 Humphrey Bogart in *The Big Sleep*

Figure 9 Robert Montgomery in *The Lady in the Lake*

Figure 10 Dick Powell in *Murder, My Sweet*

nonsense. The answer is: there is only a single character, Philip Marlowe, in all these works. It is intended that viewers are to imagine themselves seeing a detective bearing the name 'Philip Marlowe' when watching each of the various films, but viewers don't actually see the thing that *is* the Philip Marlowe 'character' exemplified across the different cases. Or, so I am inclined to hold.

The same point applies, it seems to me, to fictional actions and events in the movies. In all of the many different versions of *Les Miserables* that have been made over the years, the character, Jean Valjean, steals the Bishop Myriel's silver utensils. That is, the same fictional action, Valjean's theft of the silver, is enacted (in different versions) in every dramatization of the story. The fictional action, like the fictional characters, was originally created by the relevant passages in the Hugo novel, and it is a quasi-abstract artifact—a constituent of plot that has been variously instantiated, from film to film, in the performance of the actor who plays the miserable protagonist. The abstract character of fictional actions is especially obvious in the case of stage plays. Every fictional action in the play is newly enacted in each performance, and when different productions of the play are considered, the same 'action' may be performed in strikingly different ways. In movies, a given fictional action will usually be enacted only once and only in a single film, but the possibility of several occurrences of the same action in the same movie and of re-enactments of the same action in different film versions always exists. And, of course, there are many examples, like Valjean's stealing of the Bishop's silverware, in which repeated re-enactment across movies actually occurs.

I conclude that, whether we believe that fictional movie characters and their fictional actions and fictional circumstances exist or not, there is still going to be a problem about how it can be literally and unequivocally true that movie viewers 'see' them in the way that they see related concrete items—even as spectators at the movies. Naturally, a person can hear a melody by listening to a performance of it rendered on certain instruments. In the same manner, I suppose we can see a dramatic role by seeing suitable performances of it. So perhaps audiences can 'hear' a melody and 'see' dramatic roles on suitable occasions when the melody or the role has been performed. But hearing a melody or seeing a dramatic role in these indirect, performance-mediated ways renders these cases of perception quite different from the hearing or seeing of some piece of dry goods present in one's perceptual environment. I am therefore inclined to agree with the consensus view that we do not literally see fictional characters and other fictional constituents of the movies, at least not in the same sense that we see the cinematic images on the screen and see (indirectly) the photographed material that is depicted in those images. However, I don't think that there is some quick, decisive argument that establishes such a view. Rather, when one presses a host of questions about the nature and identity of fictional objects and actions— questions such as the ones illustrated above—it becomes increasingly hard to think of fictions as entities that are simply and directly available to us through the sense of sight. How then, on my view, can sentences like (1) and (2) be naturally used to convey and assert straightforward truths about the experience of moviegoers when they are watching a fiction film? This is the puzzle with which we began.

It is instructive to compare this case with cases in which we report the content of someone's hallucination by saying what he thereby 'sees.' This is a different and quite familiar case in which we also speak as if a person 'sees' something that does not, in the relevant circumstances, exist. For instance, a speaker says that

(3) The drunkard sees a pink elephant

or that

(4) The drunkard sees a pink elephant dancing on the driveway.

Given that there is really no pink elephant to be seen in the relevant circumstances, it is arguably the case that the propositions literally expressed by (3) and (4) are false propositions, although the propositions their speakers have intended to assert may very well be true. The envisaged uses of (3) and (4) are clear instances of the forms (α) and (β) that are not environment involving—they are, as I will say, 'narrowly subjective' uses of the forms. In cases like (3) and (4), there is nothing especially puzzling. We take it that the speaker intends to be using his words to describe what the drunkard *seems* to see, or, at least, we can naturally construe the speaker's words as constituting a purported description of this sort about his contemporaneous visual experience. Thus, what the speaker is understood to assert and communicate is (roughly) that

(3′) The drunkard *seems* to be seeing a pink elephant,

and

(4′) The drunkard *seems* to be seeing a pink elephant dancing in the driveway.

Such a use of the form of words 'X sees a Y' or 'X sees YΦ' is both common and natural. Under the appropriate reconstrual, the words are used to tell us that X is having a *visual experience* of a Y or a *visual experience* of Y Φing. If someone utters (3) or (4) and means to be reporting on the content of the drunkard's private visual experience, then the semantic content of his actual words is meant to be pragmatically qualified in the way that is marked explicitly in (3′) and (4′).[11] It is these *contextually enriched* propositions that the speaker, in the relevant context, most straightforwardly intends to communicate and assert.

In my opinion, judgments about seeing fictional objects and events in movies should be treated in a similar way, although, naturally, the specific character of the explanation will be different. That is, I will be urging that, in uttering (1) or (2), the speaker is chiefly asserting a contextually supplemented proposition about what Flannery imagines seeing in the werewolf flick, and it will be the task of the next several pages to explain the content of the relevant pragmatic enrichments. So, this is the solution that I propose to the puzzle about how the literal falsity of the sentences (1) and (2) can be compatible with the very real possibility that utterances of them commonly and straightforwardly assert something true.

---

[11] For a discussion of the general phenomenon of a semantic content being pragmatically enriched by materials derived from the conversational context, see Soames (2009), 278–297.

Scott Soames contends, "In many contexts, the semantic content of [a sentence] S—whether it is a complete proposition or not—interacts with an expanded conception of pragmatics to generate a *pragmatically enriched proposition* that it is the speaker's primary intention to assert."[12] The uses of (1) and (2) that are under scrutiny in this discussion occur in pragmatically enriching contexts that are of the sort that Soames is highlighting in the quoted passage. The propositions that narrowly constitute the literal meaning of any of the sentences (1), (2), (3), and (4) will, in the contexts envisaged, be false.

In watching the horror movie, Flannery is not having a hallucination or entertaining a visual fantasy of the werewolf creeping. Some writers, over the years, have proposed that movie viewers are characteristically under the *illusion* of seeing the contents of the movie's fictional world, but Flannery has no illusion about seeing the werewolf creeping through the maze. She has no genuine inclination to think that she is actually seeing such a thing. The thesis that spectators at movies are under an illusion of seeing the relevant narrative fictions has been widely and rightly debunked. However, it is not hard to sketch a variant proposal in a similar vein that is not so obviously mistaken. In fact, this is the proposal that I will explicate and defend. The proposal, whose content will be more carefully specified in a moment, states that movie spectators have an imaginative *impression* of its being *as if* they are seeing the fictional objects depicted in the movie they are watching. It *seems* to them that it is *as if* they are seeing a segment of the narrative world. It is in this sense then, I want to claim, that movie viewers 'imagine seeing' the movie's characters and its other fictive constituents.

Jerrold Levinson has highlighted the importance of the notion of 'as if impressions,' and as he emphasizes, the having of an impression of the sort in question need not and generally does not involve any illusion on the subject's part.[13] Certainly it can seem to me—I can have the impression—that it is right now as if I am Φing even though I am well aware that actually I am not. Suppose that as I eat my lonely dinner, I make believe to myself that I am sharing my meal with a trio of major movie stars. Perhaps, as part of the make-believe, I've arranged my dog, cat, and parrot on the dining room chairs. If things go well for me, I have the impression of its being as if I am dining with the stars,

---

[12] Soames (2009), 280. Soames also observes that a proper conception of the relation between semantic content, pragmatic enrichment, and assertion will have the consequence that "...often the semantic content of the sentence uttered is *not* itself asserted by the speaker's utterance—even when that content is itself a complete proposition, and the agent is speaking literally and unmetaphorically" (281). It seems to me that this consequence holds for the utterances of (1) and (2) and of (3) and (4) that we have been investigating.

[13] Levinson (1998), 229–230. Levinson's identification of the significance of the phenomenon of 'seeing as if' is important in the context of this debate. But, Levinson takes his remarks about 'seeing as if' to represent a way of filling out Richard Wollheim's views about the nature of 'seeing in.' As such, his proposals about 'seeing as if' are meant by him to represent an alternative to Walton's conception of 'imagined seeing.' Walton (2008), 152, denies the opposition. I am in agreement with Walton on this limited point contra Levinson, and accordingly, I have spent a good deal of space in the ensuing pages attempting to bring out why X's having an impression of its being as if she is seeing so-and-so generally constitutes a case of X's imagining seeing so-and-so.

although, given that I am not actually crazy, I know quite well that this impression of mine is make-believe. It is not true. It is just a satisfying and harmless self-pretense. Notice that in this example, I am actually doing something, i.e., eating dinner, and simultaneously forming an ongoing imaginative impression about my activity. I will be contending that imagining seeing in the movies has a similar structure. Movie spectators are doing or undergoing something, i.e., viewing the movie, and forming an imaginative impression of what their viewing amounts to—seeing the contents of the fictional world.

To introduce the basic conception, think of a case in which a character in a movie steps out of the action, looks into the camera, and makes a sequence of comments about the recent plot developments or about the broader unfolding of the movie story itself. In these circumstances, a spectator of the film—say, Gustav—commonly will have the definite *impression* that it is *as if* the character's remarks are being addressed to him (or, at least, to the audience of which he is a member). Indeed, the relevant shot or sequence will have been intended to elicit and justify that 'impression' for members of the movie's audiences. Nevertheless, spectators, having the relevant impression, are rarely under any illusion that the character is really speaking to them. They will have no tendency to believe that this is so. The 'impression' of being personally addressed in this case is an ordinary, spontaneous, and warranted *imaginative* reaction of the viewer to what is being presented on the screen. It doesn't exactly seem to viewers of the movie *that* the character is talking to them, but, to repeat, it does seem to them *as if* they are being addressed by the character. The viewers have, as I will sometimes say, the 'as if impression' of being addressed by the movie character. It is natural to think in such a case that Gustav *imagines* being addressed by the character, and, in my opinion, Gustav's imagining this content in these circumstances is just a matter of his having the relevant 'as if impression' of being so addressed.

In the sense of 'imagined seeing' that I am trying to invoke, the proposal is that instances of (1) and (2), used to describe Flannery's experience as she watches the movie, purport to describe Flannery's 'as if impression' of the character of her perceptual experience in viewing the film. The simplest version of the idea would be to say that (1) and (2) effectively communicate and assert the thought that

[In viewing the movie] Flannery imagines seeing the werewolf of London (i.e., she has the impression of its being as if she is seeing the werewolf of London),

and

[In viewing the movie] Flannery imagines seeing the werewolf creeping through the castle maze (i.e., she has the impression of its being as if she is seeing the werewolf creeping through the maze).

However, there is at least one important modification that needs to be added to this initial proposal.

Consider Gustav who has an 'as if' impression of its being as if he were being addressed by the character on screen. If the movie is, say, *Road to Morocco* (David Butler, 1942) and the character is played by Bob Hope, then Gustav's impression is likely to be warranted by the scene he is watching. But, Gustav could have essentially the same impression although it is *not* really warranted by what is going on in the film. For instance, there could be an extreme close up of the movie's protagonist who fictionally is uttering inspiring words to another character who is standing directly before him in movie space, and Gustav might have the aberrant 'as if impression' of its being as if the protagonist were speaking personally to him. Gustav may have this impression, but, in this instance, his impression is unwarranted by the scene. That is, the pertinent shots were not constructed to convey such an impression to members of the movie's audience, while in *Road to Morocco* the shots were designed to serve that function.

Suppose now that, in watching a certain shot in the movie, Flannery has the impression of its being as if she were seeing the werewolf of London creeping through the castle maze. But suppose further that her impression of what she is 'seeing' is seriously mistaken. Suppose, for example, that what is actually depicted on the screen is a black Porsche speeding along a country lane. So, Flannery's 'as if impression' of seeing, vivid as it may be, misrepresents the actual content of the shot that she is watching. In a certain sense, her 'as if impression' of seeing a werewolf creeping fails to be *warranted* by what she is actually perceiving in the film.[14] That is, the shots before her eyes were not designed to elicit in normal viewers of the movie the impression of its being as if they were seeing a werewolf in the castle maze. When a spectator's 'as if impression' of seeing X Φ fails to be 'veridical' in this way, one may be reluctant to accept, without qualification, that the spectator is 'seeing' (in the movie) X Φ. It is unlikely that Flannery, in witnessing the Porsche-depicting movie shot, could naturally be said to be seeing a werewolf creeping through a maze. No doubt it *seems* to Flannery that this is what she is seeing in the shot, but, it is not something that she actually does 'see.' She doesn't 'see' this even in the movie. Her impression of seeing a werewolf is not an apt imaginative response to the actual contents of the film images she is viewing.

---

[14] Plainly more needs to be said by way of explaining what it is for a shot, sequence, or scene to *warrant* an imaginative 'as if impression' of seeing (or hearing) *so-and-so* in the movie that has been prompted by watching the film segment in question. I have suggested in the main text that the impression is warranted by the segment if and only if the segment was designed by the film-makers to elicit an impression of just that type and content. However, there are complications and qualifications that deserve to be worked out, but it seems counterproductive in the present setting to try to work out this very tricky issue in elaborate detail. A possible account can be given in Walton's terms. The imaginative impression of the segment is warranted just in case the viewer is playing an *authorized* game of make-believe in which the movie serves as a prop, and the impression is 'prescribed' for the viewer, given the 'rules of generation' for that game and pertinent facts about the character of the segment. This possible explication has the virtue of placing the concept of a warranted 'as if impression' in more familiar theoretical terrain, but it is unlikely to answer all the questions that will quite naturally arise. For some readers, it may raise as many questions as it answers. See Walton (1990), especially 25–43.

If we want to capture this restriction on our use of (1) and (2), then we should add a 'veridicality' condition to the treatment of them that I have outlined just above. We should say that (1) and (2) are used primarily to assert the strengthened claims that

(1′) [In viewing the movie] Flannery aptly imagines seeing the werewolf of London (i.e., she has the *warranted* impression of its being as if she is seeing the werewolf of London),

and

(2′) [In viewing the movie] Flannery aptly imagines seeing the werewolf creeping through the castle maze (i.e., she has the *warranted* impression of its being as if she is seeing the werewolf creeping through the castle maze).

It is important here that it is no part of the claim that (1′) and (2′) paraphrase some literal sense of the form of words in (1) and (2). Rather (1′) and (2′) are related to (1) and (2) in essentially the same way that (3′) and (4′) are related to (3) and (4). They render the pragmatically enriched proposition that the speaker primarily intends, in the relevant context, to affirm. As I argued earlier, the literal meaning or the semantic content of (1) and (2) are given by propositions that are strictly speaking false.

Ordinary uses of instances of (α) and (β) that make no reference to movie viewing generally will be, as I explained before, 'environment involving,' although 'narrowly subjective' uses are familiar enough. If Ellen sees Sam raking leaves, then there is a raking of leaves by Sam in her environment, a raking that bears the right relation to her concurrent visual experience. A similar point applies, I believe, to instances of (α) and (β) that purport to describe what a spectator is 'seeing' in a movie shot or sequence. That is, (1′) and (2′) also characterize, so to speak, an 'environment involving' use of these judgments, although, in this case, the 'environment' that is involved is provided by the fictional world of the movie in question. This, or so it seems to me, is the normal understanding of (1) and (2). If it is true that (2), then the shot or sequence that Flannery is viewing must depict a werewolf creeping through the maze, and that shot or sequence must prompt and be suitably designed to match her concurrent 'as if impression' of what it is that she is seeing. Various additional refinements and amplifications could be investigated in the light of certain more nuanced complications of a similar ilk, but I assume that the basic import of the overall hypothesis that I am proposing is clear enough.

The last few paragraphs are meant to introduce the sort of imagined seeing I am trying to single out; still, it is worth saying something more about the use of the 'imagined Φing' construction I have in mind. This project of amplification is yet another juncture at which the account is difficult to formulate with adequate refinement, but it is crucial to say something positive and suitably qualified about what 'imagined seeing' is supposed to amount to in my projected version of the Imagined Seeing Thesis. Otherwise, the version of the thesis I am defending will almost certainly be misunderstood. The phrase 'to imagine seeing' has several distinct uses, most of which are irrelevant to the thesis that I endorse.

For example, in watching a crowd scene in a movie, I might 'imagine seeing' my wife's face among faces of the people in the crowd. This is simply a case of misperception inflected by my imagination—my apparent seeing is distorted and mistaken. If we were to focus on this kind of use, then we could well be tempted by the thought that imagined seeing must generally involve illusion of some sort. Or, the following is an example of still another type of use. In watching a jungle movie, Gareth may view a scene in which the hunter/hero sees a lion coming toward him across the clearing. This scene could prompt him to visualize himself standing in the movie hero's position and looking at the lion as it approaches him. In this instance, the movie has indeed led Gareth to 'imagine seeing' the lion approaching him, but not in the use of 'imagine seeing' that is in question here.

In the target sense, already adumbrated, no inner act of visualization needs to be involved. Indeed no *act* or *activity* of the imagination has to occur at all—at least if 'act' and 'activity' are used in some minimally full-blooded sense. Thus, if my proposal can be adequately filled out, it yields a version of the Imagined Seeing Thesis that avoids a range of the most familiar objections to the initial proto-conception. Many authors have rejected the notion that our experiential relation to fictional things in the movies is properly described in terms of 'imagined seeing' at all, but it is my conviction that these critics have missed the sense in question. Or, at a minimum, the critics have been puzzled about what sort of imaginative phenomena such a description is supposed to cover. This is what the ensuing remarks are meant to clarify further.

There are different modes in which a person may have an 'as if impression' of himself Φing or being Φ'd. For instance, Rudolph may have the impression, on the basis of sketchy indicators, of being cheated by his partners in a card game. The 'as if impression,' in this instance, may involve nothing more than Rudolph's very tentative intuition (hunch) that he is being cheated by the other players. In this instance, Rudolph's imaginings and private fantasy play no notable role in the prompting of his impression. Rudolph isn't *imagining* himself being cheated. In the present example, he is being cheated, and he has acquired the suspicion that this is so. Or again, the following is a similar but more ambiguous case. Rolph is having an especially vivid and realistic hallucination of there being a green cube before his eyes, but he knows full well that he is hallucinating. He doesn't imagine for a moment *that* there really is a green cube in front of him. Still, Rolph does have the impression of its being as if he is actually seeing a green cube, and his impression arises solely from the fact that it really is, in his experience, as if he were seeing a green cube. Rolph's impression is directly responsive to that fact. As before, no element of fantasy or fancy plays a role in causing the 'as if impression' that he is having or in influencing its specific content. Despite the existence of Rolph's definite 'as if impression,' it seems doubtful to me that Rolph actually *imagines* himself seeing a green cube before his eyes. At some level, his impression is simply registering the phenomenal situation that he experiences.

Contrast these cases with the case of Randolph. As he is walking through the basement of a tall building, Randolph is seized by the impression of its being as if the building is starting to collapse around his ears. He has this impression, we will suppose, even though he is completely certain that his paranoid sense is false. In Randolph's case, however, imagination or fantasy does play a key role in producing his impression of an imminent building collapse. Presumably, his impression is partly caused by imaginings encouraged by certain of his claustrophobic fears. Randolph does *imagine* the building's being about to fall upon him.[15] The contrast between the cases of Rudolph and Rolph, on the one hand, and the case of Randolph, on the other, indicates that we can draw a distinction between *imaginative* 'as if impressions' and those in which the subject's imagination plays no significant role. No doubt the distinction is somewhat crude, but it has an intuitive basis nonetheless.

These considerations allow us to refine the Imagined Seeing Thesis with one further qualification. A critical source of Gustav's impression that he is being spoken to by the on screen character *is* an imagining—an imagining that arises in an apt and familiar way out of his normal imaginative engagement with the film. Gustav's 'as if impression' of being personally addressed by the screen character is therefore an *imaginative* one. Similarly, it seems to me that Flannery's impression of seeing the werewolf creeping through the maze is notably comparable to Gustav's in just this way. Her impression of seeing fictions in the movie is likely to be involuntary, and it is likewise a warranted imaginative response to segments of the visual narration of the film. Her impression of seeing the werewolf and his behavior in the movie is a spontaneous and appropriate upshot of her imaginative processing of the images presented to her in the film. The film-makers will have counted on members of the audience to form the relevant 'as if impressions' in relation to the dramatic action. In fact, another related phenomenon occurs when the werewolf comes into view, and Flannery has a vivid impression of imminent danger for the heroine. This involves an imaginative *emotional* response to the movie, justified by what the movie depicts, a response that arises spontaneously out of Flannery's imagined seeing of the fictional scene.[16]

So, this is the version of the Imagined Seeing Thesis that I have advocated. Normal viewers of fiction films characteristically have an imaginative 'as if impression' of seeing the narrative objects and events of a fiction film. They have the continuing impression that it is as if they were witnessing segments of the fictional world.[17] It is in *this* special albeit somewhat elusive sense that Flannery *imagines* seeing the werewolf creeping through the maze, and more generally, that movie viewers *imagine* seeing the fictional objects and events that are presented to them on the screen. Plainly, my justification for this account rests on the explanation that I favor of our ubiquitous talk of 'seeing'

[15] If we think that a hallucination is always a product in some sense of the imagination—the capacity to form perceptual images—then there may be a sense in which we do accept that Rolph imagines seeing the green cube before him. But this *is*, I believe, a different sense of the phrase.

[16] See Walton (1978), 5–27.

[17] Indeed, as I will argue later, the viewer has the impression that it is as if she were seeing a segment of the fictional world *by* seeing 'motion picture-like images' that have been derived from that portion of the world. This, of course, is the Mediated Version of the Imagined Seeing Thesis.

fictional characters and their actions and circumstances in a movie. Thus, the speaker who affirms (1) and (2) and conveys a true thought thereby, means to be describing the content of the warranted 'as if impression' of seeing that Flannery has had in watching the 'werewolf' sequence. It is an impression whose specific content is validated or not depending on what she sees more narrowly on screen. The words of (1) and (2) are naturally construed as claiming rightly that Flannery, suitably engaged in her watching of the movie, is having the immediate imaginative impression of seeing the werewolf and/or of seeing the werewolf's fictive behavior in the maze, and it strictly implies that Flannery's impression is warranted by what the film she is watching actually depicts.

It is noteworthy that Flannery's impression of looking into the fictional world of a movie can be disrupted. It seems to be grounded in Flannery's maintaining some kind of suitable imaginative engagement with the narration and narrative of the film. Thus, her impression of seeing the werewolf creeping through the maze can be lost or diminished if, for example, clumsy editing, stylized acting, or egregiously artificial special effects break the spell. Incompetent back projection can dim a viewer's initial impression of seeing a pair of characters who are together in a car while driving through the countryside. The potential vulnerability of a viewer's continued impression of looking into the movie's fictional world reinforces the idea that the provenance of such an impression depends crucially on the viewer's imagination and the extent to which it imbues and articulates her experience of the image-track (and her apprehension of the sound-track).

Context matters as well. Compare seeing an extended shot from, say, *Vertigo* and seeing subsequently the very same shot in the setting of a documentary about the making of *Vertigo*, especially where, in the documentary setting, some of the artifice involved in executing the shot has been effectively exposed. It is probable that we will see the shot in very different ways in each instance, and some significant diminishment of the 'as if impression' of simply looking into a fictional world is likely to result from the documentary context. Naturally there are many movies that invoke the 'as if impression' of seeing into a fictional world only to subvert it in one of several ways. We are not likely to grasp the various possible artistic aims that motivate such subversions of the spectator's normal imaginative stance toward fiction film unless we already grasp the aesthetic force and significance of what we might call the 'as if impression' of perceptual realism within the traditional cinema.[18]

---

[18] For a fairly complicated example of how these issues can ramify in aesthetically interesting ways, see my discussion of von Sternberg's *The Scarlet Empress* (1934) in Chapter 8. I discuss the way in which the viewer imagines seeing the movie character, Catherine the Great, by actually seeing Marlene Dietrich play the role. But our imagined seeing of the character is deeply inflected by seeing the character in terms of Dietrich's familiar screen persona. Catherine the Great in this movie is supposed to be imagined in terms importantly supplied by that persona. This presupposes the fact that viewers, as they *imagine seeing* the character Catherine, are *actually seeing* Dietrich, *albeit* indirectly, and generally they will be *aware*, if only *subliminally*, that this is so. In general, the phenomenology of seeing a stretch of a fiction film is enormously complicated, and the Imagined Seeing Thesis is meant to capture only an aspect—although a basic aspect—of our characteristic

A number of authors, writing in this area, have rejected the Imagined Seeing Thesis, maintaining instead that our experience of film can be adequately described without invoking the concept of 'imagining seeing' at all. Here is a short affirmation of that point by Noël Carroll. He says:

My own view is that there is no seeing imaginarily involved. Spectators see cinematographic images on screen which they use to imagine what is fictionally the case. Watching *The General*, they see a moving photographic picture of a locomotive and they imagine that the engine, The General, has been hi-jacked by Union spies. They do not imagine seeing the event . . . We do not imagine seeing Johnnie Gray [the character] and his locomotive. We see images of Buster Keaton doing this and that, and imagine that Johnnie Gray is doing thus and so.[19]

According to Carroll, all that the viewer strictly speaking sees are the movie's images and the photographed material presented in those shots. On the basis of what is thereby seen, and guided by a contextual sense of the narrative developments up to the relevant point, the viewer imagines that so and so is going on in the story now. Colin McGinn in *The Power of the Movies* emphatically embraces the same position. (See the passage I quoted earlier in this chapter.)

Carroll certainly accepts that we do not, strictly speaking, see the characters and their actions, and he also maintains quite explicitly in this passage that viewers also do not imagine seeing these fictional items either. But consider the segment from *M* that I mentioned earlier. My remarks about the segment already indicate why this position is too impoverished to succeed. Viewers see the projected segment and they are thereby prompted to *imagine* that (i) the murderer meets the little girl; that (ii) he purchases a balloon; and, a little later that (iii) he kills her. However, the approach favored by Carroll and McGinn offers us no way to mark the obvious distinction. That is, the viewer 'sees' or (better) imagines seeing the purchase of the balloon (and perhaps the meeting), but, as the movie is actually constructed, the viewer does not 'see' or imagine seeing the murder of the little girl. In terms of truth in the fiction, (i), (ii), and (iii) are on a par, but in terms of the way in which viewers have access to the fictional contents, they are not. No satisfactory account of our experience of fictions in films can fail to mark this distinction.

Gregory Currie also denies that we see or, more narrowly, imagine seeing fictions in movies, but his positive account has resources that allow him to draw something like the distinctions underscored above. That is, he distinguishes between simply imagining that P on the basis of seeing a movie, and more determinately *perceptually imagining* that P. Roughly, a viewer perceptually imagines an object or event X on a certain occasion just in case she imagines something adequately rich and vivid about the appearance of X, her imagining on that occasion is prompted by her actual perception of some visual

movie viewing experience. Although the case of *The Scarlet Empress* is especially complicated, similar complications are very often involved in the imagined seeing of many movie fictions.

[19] Carroll (2006), 184, fn 7.

representation of X,[20] and the content of the imagining is counterfactually dependent in a sufficiently sensitive way on features of her actual perception of the movie's representation of X. In Currie's terms, one can observe that M contains shots that mandate perceptual imaginings about the murderer's initial encounter with the young girl and about the buying of the balloon, but that it includes no shots that prescribe that the viewer is to *perceptually* imagine the murder of the little girl. This approach then satisfies the constraint that, as I would put it, the viewer imagines seeing the meeting and the purchase of the balloon, but not the killing. Is the difference here something more than a matter of terminology? Is there a significant difference between the concept of 'imagined seeing' in the movies, as I have developed it, and the concept of 'perceptual imagining' as it is explained by Currie?

It seems to me that there are certainly differences between Currie's concept and mine, but it is much less clear that most of the differences between us turn out to be significant in the present debate. As I discussed in Chapter 2, Currie maintains that if viewers of a movie were to imagine seeing a particular segment of the fictional world, then their imagining would have to involve imagining themselves to be located in the implicit space of the scene and observing the visible scene from there. He maintains, in other words, that the Imagined Seeing Thesis must be understood in the Face-to-Face Version and that the Face-to-Face Version is simply false. His concept of 'perceptual imagining' is specifically crafted to avoid the implication that viewers must project themselves imaginatively into the movie's fictional space. Now, of course, if Currie were right that imagined seeing has to be thought of as a kind of 'face-to-face' seeing, then there plainly would be a significant difference between the distinct but kindred concepts. However, the main point of the middle part of Chapter 2 was to argue that the Face-to-Face Version of the Imagined Seeing Thesis is false and to argue that it is perfectly coherent to suppose that viewers imagine seeing fictions from an 'unoccupied visual perspective,' i.e. that they imagine seeing a given scene without imagining about themselves that somehow they have been suitably positioned to have that scene directly before their eyes. As I have framed the concept of 'imagined seeing' in the present section, it does not carry the objectionable implication, and therefore it doesn't differ in that regard from what Currie calls 'perceptual imagining.'

In the next chapter I will take up this central question one more time, because my exposition of an alternative to Currie's position in Chapter 2 was significantly incomplete. In effect, I delineated *two* possible ways in which a commitment to the Face-to-Face Version can be avoided. One of these is the to adopt some Mediated Version of the Imagined Seeing Thesis, and that is the strategy that I wound up endorsing in the original version of Chapter 2. But I failed to explain my grounds for settling on that endorsement. I had already sketched a position, apparently more

---

[20] A person can perceptually imagine something about an actual item X, and this will require that the person's imagining is prompted by X and is counterfactually dependent on the person's perceptual experience of X. However, we are concerned here only with perceptual imagining at the movies.

modest than the Mediated Version, which also repudiated the obvious implausibility of the Face-to-Face account. According to the position, viewers do imagine seeing segments of the movie's fictional world, but it is altogether indeterminate for them how they do so. It is indeterminate for them whether they imagine seeing the fictional world either face-to-face or in some mediated fashion. And yet, I gave no reasons for rejecting this 'Modest Version' of Imagined Seeing and correlatively no reasons for favoring some Mediated Version over it. In the next chapter, I try to rectify the oversight. Clarifying this matter is important for defining more carefully the specific position that I have meant to be endorsing in the previous chapter and in this one.

4

Le Grand Imagier in Review

I. The Modest Version of the Imagined Seeing Thesis

In "*Le Grand Imagier* Steps Out" (Chapter 2) I spent a fair amount of space deflecting the charge of incoherence that Gregory Currie originally mounted against the Imagined Seeing Thesis. This is one of several deep puzzles about the nature of our access to the fictions in fiction films, puzzles that any account of movie spectatorship should address. Of course, philosophers have spent a fair amount of space attempting to give an account of Truth in Fiction, aiming to explain at least roughly what it is for a proposition to be true in a work of fiction. They have searched for an account that works for literary fiction and a corresponding account suitable for cinematic fiction. However, less space and effort have been devoted to questions about our Acquaintance with Fictions and the nature of our Knowledge of them. The present chapter will be devoted to several of these questions as they arise for the case of movies—epistemological problems about our access to fictional items and fictional truths in the cinema. As I proceed, I will match and contrast some of the results that I defend in this domain with counterpart considerations about dramatic fictions in radio broadcasts. In general, different forms and media have to be treated somewhat differently. This is what one would expect, although certain results, as we will observe, will carry over from one case to another.

I will begin by investigating again, more rigorously and systematically, Currie's basic objection to the Imagined Seeing Thesis. There are two good reasons for doing so. First, my discussion of Currie's challenge in Chapter 2 is pretty compressed, and, as I indicated at the end of the last chapter, I have been guilty of running together two central facets of the problem that Currie's challenge raises. It is crucial, of course, to distinguish the Face-to-Face Version of the Imagined Seeing Thesis from elaborations of the Mediated Version, but it is also crucial to distinguish both of these from what I am now dubbing 'the Modest Version.'[1] The difference between the third option

---

[1] Although I will go over the terminology more carefully in the present section of the present chapter, it is best to set the basic categories straight at the outset. The Modest Version of the Imagined Seeing Thesis says that movie viewers imagine seeing into the fictional world of the movie *and* that it is fictionally indeterminate for them whether the seeing they imagine is face-to-face or mediated in some way. The Face-to-Face Version grants that viewers imagine seeing segments of the fictional world from a position face-to-face with the segments in question. The Mediated Version asserts that viewers imagine seeing segments of the fictional world and that the seeing they thereby imagine is mediated or indirect in some fashion. The Mediated

and the second marks a major epistemic consideration that I have so far failed to highlight appropriately. As the chapter proceeds, I will be rejecting the Modest Version for reasons yet to be introduced and defending a highly qualified elaboration of the Mediated Version. It will be a notable theoretical advance to be clear about the differences between this 'mediated' Version and the simpler but inadequate Modest Version. Second, Currie's objection has continued to have considerable currency. For instance, Noël Carroll has reiterated and endorsed it in a recent article on narration in film. So plainly there is more to be said about why I maintain that Currie's objection is unsuccessful. It is my sense that 'imagined seeing' has come to be out of favor, but the reasons I have seen for this disfavor are mistaken. In saying more about this and related matters, we will conspicuously advance our comprehension of various facets of the epistemology of fiction film.

Here is the lively way in which Carroll frames the issues:

Watching a gun battle in *3:10 to Yuma*, I find myself curiously unscathed, nor do I imagine myself ducking bullets. Yet if I were imagining I was seeing a gun fight close up, wouldn't I have to imagine that my life was endangered? Can I be imagining that I'm seeing a gun battle from a vantage point inside the line of fire and not imagine bullets bursting midair around me? And if I were imagining that, how would I continue eating my popcorn so nonchalantly because I don't imagine myself amidst a blizzard of flying steel and if I don't imagine that I am amidst the fire fight, how can I plausibly imagine that I am seeing it?[2]

In this passage, Carroll is arguing from the following assumptions.

(A)   If movie viewers imagine seeing a fictional situation in a given shot, then these viewers imagine seeing that fictional situation from a certain determinate visual perspective.

Usually, the visual perspective of the shot will effectively define a fictional vantage point (VP) for the shot—a location *in the implied fictional space* of the shot from which the situation is presented. It is the fictional location that yields the visual perspective displayed on screen.[3] Thus, Carroll, like Currie before him, also assumes that

---

Version itself can come in a range of elaborations. Strong elaborations would specify the nature of the imagined mediation. A weak elaboration would hold in turn that the means or mechanism that constitutes the mediation is, in general, fictionally indeterminate. This, in the end, is the position that I accept.

[2] Carroll (2009), 199.

[3] The formulation makes the simplifying assumption that the shot in question involves no camera movement. Of course, this is a gross oversimplification, but I do not think that it significantly affects the issues presently under discussion. A formulation that dropped this restriction would quickly become extremely complicated. Also, we have to distinguish the real physical vantage point that the camera occupied at the time the shot was taken, and the vantage point in the fictional space of the story from which the specific configuration of fictional items has apparently been presented. Very often, it is possible to define the vantage point in fictional space only in more or less approximate terms.

(B)   If viewers imagine seeing a certain fictional situation from a determinate visual perspective, then this entails that the viewers imagine themselves being located within the fictional space at VP and seeing the situation from that position.

Condition (B) is the Face-to-Face constraint on imagined seeing, and its acceptance defines what I have called 'the Face-to-Face Version of the Imagined Seeing Thesis.' Many writers seem to have assumed that this restrictive constraint is an inevitable part of the Imagined Seeing Thesis, and they have argued that imagined seeing, understood in this fashion, leads to implausible and even absurd consequences. That is, they also accept

(C)   If viewers imagine seeing a certain scene from an implicit vantage point VP within the fictional space of the narrative action, then they are committed to imagining themselves as being involved in whatever fictional circumstances are represented as obtaining at VP.

Thus, using Carroll's example, if the movie represents it as being the case that a fight is raging around the vantage point VP, then the viewer of the relevant shot is committed to imagining herself as being in the midst of that battle. If the movie shows us that it is raining around VP, then the viewer at VP is committed to imagining being soaked in the depicted rain.

In fact, Currie originally presented a closely related objection to the Imagined Seeing Thesis that equally rests on (A), (B), combined with a slight variant of (C). Currie thinks that the Imagined Seeing Thesis has the consequence that viewers who see a *sequence* of shots that are taken from *different* vantage points are committed to imagining themselves as absurdly mobile witnesses of the scene. Taking a sequence from *The Birds* (Hitchcock, 1961) as his example, Currie says, "... the transitions between the first three shots would require [the spectator] to imagine her position shifted instantly through ninety degrees twice, around the edge of the bay... The transitions between [shots] 5 and 14 would then have her imagine herself shifting back and forth nine times between Melanie's own position ... and different points on the shore, all within the space of a minute or two."[4] Because Currie thinks that Imagined Seeing is committed to the Face-to-Face Version, he maintains that Imagined Seeing has the immediate consequence that a spectator who sees two or more successive shots, each with different vantage points in fictional space, must imagine himself as having *moved* or having *been moved* instantaneously from one position to the other. In Currie's example from *The Birds*, the implausible circumstances (the viewer's having suddenly changed positions in fictional space) are supposed to be a consequence of the sequence

---

[4] Currie (1995), 177. Carroll (2009), 199–200 raises the same objection. Walton (2008) discusses this passage critically on 119–120.

of shots, given that the viewer imagines being located at the vantage point in each instance.

Currie and Carroll contend—rightly I think—that

(D)   Movie viewers do *not* normally imagine themselves embroiled in the fictional circumstances depicted or implied by the shots or shot sequences, and it is intuitively implausible that they have any sort of rational commitment to so imagine.

In other words, the consequent of (C) is false, and this entails, by way of (B), that viewers don't imagine seeing fictional situations from some determinate perspective. But then, by (A), it follows that they don't imagine seeing the objects and events of the fiction at all. If the argument were sound, it would destroy the Imagined Seeing Thesis in every possible version.

Assumption (A), with minor qualifications, is a triviality,[5] and it is not something I dispute. I also agree with (D). Thus, it is the principles (B) and (C) that are the contentious components of the argument. On the one hand, Kendall Walton seems to accept (B)—the Face-to-Face constraint. However, he plainly denies that imagining oneself located at the vantage point really gives rise to the problematic commitments described in (C). He says, for instance,

And perhaps imagining seeing, or the kind of imagining seeing depictions provoke, is imagining seeing from one or another particular perspective. Even so there is no paradox. What Currie finds strange is not the idea that spectators of film imagine seeing from a given perspective, but that they imagine certain *consequences* [my emphasis] of their seeing from the perspective in question; their being in the water, being immune to bullets, changing position, and so on. Imagining seeing from the relevant perspective does not require imagining these consequences.[6]

---

[5]   I will consider the relevant issues later. Basically, they turn on a crucial ambiguity. The statement
(a) Jones sees the fictional items in the scene from a certain visual perspective,
may mean
(b) Jones sees the fictional items in the scene *and* sees them as standing in a certain set of *visual relations*—relations to one another and to the surface of the picture plane.
But it can also mean
(c) Jones sees the fictional items in the scene *and* imagines himself occupying a designated location *within* the fictional space in question and seeing the fictional items *from that position*.
The first of these readings normally has a simple, regular, and unproblematic application to the viewer's experience. The second of these readings very rarely does. Thus, the ubiquitously applicable first reading simply does not imply corresponding instances of the second, but it is extremely easy to run questions of the truth and falsity of (b) and (c) together. This is because the phrase "visual perspective" can define the pertinent visual relations of the visual position from which a suitably placed perceiver might have the depicted visual experience of both the items in the scene and the visual relations that they exemplify.

[6]   Walton (2008), 122. And yet, in the very next line he suggests an account of 'seeing from a perspective' of the sort that I favor, and this involves rejecting, as I do, thesis (B). So I am unsure about the difference between us on this issue. Also, I agree with him that it is not in general true that if an audience imagines and is meant to imagine that P, then the audience imagines or is even meant to imagine all the propositions that are thereby implied, suggested, or obviously presupposed by P. Call this thesis (C+). However, notice that the 'consequences' that Walton mentions are *consequences of what the viewer imagines* when, as it is

However, it seems to me and I will argue that the real trouble resides in (B). Viewers are not committed to imagining that they are relevantly implicated in the contextually determined fictional circumstances, *because* they simply don't imagine themselves being at the relevant vantage point in the first place. More broadly, they usually don't imagine themselves being stationed anywhere within the movie's fictional space at all.

It is worth noting in passing that assumption (C) does have a certain factitious plausibility if we conceive of 'imagined seeing' in the wrong way. In general, it is *possible* for the viewer of a perspectival picture to form an inner visualization of herself as standing at the picture's vantage point and looking at the depicted situation from that position. Now, if the viewer were to undertake this imaginative exercise, then she would be (at a minimum) under some rational pressure to visualize herself as subject to whatever circumstances (e.g., the tumult of battle, the pouring rain) that she takes to be fictionally realized at the vantage point. That is, (C) might well seem to be correct if 'imagined seeing' were wrongly modeled on this sort of inner self-visualizing. But, as I tried to bring out in the previous chapter, this is a terrible model for the imagined seeing that, on my view, regularly does take place in movie audiences. Although the viewer's imaginative projection of herself into the space of a sequence or scene is something viewers *can* potentially accomplish, it is in fact a specialized and very rare performance. As a rule, movie viewers don't imaginatively project themselves into their movies in this way. Therefore, imagining seeing, properly understood, does not involve an imagining, by an audience member, of being located at the optical vantage point of the shot.

It is instructive to consider how an argument, analogous to the Currie/Carroll objection, might be constructed to apply to a related but simpler type of case—the case of fictional stories dramatized on the radio. By doing so, we begin to generalize the issue of how audiences imaginatively perceive the fictions with which they are, in some sense, presented. In the case of radio plays, I assume that listeners *do* imagine hearing the fictional utterances and sounds that occur in the course of such a dramatization. However, I suppose that it could seem that this simple, naïve assumption might also seem to be threatened equally by a suitable variant of the Currie/Carroll objection. Counterparts to (A) through (D) above might seem to show that the very idea of 'the imagined hearing' of fictional sounds in radio programs turns out to be incoherent. However, if we try to work out the counterpart objection, it becomes plain that any reasonable analogue of assumption (B) will be false, and the reasons that this is so suggest a good deal about why (B) itself is wrong. Of course, there are many potentially

supposed, the viewer imagines herself positioned at the vantage point in fictional space. I am repudiating the idea that the movie viewer imagines any such thing, and hence rejecting that the 'consequences' that Currie and Carroll identify are genuine consequences of anything that the viewer actually imagines or is supposed to imagine in watching the film. I accept (C+) in its full generality, but I reject the more restricted (C) because it presupposes the truth of the incorrect assumption (B). Whether Walton and I actually disagree over this point is not so important. What is important is that there are at least two different ways of rejecting the Currie/Carroll argument against the Imagined Seeing Thesis.

relevant differences between 'seeing' movie fictions and 'hearing' radio fictions, but I will explain why these differences do nothing more than give (B) a spurious plausibility.

To render the example somewhat more concrete, suppose that members of a radio audience are listening to a creepy mystery program on the radio. At a particular juncture of the program, listeners may imagine hearing the patter of fictional rain upon a fictional church roof. Concurrently, they may also imagine hearing the voices of the hero and heroine, the thunder of a violent rainstorm, and the harsh whistling of the wind through nearby trees. But of course, what these listeners are actually hearing are dramatic performances and sound effects broadcast over the radio. The program's listeners imagine hearing those very real broadcast sounds *as* the sound of rain on a roof, *as* peals of thunder in the vicinity, and *as* the whistling of wind in churchyard trees. Similarly, the listeners actually hear the verbal performances of the actors, and imagine hearing their utterances *as* the fictive speech acts of the fictional characters they play.

In the normal case, it just won't make sense to wonder *where* the radio listeners imagine themselves to be situated as they 'hear' the fictional thunder, rain, and wind. It usually will not make sense even to wonder if the listeners imagine themselves stationed within the church and hearing the sounds from within that edifice or whether instead they are somewhere outside the church and listening from that unsheltered spot. Nothing in what they hear and nothing in background information from the story context that helps to adumbrate the spatial layout of the scene will permit the audience to make a reasonable discrimination of a fictional position for them even as broad as this.[7] At the same time, this is not to say that 'nothing' will have been conveyed to the listeners about the fictional spatial configuration of objects and events in the dramatic scene. It may sound as though the thunder is coming from somewhere beyond the church and that the whistling of the wind in the trees is somewhere adjacent to the splatter of the rain upon the church roof. We could therefore say, if we chose to do so, that the constellation of simultaneous story sounds exhibits 'an auditory perspectival structure' for the listeners, although it should be understood that the extent of the structuring may, in particular cases, be pretty schematic. Nevertheless, the various cues that convey information about the spatial configuration of the fictional sounds will usually not come close to specifying any reasonably definite position or locale within the scene that defines, as it were, an 'auditory vantage point' from which the imagined hearing of the sounds is (fictionally)

---

[7] This is not to say that there can not be something like an 'auditory vantage point.' Listeners may be prompted to imagine hearing the voices of certain characters, hearing them as they sound from the bottom of a deep and narrow well. Perhaps the voices are to sound as fictionally they sound to another character that is lying at the bottom of the well. My point in the text is that this is far from the normal case, and, even in a case of this kind, listeners do not imagine *themselves* to be at the bottom of the well and hearing the voices from there. If they did, would they imagine being stuffed in the well with the character who fictionally *is* lying there?

to occur. One can allow then that, in listening to the program, listeners imagine hearing an array of sounds, and they thereby imagine hearing that array as having a certain rough auditory 'perspective.' But to say that the fictional sounds are heard from such a perspective is *only* to say that, as the listeners imagine hearing the various sounds, they apprehend them (or, more specifically, their fictional sources) as standing in certain fairly sketchy spatial relationships to one another. Having an auditory perceptual structure amounts to nothing more than this, and the condition on the audience's experience provides no encouragement to the idea that audience members imagine themselves listening from somewhere *within* the dramatic space.

This is the crucial point. Reasonable counterparts to (A), (C), and (D) above seem to hold for the case of radio dramas. Comparable to (A) is the fact that, in 'hearing' the fictional sounds of the program, listeners 'hear' those sounds from a (rough and ready) auditory perspective. Similarly, an analogue for (C) seems correct. *If* listeners to the mystery program described above *were* to imagine themselves in the vicinity of the storm-soaked church, then they *would* imagine or have reason to imagine the rain in their faces and the windy chill around their ears. But suppose we were to try to construct an analogue for (B)—for the Face-to-Face constraint—that applied to the radio listener's experience of the program. First, as noted above, we would have no systematic way of defining an 'auditory vantage point' to match the formulation in the consequent of (B). But second and more important, even if the hypothetical analogue of (B) were taken to be much more loosely specified—making reference to a *region* in fictional space, for instance—thesis (B) still would remain utterly incredible. Thus, let the analogue be, for example,

(B★) If members of the radio audience imagine hearing the program's narrative events, then they must imagine being *somewhere* in the program's fictional space and hearing the constellation of sounds from there.

This principle, in my opinion, lacks all intuitive appeal. Now, what I am calling 'the Modest Version of the Imagined Seeing Thesis' suggests that a similar diagnosis is feasible for the more complicated case of imagined seeing at the movies.

Of course, there are important differences between the two cases, but none of the resulting contrasts affects the essential point. It is true that a shot (or a temporal slice of a shot in motion) in a standard narrative film will typically present a fictional situation from a highly specific visual perspective. Facts about the character of the visual perspective combined with facts about the fictional spatial layout of the overall dramatic scene will standardly assign a fictional vantage point to the shot—the vantage point from which the narrative situation has been depicted in the shot. One might be tempted to suspect that these facts about the specificity of the audience's viewpoint in looking at movies make a crucial difference here. Don't these facts establish that imagined seeing in the movies must involve imagined seeing of the story action from the vantage point implicitly associated with the shot? In the case of radio dramas, as

I have indicated, the broadcasting of the fictional sounds does not, as a rule, establish specific auditory counterparts of the visual vantage points in film.

In watching a movie shot, (a) the viewer imagines (and is meant to imagine) seeing the objects, events, and circumstances depicted in the fiction. (b) She also thereby imagines seeing this collection of fictional items as displayed in the spatial relationships exhibited in the shot.[8] And finally, (c) she thereby imagines seeing the fictional manifold as visually presented from some definite visual orientation in relation to the frontal plane of the screen. However, information of these three kinds seems to give us everything that is constitutive of the fact that she imagines seeing the items *from a (relatively) determinate visual perspective*. If that visual perspective is associated with a particular vantage point VP in fictional space (as very often it will be), then the viewer will correlatively imagine seeing these items from the vantage point in question. But, all that this point amounts to is that, when the viewer imagines seeing the items from VP, she imagines that the way that the fictional items appear to her within the shot corresponds to the way in which fictionally those items *would* appear to a suitable observer *were* he or she to occupy the position VP within the fictional space of the scene. Or, more guardedly, the shot corresponds to the way in which fictionally those items would appear to be *spatially configured and oriented* in relation to a *hypothetical* (and possibly fictional) *witness* who occupied the fictional position VP.

Therefore, we should grant that movie viewers do imagine themselves seeing a fictional situation from a definite 'visual perspective' and usually from, so to speak, an associated 'vantage point' as well. However, in accepting these descriptions, we have no reason to allow that viewers thereby imagine themselves to literally *occupy* either the perspective or the vantage point. That defective idea, of course, is the idea that is captured in the Face-to-Face constraint. The perspectival visual structure in a movie shot is determined in terms of a complex, interacting system of visual information and cues, and the structures that are created in this manner are characteristically much richer than the auditory perspectival structures created in the course of a typical radio drama. Nevertheless, I maintain that the greater complexity of visual perspectives over auditory perspectives does not essentially change the central facts about the ways in which we are imaginatively engaged with the fictional spaces that movies and radio respectively construct. In both instances, we imagine perceiving the relevant entities and events and we imagine perceiving them as standing in certain spatial relations. Moreover, in both cases, these imagined perceptions are based on our imagined seeing or imagined hearing of the fictional objects and events that have been depicted. But, to repeat a final time, we can explicate the content of these claims in a way that does not entail that we imagine our having been situated somewhere within the fictional space of the story. The pertinent strategy of explication is clearer perhaps when we consider

---

[8]   This passage needs a qualification to allow for certain effects of shooting the scene with distorting lenses. Among the effects may be a distortion of some aspects of the spatial relationships between the items depicted in the shot.

the simpler case of 'hearing' fictional sounds when listening to a radio drama, but I'm proposing that the strategies are essentially the same.

It is little wonder that such questions are so perplexing. First, the facts about how even a mainstream fiction film establishes the fictional space of a scene or segment can be pretty complicated. Second, many of the crucial terms that we employ to describe our epistemic relation to that fictional space become systematically ambiguous. For instance, the camera used to shoot a given shot is actually located at a certain point in physical space and thereby establishes quite literally a 'vantage point' within that real space. But, the shot in its narrative context will usually establish a fictional vantage point within the fictional space of the enacted scene, and yet, it is nevertheless part of the movie story that no camera occupies that fictional vantage point. Moreover, as I have been urging, neither do viewers of the movie occupy such a vantage point— even in their own imaginations. It is easy to lose sight of the fact that the space of the fictive drama and the vantage points that open upon a time-slice of a narrative history are just as fictional as the characters and situations that progressively forge the developments of plot.

These are the reasons that I conclude that the Face-to-Face Version is false— I conclude that it is possible and desirable to endorse the Imagined Seeing Thesis without supposing that viewers imagine themselves seeing the fictional scene 'face-to-face' from within the fictional space that encompasses it. If movie viewers characteristically do not imagine themselves within the fictional space of a shot or sequence at all, then *a fortiori* they also do not imagine either that they are embroiled in the circumstances that might otherwise assault them in those fictional locales. There is also no reason for us to construct an explanation, even in the imagination, about how it is that movie viewers might seem to shift their fictional vantage point instantaneously from one shot to another. The movie's viewers do not move, even fictionally, because the vantage point in each of the shots has not been fictionally occupied by them.[9] The Modest Version, which holds that the seeing that we imagine is neither direct nor mediated, captures all of this, but, as I will argue shortly in rejecting any mediation in the imagined seeing, it goes too far.

Nevertheless, I believe that there is still another tempting motivation for the Face-to-Face Version that needs to be addressed. If it is true after all that members of the audience imagine themselves seeing the fictional situations in a movie, then one might say, must it not be true that they implicitly imagine *something* about *what makes it possible* for them to be seeing the pertinent fictional objects, events, and situations? And yet, how can they imagine themselves to be seeing these narrative elements unless they imagine themselves as being, so to speak, within eyeshot of the fictive items and occurrences on view? Once we allow ourselves to insist upon an answer to such a

---

[9] Naturally, if the shot is an optical POV shot from the visual perspective of a character, then the vantage point is fictionally occupied by the relevant character. I discuss optical POV shots and other types of 'subjective' shots in Chapter 6.

question, it is almost inevitable that we will agree that viewers must imagine themselves seeing the fictional items 'before their very eyes.' Suppose, however, that we were to insist on the same question in connection with the radio dramas considered earlier. It will seem almost equally inevitable, I suppose, to agree that if listeners imagine hearing the narrative action of the program, then they must be imagining themselves as being within 'earshot' of the fictional sounds they hear. So one will be forced along this route to the conclusion that radio audiences imagine themselves being within the fictional space of the radio show's dramatic action after all. I assume that this conclusion has almost no intuitive appeal.

It was a major theme in Chapter 2 that philosophers need to resist the temptation to believe that such seductively 'natural' questions must always have a well-motivated and intelligible answer. Sometimes they do, but often enough they do not. It is a striking feature of the imagination that we may imagine Φing (e.g., turning into a frog) without imagining, as part of this, that even the most basic conditions for Φing in the actual world have been satisfied in the state of affairs imagined. Indeed, we may imagine Φing without presupposing that what we thereby imagine is fully intelligible in the first place. To repeat, this was a point that I stressed at some length in the second chapter. However, the methodological issues here are difficult. Any position on the questions we have been discussing will wind up appealing at some stage of the argument to the ungrounded character of *some* of the fictional and imaginative truths that audiences more or less primitively accept. We should not assume that an imagined explanation of *how* the audience perceives the target fictions that are somehow available to them in the work can be constructed to rationalize philosophically the 'access' to the fictions that the viewers or listeners unreflectively enjoy.

Previously, I presented some literary examples of this point. In a novel whose plot is told by a certain kind of omniscient narrator, we imagine that the narrator has more or less unrestricted knowledge of the inner and outer lives of the characters. This is something about the work's narration that we simply accept as such, without relying on a work-internal explanation of how it might be so. Indeed, we regard any requirement that there has to be such an explanation as silly and beside the point.[10] Or, here is a still more colorful example from Chapter 1. In the famous animal novel, *Black Beauty*, the narrator is a horse—the eponymous Black Beauty. We accept throughout our reading of the novel that the words of the text are the words of Black Beauty recounting the adventures of his life, and it would be incredibly perverse to worry about how it was possible for a *horse* to have composed his own autobiography. Any attempt at an explanation of the rock bottom conventions of narration upon which this novel relies surely would not appeal to the uncanny linguistic abilities of the narrating horse. Such an answer to such a 'silly question' would actually be an exercise in sheer nuttiness.

---

[10] For the seminal discussion of these matters, see the section "Silly Questions," in Walton (1990), 174–183.

In fact, one reason that I have developed the example of radio dramatization at some length is because it strikes me as still another persuasive example of this same point. We imagine hearing the narrative action of the program, but we imagine nothing about what could be giving us auditory access to those fictional sounds. What in the world might we imagine on this score? We know the work-external basis of our imagined access, and there is nothing more that is called for epistemically. In the next section, we will have further instances of the implicit ungrounded character of story-presenting frameworks in fictional works. The hard thing, of course, is to discriminate between the cases in which such appeals to the ungrounded character or indeterminacy within the fiction are legitimate and the cases in which they are not.[11] I suspect that, despite the strength of my own intuitions—even my firm intuitions about the case of radio plays— the point may nevertheless be somewhat controversial. Therefore, I am afraid that we are forced to make the requisite discriminations pretty much instance by instance. I cannot see what *general* principles might be available to us and would do much to adjudicate plausibly the variety of examples with which one can be confronted.

II. The case for the Mediated Version of the Imagined Seeing Thesis

I will be arguing shortly that we do have reasons to enrich the Modest Version in a significant way, arriving at a variant of that position—the view that, in earlier chapters, I have dubbed 'the Mediated Version of the Imagined Seeing Thesis.' Understanding the Modest Version is important to grasping what is wrong with the Currie/Carroll objection, but there are also other critical considerations about film spectatorship that the 'modest' view, without supplementation and qualification, is not well positioned to accommodate. Reflection on these additional considerations provides grounds for shifting to an enrichment of the Modest Version, an enrichment that maintains that the seeing that movie viewers imagine themselves doing is somehow *mediated*. But, as we will see in the course of that discussion, it is important that this desirable enrichment should also be developed in 'modest' fashion. It is easy to go ham-handedly too far. For reasons that will emerge as we proceed, calling this enrichment 'the Mediated Version' may be somewhat misleading, but I will try to explain both the appropriateness and the dangers of this label.

In an earlier discussion of the subject, I stated the Mediated Version in the following shorthand way: "It is fictional in our imaginative engagement with [mainstream] narrative films that they consist of 'motion picture-like shots' that have been derived in a fictionally indeterminate manner from pertinent segments of the fictional narrative worlds."[12] Hence, when film viewers imagine seeing constituents of the narrative

---

[11] I also examine these issues further in Chapter 5.

[12] Of course, the Mediated Version was first introduced and somewhat tentatively endorsed in Chapter 2.

world, they imagine themselves seeing those fictional constituents *through the mediation* of the on-screen moving images, images that *fictionally* have been transparently derived from the dramatized situations of the story. To say that an image (or series of images) is *transparently* derived from a situation X is to say that X is an *actual* situation that the relevant image depicts and that the constellation of visual properties present in the image bears a suitably rich, systematic, and natural counterfactual dependence upon the visual properties actually displayed in X.[13]

As a rule, still and moving picture photographs *are* transparently derived from their photographed subjects,[14] but other types of images, including other types of moving images,[15] are transparently derived from their relevant causal sources as well. Mirror images and other images that have been appropriately produced in reflective surfaces, e.g. sheets of steel and pools of still water, are also 'transparent' to what they reflect. So are images on a monitor that have been transmitted without resemblance-obliterating distortion through closed circuit surveillance systems or by means of live television transmission. Therefore, the class of transparently derived images includes 'documentary' motion picture shots, but the extension of the concept is much broader than this, and, in fact, it is significantly open-ended.

The shots of a fiction film have often been transparently derived from the actual objects and events that were photographed in taking the picture, but, of course, such shots are *never* transparently derived from their *fictional* subjects. However, it *is* a central claim of the Mediated Version that viewers characteristically *imagine* (and normally are meant to imagine) that the shots of a movie (whose contents are not, in some mode, subjective)[16] are moving images that have been transparently derived from the depicted segments of the movie's fictional world. Alternatively, the claim is that it is fictional for

---

[13] For more on the transparency of certain images and on the idea that an image has been transparently derived from a certain visual source, see Chapter 2. For seminal discussions of these issues, see the essay, "Transparent Pictures" in Walton (2008), especially 98–101, and Currie (1985), 53–56. In Chapter 2, I spoke in this connection of a 'natural iconic image of X.' But I have come to think that the terminology is misleading. It seems to suggest to too many ears that movies are supposed to involve images of two distinct types, i.e., the actual movie images and the naturally iconic ones. The only images that are involved are the actual movie's images, and, according to the Mediated Version, viewers of the movie imagine *about them* that they have been transparently derived from the movie's fictional world. Setting aside computer-generated images (CGI), these actual images *have* been transparently derived from the photographed material that was before the camera at the time.

[14] Of course, this will not be true of a CGI, and CGIs are notoriously becoming more and more common in fiction films. I will ignore this complication—important for many issues, but not, I think, in the present context.

[15] Here and henceforward I follow Carroll's generalized use of the phrase "moving image." See, for instance, Carroll (2003), 1–9, especially 9. Carroll has introduced and defended this broad use of "moving image" in several other places.

[16] This qualification is patently important, but its scope and content are not easy to explain. In an ensuing chapter, I make an attempt at explaining a number of senses in which a shot or sequence may be 'subjective.' Subjective shots and sequences, contextually marked as such, cancel the normal presumption that the contents of the shot have been transparently derived from the 'basic' narrative world of the fiction. Getting clear about these matters constitutes a huge and very important part of the problem of understanding 'audio-visual narration in fiction films.'

the movie viewer that the image-track constitutes a transparent record of the events of the enacted story.

Moreover, it is a crucial additional part of the Mediated Version that, as a rule, it is *fictionally indeterminate* just *how* the on-screen images of the story events have come to be transparently derived into images presented on the screen. Therefore, it is no part of this overall view that the transparent derivation had to have been achieved by some motion picture photography conducted by fictional film-makers in the fictional world. Characteristically, it is fictional in the work that no motion picture camera was present in the vicinity of the narrative action, although, of course, there are many exceptions to this norm.[17] In any case, I am assuming that it is trivial that Walton's Transparency Thesis will hold in relation to any images that have been transparently derived. If an image K (moving or otherwise) is transparently derived from an actual situation X, then any competent perceiver who sees K will thereby also *see* X, i.e., see it indirectly—through the mediation of the image K. Correlatively, if a spectator sees an image that she imagines to have been transparently derived from a fictional source X, then she thereby *imagines seeing* X actually but indirectly, i.e., she imagines seeing it through the mediation of K. It is at the very heart of the Mediated Version of the Imagined Seeing Thesis that moviegoers imagine seeing the fictional action of the story *by* viewing images of that action—the action from which those very images have been transparently derived. That is, they imagine, falsely but quite legitimately, *about the actual shots of the film*, that those have been transparently derived from certain visible constituents of the fictional world that the film creates.[18]

Finally, the Mediated Version of the Imagined Seeing Thesis emphasizes that, when viewers imagine seeing fictions in the movies, they also imagine that their imagined experience of *seeing those fictions* is characteristically marked or otherwise inflected by the mediated aspect of the imagined experience. For instance, in watching a black and white fiction film, I imagine that I am seeing a fictional world whose objects are colored but are presented to me in black and white. The black and white presentation is simply grasped as the result of a mediation between me and the 'objective' fictional world. Naturally, such an imagined seeing in the movies differs in this way from my normal experiences of seeing the actual world in the colors that it instantiates and in the

---

[17] That is, it is common enough to have a shot or sequence which fictionally does have a provenance from within the fictional world—a source that is contextually marked or otherwise identified.

[18] In an extremely interesting article, Robert Hopkins (2008) contemplates a view that I would reconstruct as the Mediated Version of the Imagined Seeing Thesis. That is, he considers the possibility that there are two fundamental aspects to our 'seeing' fictions in movies. (i) We 'see' the fictional events and situations of the movie story without attending to the facts that are visible on screen about the acting, staging, etc. ('the theatrical dimension') that dramatically portray the fictional circumstances. (ii) We also see the fictional events and situations, as he puts it, 'photographically.' Hopkins neither endorses nor rejects (i) and (ii), but he sees this pair of theses as potentially very important to a theory of our perceptual/imaginative experience of movies. Hopkins sets up these issues quite differently than I have, and it would take a full essay to compare what he calls 'collapsed photographic seeing' with 'mediated imagined seeing,' as I have presented that notion. However, I think that the comparison is intriguing, and it would be well worth working it out. See Hopkins (2008), esp. 155–156.

way that they are exemplified. I will elaborate this point with additional examples a little later on.

There is a rough but important distinction that we want to recognize in this connection. Granted that movie audiences imagine seeing the fictional constituents of the movie's drama, we can ask what they imagine about the *way* in which they are seeing these items. We can ask this, and yet the query is, as it stands, ambiguous. It could ask: what is the *means* or *mechanism* that viewers imagine as the causal source of their imagined perception of the fictional constituents in the narrative shot or se- quence? However, the query could also mean: what is the *qualitative* (or: *phenomenal*) *character* of the perceptual experience of the fictional world that viewers imagine themselves, in watching the movie, to have? If the query is interpreted in the first way, then I believe that, except in very special contexts, movie viewers simply imagine almost nothing on this score. Viewers imagine themselves looking into the movie's dramatized universe, but, as a rule, they are imaginatively oblivious about how their fictional seeing into the narrative world might have been causally produced. The question just doesn't arise for them. This is a point I emphasized above. On the other hand, it seems to me that they do normally imagine this much about their seeing of the movie fictions: they imagine that they are seeing them indirectly, i.e., seeing them through the mediation of suitable moving images, and it is the nature of the mediation that typically serves to partially determine the qualitative character of the way in which the fictional items are perceptually present on screen to the film's audience.

It is true that what viewers imagine about the phenomenal character of their visual experience of the fictions in the movie is normally determined in a pretty straight- forward way by the actual qualitative properties of the shot or sequence before their eyes. Naturally, we imagine seeing the colored world of the fiction presented to us in terms of black and white, because, of course, the movie itself was shot in black and white. The 'explanation' of how our imagined seeing of the cinematic world is qualitatively inflected by the actual properties of the actual shots will therefore usually be straightforward and usually be quite trivial. The relative triviality of the way we incorporate much of the actual qualitative display of the image-track into the qualitative character of our experiences as we imagine seeing the represented fictional world tends to obscure the near ubiquity and the aesthetic importance of this imaginative phenomenon.

Moreover, there is nothing special here about the case of cinema. The same trivial dependence occurs in a similarly recessive fashion in our imaginative relations to literary fiction. For instance, the fictional prose style of the narrator trivially depends upon the actual style of the prose the author has historically constructed. For instance, in reading Henry James's *The Sacred Fount* (1901), we imagine that we are being informed of the nameless narrator's investigations of the romantic entanglements at a country house, a story which he fictionally relates in a distinctive, elegant, and notoriously convoluted prose style. But, of course, it is just because the sentences that James *actually* produced in constructing the novel—the sentences we actually read—give rise to the fact that readers *imagine* themselves *learning* of the narrator's investigations through the *mediation* of this distinctive and convoluted prose style. Readers imagine that their learning of the narrator's investigations has a certain specific qualitative character, and that character arises mostly from the actual text before our eyes. We actually know, and we don't merely imagine, that we are reading prose that manifests the familiar Jamesian style, but we do merely imagine that we come to *know* of the narrator's circumstances by *being told about them* in this peculiarly Jamesian manner.

Here is a broader way of looking at the issues that are at stake in this connection. There is a basic distinction between two types of on-screen items and visual qualities in movie fictions—those that are diegetic and those that are not. I try to explicate the nature of the distinction below, and I stress that the diegetic has an epistemic status in our imaginative experience of the film different from that of the non-diegetic. Finally, I argue that an adequate account of this difference in epistemic status is difficult to formulate simply and naturally unless we are prepared to accept the Imagined Seeing Thesis in its Mediated Version.

Here is one very simple example of the distinction—an example of an entirely familiar sort. In the opening of *Psycho* (Alfred Hitchcock, 1959), there is a shot that scans over downtown Phoenix where, as it will shortly emerge, the characters, Marion Crane (Janet Leigh) and Sam Loomis (John Gavin) are meeting in a hotel for an afternoon assignation. At the beginning of the shot, we see the words,

PHOENIX, ARIZONA

on screen, and then the inscription moves swiftly to the left and off the screen. As the camera apparently continues panning across the same Phoenix skyline, the time specification

FRIDAY, DECEMBER THE ELEVENTH

appears on screen until that also exits screen left and is succeeded by the inscription

TWO FORTY-THREE P.M.,

and that caption disappears in this instance to the right (see figures 11 and 12). In viewing this shot, we imagine discovering the hotel and then the hotel room of the illicit lovers, but naturally we do *not* imagine seeing the words that make up the inscription as if they were located somewhere in the movie's fictional space, e.g., as floating around somewhere outside the Phoenix hotel. Rather, it seems to me, we imagine this shot as constituting what becomes a visual record of the couple in the hotel, and we imagine that the place and time-identifying captions have been inscribed upon that visual record of the narrative action.

By imagining the actual shot as if it were a visual record transparently derived from the fictional lovers' tryst, we are thereby licensed to imagine ourselves as *actually seeing the meeting of Marion and Sam*, although our seeing of the incident is imagined to be

Figure 11 Opening of *Psycho*—the Phoenix skyline

Figure 12 Opening of *Psycho*—the hotel room window

indirect. That is, it is imagined that the seeing is mediated by the recorded moving images that fictionally purport to register the lovers' behavior. The characters and the constituents of their fictional circumstances (the hotel setting) are, as I will say, *diegetic* items in the shot. At the same time, the inscriptions are plainly *non-diegetic*. The words on the screen are not imagined to be among the elements of the fictional space or the course of narrative action presented in the film image—they have been inscribed by some agency *onto* the imagined transparency of the film image to the dramatized situations. But this means that we *imagine* seeing the characters, Marion and Sam, and their actions in the Phoenix hotel (the diegetic items) *by means of* seeing a shot (actually a sequence of shots) that has (have) been transparently derived from these depicted fictions. It is in this sense that we imagine about ourselves that, in seeing the lovers and their behavior, we are seeing them only *indirectly*.

I want to emphasize that the Modest Version does not permit us to say even this much. It declines to specify anything about *how* we imagine seeing the world of the story. As we saw, it denies that we imagine seeing the elements in the diegesis face-to-face, but equally it does not allow that we imagine seeing the diegesis in some indirect or mediated fashion either. For this reason, the Modest Version fails to characterize how we experience the distinction between diegetic and non-diegetic items in our imaginative apprehension of the shot. And yet, this distinction marks a basic type of perceptual discrimination, one that we almost effortlessly make all the time in watching movies. It is for this reason that the Mediated Version of the Imagined Seeing Thesis is to be preferred.

The point can be generalized. It is possible to draw a closely related distinction between the diegetic and non-diegetic *visual qualities* that are manifested in a given shot or sequence. (Although it is a tricky matter to give the distinction a fully adequate, general formulation.) To sketch the distinction as it applies to visual qualities, let us briefly consider another hypothetical example. S is to be a shot that occurs in the setting of a fiction film F. In making S, the film-makers have photographed the performance of a pair of *actors*, Jones and Smith, who enact the fictional murder of one *character* in the story by another. The characters involved are Sludge (the murderer) and Fudge (the victim) respectively. Now, if we talk about the 'content' of a given shot S, there is an immediate ambiguity. On the one hand, S visually records the physical appearance and behavior of Jones and Smith as they enact the murder, and it registers parts of the setting (a studio set, for instance) in which their performances have actually been executed. Let us say then that shot S *visually records* information about, e.g., the actors, Jones and Smith, and their enactment of the murder on a set. S is a motion picture photograph of these real people, events, and situations. But now, when S has been integrated into the larger context of the movie F—when it has been added to F with the intention of advancing however slightly the story that F is telling—we can say that, in the film F, S *depicts* particular story content, e.g., Sludge murdered Fudge in a dark alley in nineteenth-century Dublin. Correlatively, it depicts the diegetic constituents of that story content: the fictional characters, Sludge and Fudge, the fictional murder, and the fictional circumstances of the action, e.g., a dark Dublin alley. These, of course, are the diegetic *items* in S.

What is more, S manifests a dense and complicated constellation of visual qualities. Many of these visual qualities represent facts about ways in which the diegetic items in S fictionally appear within the narrative world. Viewers not only imagine seeing

Sludge murder Fudge, but they also imagine seeing a range of facts about how Sludge and Fudge looked at the time of the murder and, in addition, about how the murder itself appeared from certain specific visual perspectives.[19] The visual qualities of the shot that serve to specify this kind of information about the appearance of objects and events within the world of the story, by exhibiting those qualities on the screen, are the diegetic visual qualities in the movie image.[20] However, let us stipulate some additional facts about the visual character of the hypothetical shot. We stipulate that S is (i) in black and white, (ii) in soft focus, (iii) in slow motion, and (iv) it ends with a gradual fade to dark. Each of (i) through (iv) corresponds to important visual qualities that are also instantiated in the shot, but in the normal case these qualities will *not* represent visible properties of the diegetic objects and events themselves.[21] These will count as the non-diegetic visual qualities in S. Competent viewers, seeing the shot in black and white, do not imagine for a moment that they are seeing a segment of a monochromatic fictional world. And, seeing the soft focus of the shot, they do not imagine that the narrative constituents of the movie are objectively bright and blurry or even that they look bright and blurry to real or hypothetical perceivers in the fictional environment. These visual qualities are apprehended as merely visual *inflections* of the movie's medium or as visual *traces* of the mode and manner in which the shot was executed. Thus, construed along these lines, we have a broad distinction between the diegetic and non-diegetic visual qualities that occur in a given movie sequence.

Although we clearly do make something like the distinction that I have just sketched, the distinction is not so easy to characterize in general terms. Indeed, there are important cases in which it is not even easy to apply. Consider, for instance, movies made in early Technicolor. The 1939 version of *Robin Hood* (Michael Curtiz) is a good example. Do we imagine that the fictional world of this *Robin Hood* is actually colored in a more naturalistic fashion than what we see on screen and that the vivid, highly saturated colors are only a visual trace of the Technicolor photography? Or do we imagine that the fictional world of *Robin Hood* is itself more brilliantly and fantastically hued than the world of ordinary experience—that its colors are somewhat incredible but to be accepted nevertheless as part of the 'real' look of the world? In this particular case, I lean to the view that viewers tend to favor something like the second alternative. They imagine Robin Hood's domain to have a hypernatural vividness in both color and dramatic excitement. But if *Night and the City* (Jules Dassin, 1950) had been similarly photographed in the same sort of Technicolor stock, I almost certainly would have favored the first type of impression for that hypothetical color version. It would be hard to accept the world depicted in *Night and the City* as a colorful world of

---

[19] Of course, the shots may show us how something looked inter-subjectively (to normal perceivers) or to a particular viewer or group of viewers contextually indicated in the scene.

[20] Of course, essentially the same distinction between diegetic and non-diegetic *auditory* attributes can be made in a very similar fashion.

[21] And certainly this can happen. One can use slow motion photography to depict the characters as moving slowly and a fade to dark could be used to depict real darkness falling over the scene.

fantasy. It would be easier to assume that some surrealistic and allegorical commentary was intended. Nevertheless, I don't assume that there is a sharp basis for my inclinations concerning these examples, and, in many other cases, the question will just seem silly. Indeed, the distinction between diegetic and non-diegetic *color* in movies is often hard or even impossible to make. However, the existence of indeterminate examples of this ilk does nothing to undercut the idea that there is a general distinction to be drawn, within the visual attributes that are present on screen, between those that display the fictional look of the narrative world and visual inflections or traces of the compositional manner in which that world has been rendered in the image-track.

A related qualification is in order. Certain visual qualities in certain shots or sequences may be diegetic or not in a narrower or in a broader sense. Suppose we have a movie mostly done in color, which contains flashback sequences in black and white. The flashback sequences will not be narrowly diegetic in that viewers are not to imagine that the objects and events existing at the designated past times were really just black, white, and gray as they appear on screen. But the black and white sequences may be intended to indicate that the narrative situations they portray are situations that occurred in the past relative to the baseline present of the story. In a broad sense, this is fictive information about an aspect of the story and so could count as broadly 'diegetic' for that reason. Moreover, various qualities that are not even broadly diegetic in a given sequence or stretch of the film may be used to present or to suggest some kind of commentary on aspects of the narrative development narrowly construed. In other words, the non-diegetic, as I have construed it, may introduce visual properties that are visually expressive or visually metaphorical in a host of interesting ways. The tinting in silent films, for example, often used the color of the tinting for figurative and/or other purposes. There are a multitude of subtle possibilities that arise in this connection, but I will not attempt to list or analyze the considerable complexity that arises in this domain.

The crucial observation is that we accommodate diegetic versus non-diegetic properties in very different ways in our imaginative engagement with the film. For a striking illustration of the contrast, imagine two fiction films, *Monochrome* and *Monochrome**. In *Monochrome*, it is fictional in the movie that the world of the story has been rendered colorless by an evil genius. Fictionally, all the objects and events in the story really are either black or white or shades of gray, and we imagine seeing each item as having the monochromatic hue that it exemplifies on screen.[22] *Monochrome**, on the other hand, is a normal black and white movie in which, as usual, it is fictional that the denizens of its story world are actually colored in some natural way. In watching

---

[22] In *A Matter of Life and Death* (Powell and Pressburger, 1946) Heaven (in which a fair amount of the action is set) is fictionally without color. Thus, in the scenes in Heaven, the black and white photography is supposed to render the monochromatic visual appearance of the celestial place. By contrast, it is fictional in the movie that Earth is more or less normally colored, and the Technicolor photography used to present scenes on Earth shows us the relevant colors.

Monochrome★, we imagine seeing a world in which things do have colors although we don't imagine seeing the particular color of the individual items. In fact, *Monochrome* and *Monochrome★* might even contain some shots or sequences that are visually indistinguishable. However, what we will imagine ourselves to be seeing when we view a given shot in *Monochrome* will be different from what we imagine seeing in the very same shot in *Monochrome★*. Consider the difference between a viewer's imagining seeing an object that she rightly knows to be emerald green but which is presented to her as a shade of very dark gray and her imagining seeing the particular green of the very same object placed in the same setting. As far as I can see, the Modest Version has no way of explaining the difference in our overall imaginative experience of these movies, although the difference, once it is pointed out, is simple and obvious enough. After all, it arises as a difference in how audience members imagine their seeing of the story to be mediated in relation to the range of visual qualities that appear in the projected image-track.

Most visual qualities that customarily function in a non-diegetic manner, e.g., soft focus, slow motion, spatial distortion through the choice of lens or manipulation of focus, fade to black, etc., can also occur as standing for diegetic visual qualities in suitable narrative and narrational surroundings. Thus, a shot in slow motion can depict a situation in which the operations in the narrative world are really suffering some unnatural retardation. Therefore, the same kind of contrastive thought experiment can be run for all these visual qualities as well. Roughly, the diegetic visual qualities of a movie are experienced as *located in* the narrative world and embodied as visible attributes of the diegetic items. The non-diegetic visual qualities are experienced as arising from the compositional character of the image-track and as *projected onto* the movie's narrative world. The Mediated Version of the Imagined Seeing Thesis is called for to articulate the intuitive results of the imagined contrast in each such instance.

Here in summary is the basic puzzle and the solution to it that the Mediated Version proposes. I have argued especially in Chapter 3 that we imagine seeing segments of a fictional world in watching fiction films. This *is* the Imagined Seeing Thesis. Moreover, the seeing of fictions that we imagine ourselves to experience is regularly imbued (sometimes thoroughly) with non-diegetic visual qualities that are present on screen within the movie viewed. This means that, e.g., the spectator's seeing of Fudge's murder in the movie F is very liable to be qualitatively unlike any face-to-face seeing of Sludge or Fudge or, for that matter, any direct witnessing of a real murder of one character by the other. How is it then that a viewing experience that is qualitatively so different from our ordinary seeing of murders in a plausible real world environment can be imagined as a genuine experience of a *seeing* of Fudge's murder? Of course, both the Modest and the Mediated Version agree that the imagined seeing of the movie murder is not imagined as a face-to-face seeing and, more generally, that ordinary seeing and cinematic 'seeing' are qualitatively quite different from one another. But the Mediated Version goes on to remind us that in ordinary life we also see objects and events indirectly—that we see them through the mediation of various kinds of transparent images, still and moving. And finally, it proposes that it is some kind of indirect seeing of Fudge's murder that we imagine ourselves to be experiencing in watching the movie. It is an indirect seeing that is fictionally mediated, so to speak, by the very shots before our eyes, when they are suitably imagined. There is, therefore, no expectation that this mediated seeing should be qualitatively much like a face-to-face viewing, and it is to be expected that our mediated movie 'views' of movie fictions will include a range of non-diegetic items and that they will be thoroughly inflected by a host of non-diegetic visual qualities.

In some film segments, the character of the means or method of mediation is made relatively determinate and explicit at least for the duration of a shot or sequence. For example, we are seeing the Green Slime come into the cabin *through the mediation* of a surveillance camera on the spaceship that is recording the (fictional) space of the ship's cabin. Or alternatively, when we see a subjectively inflected point of view shot of the same action, we are seeing the Green Slime through the mediation of the visual experiences of human observers fictionally looking through binoculars upon the scene. However, as I've stressed, in the standard case—the default case—we are seeing the fictional action through the mediation of a stretch of moving imagery whose provenance is fictionally more or less totally indeterminate. Similarly, young children, knowing that they are seeing something real depicted in, for instance, an instructional film, will know that they are seeing the photographic subjects as mediated by the medium that depicts them, but they may know next to nothing about the nature of that medium and how it works.

Back in Chapters 2 and 3, I argued at great length that it is no part of our conception of what it is for viewers to imagine seeing in the movies that they imagine themselves within the movie's fictional space. It is, of course, an immediate virtue of the Mediated Version of the Imagined Seeing Thesis that it alleviates any temptation to believe otherwise. Suppose that I actually see a certain situation in a mirror, where the mirror that I'm looking into reflects an image of a certain situation that has been relayed to it by a series of mirrors whose initial member directly reflects the situation that I am seeing in the mirror before me. In this case, I do not see the situation from the implicit vantage point of the mirror image that is in my line of sight, and, if I know the basic facts about the way that the relay of mirrors has been set up, then I don't suppose that I do. Similarly, if I imagine seeing the murder of Fudge in the film F, then I imagine that my seeing is a *mediated* seeing and that it is mediated by my seeing of transparent visual images of the murder, images that are now projected before my eyes. Thus, the seeing of the murder that I imagine takes place 'in my head' and it occurs at whatever position I occupy in the movie theater. I have little or no temptation to imagine myself seeing the murder from any other place. In this respect at least, the Mediated Version agrees with a key consideration about the phenomenology of spectatorship that motivates (mistakenly) Currie's contention that we don't imagine seeing movie fictions at all. Naturally, what I imagine about my viewing position and the visual character of the shot is factually correct, and what is falsely imagined about the actual shot is that the 'visual information' that it incorporates is transparently derived from a fictional murder that it portrays.

The Mediated Version also offers a direct and plausible answer to another question. Consider the case when we watch a theatrical fiction enacted in front of us on stage. In viewing such a performance, do we imagine seeing the fictional action depicted in the play? If the play itself or the acting or the staging of the play is not too stylized or abstract, then I am inclined to answer this question affirmatively. However, if this point is granted, then one wants to insist nevertheless that the imagined seeing of the dramatic action in a movie is essentially very different from the imagined seeing of the dramatic action in the performance of a staged play. Of course, there are a lot of differences between movie viewings and the viewings of stage plays, but it is arguable that the Mediated Version captures one obvious and fundamental dissimilarity that exists between them. In watching a fiction film, the viewer's imagined seeing of the fictional action is mediated by her imagined seeing of 'motion picture-like' images—or, at least, of 'moving images (of an indeterminate kind)'—of the fictional action. No such mediation is involved, actually or imaginatively, in the case of theater.[23]

Theater is an interesting case in this regard. I am inclined to think that we imagine seeing the characters and their fictional deeds *directly*, but I do not think that we imagine seeing these things *face-to face*. That is, when we are watching a play, we also do not imagine ourselves located somewhere in the fictional space of the drama and seeing from that place.[24] Movie viewing and play viewing are the same in this regard. Indeed, the point is even more apparent in the case of theater. Our impression of a determinately bounded fictional space for a scene in a play tends to be much less specific than our impression of traditional cinematic spaces, and our sense of our relation to the theatrical spaces is correspondingly less sharp. However, as I have just contended, we normally do not imagine our seeing of the action as if it were somehow mediated by some determinate mode of intervening visual medium. In any case, there is a good deal about the seeing of theatrical fictions and dramatic spaces that deserves to be thought through in this connection, but I will not pursue the matter here.

Hence, the Mediated Version of the Imagined Seeing Thesis differs from the Modest Version in the following way. The Modest Version asserts that viewers imagine seeing fictions in movies, *and* it also asserts that, as a rule, it is imaginatively and fictionally indeterminate to movie viewers what makes it possible for them to be seeing into the

---

[23] As my daughter Flannery reminds me, these remarks are much too brief. Very often the sets of a theatrical play—even a play that aims at 'realism'—will be somewhat more abstract and schematic than movie sets. Am I suggesting here that the spectator at the play has to give more 'work' to his/her imagination in order to 'imagine seeing' the situation realistically? Or, is it that the depicted situation will always give the impression of being relatively more sketchy? I confess that I don't know how to answer briefly the questions posed by this shrewd observation.

[24] Here I believe I am in agreement with Bernard Williams's views about seeing fictions in a staged play. See especially Williams (1973), 35–36. I think I am also in agreement with what he says about seeing fictions in the cinema, but, since he is much briefer on this subject, it is harder for me to be sure. In any case, I have been much impressed and influenced by this classic essay. I discuss this influence in the Introduction.

movie's fictional world at all. The Mediated Version certainly agrees about the first conjunct but, insofar as it agrees with the second, it does so only with a significant qualification. (α) It allows that it is characteristically fictional for viewers that they imagine seeing objects and events in the movie's fictional world and see them somehow in an indirect or mediated way, but (β) it also insists that, as a rule, it is fictionally indeterminate what the nature of the mediating medium might be and indeterminate how the mediation works to inflect the movie viewers' perception of the fictional world. Thus, for example, as I have repeatedly insisted, it normally *is* determinate in the viewer's imagination that she is *not* seeing the narrative action *by* seeing *movie shots* of that fictional action. She *is* seeing the action indirectly, but the mode and method of the indirection that her seeing might exemplify is left in limbo. Plainly, this is a delicate matter. It is hard to be sure that (α) and (β) are coherent together, and the viability of the Mediated Version depends upon the conceptual bet that they are. I accept the bet.[25]

It is true that the 'iconic' transcriptions of the fictional world that we imagine seeing in a movie are apprehended as having a number of significant properties in common with the standard products of motion picture photography. It is because of these resemblances that I have sometimes spoken as if movie spectators see, in the first instance, 'motion picture-like' images of the fictional world. First, spectators accept that (i) a shot of a movie murder has a visual appearance that is counterfactually dependent upon the fictional appearance of the enacted killing—counterfactually dependent in extensive and systematic ways. More specifically, spectators imagine that visual information about the episode has been stored and transmitted pictorially in the cinematic image.

Second, (ii) since the shot that is imagined as transparently derived from the fictional world just is the relevant shot that the film-makers actually created photographically, it is trivial that the shot appearing on screen will qualitatively match more or less the shot as movie viewers see it in the imagination. The actual shot and the shot as viewers imagine it to be differ only in that we imagine the actual shot as having a kind of causal origin that we know it really did not have. No one photographed the magical Land of Oz. The similarities such as those that are described in (i) and (ii)—similarities that we imaginatively accept—do not contradict the dissimilarity concerning causal etiology that we simultaneously embrace as well. Although genuine motion picture shots are

---

[25] Earlier I pointed out that Colin McGinn (2005) maintains that movie viewers, prompted by seeing the photographed subject matter, *imagine* the associated fictional items. I suggested that his views ought to be emended to grant that viewers *imagine seeing* the fictional items. If McGinn were to accept this emendation, then what he says about 'reciprocal seeing' would seem to involve an endorsement of the Mediated Version. For instance, he remarks, "Thus the seeing has a kind of inner complexity, bringing two objects into close relations: the image and what it is an image of. It isn't just that you see the image *and* you see the object it represents; you see the object by *means* of the image" (46). I think this should read, "Thus the imagined seeing of fictions has a kind of inner complexity, bringing two objects into close relations: the image and the fictional object that it represents. It isn't just that you see the image *and* you imagine seeing the fictional objects it represents; you imagine yourself seeing the fictional object by *means* of the image."

the product of motion picture photography (ignoring CG imagery), we accept that the 'motion picture-like shots' we imagine have not been photographed and that it is not specified, even implicitly, how the imagined visual renderings might have come to be. We accept that the question of their provenance has no work-internal answer and regard it as a pointless misunderstanding to insist that some sort of answer needs to be supplied. So this is the heart of the Mediated Version that I am defending, and it is important to underscore the following point one final time. The position here is not that the make-believe visual records we 'see' in a movie are imagined to have been created in some 'magical' or otherwise 'supernatural' fashion. We do not have the impression that these visual records have been produced out of the fictional world by some 'inscrutable' technique. It is just that we imagine *nothing* about how fictionally they came into existence, and we are fully justified, as normal consumers of traditional fictional cinema, in doing so.

In Chapter 2, I highlighted the wonderfully suggestive example that David Hills made to me in private communication. In the old Flash Gordon serials, the Emperor Ming possessed a view screen that allowed him, by suitable adjustment of the dials, to see what was currently going on at any point of his planet. But what were members of the young Saturday afternoon audiences supposed to imagine about how such a wonderful device was supposed to work? There was absolutely nothing suggested in the Flash Gordon episodes about how the relevant information could be so extensively selected and transmitted. Again, the audience members weren't expected to imagine anything on this score. They were expected to accept the fiction of the device without worrying a bit about how such a thing might work. Of course, this is an example of a surprising, ungrounded fictional truth that arises only *within* the narrative, but I do not see why there cannot be similarly ungrounded fictional truths that arise from the rock-bottom character of the cinematic narration itself. In fact, I think that this is an utterly common phenomenon, and, along the way, I've indicated further examples of this point.

It is a fundamental convention of fiction films that facts about the actual look of the screen imagery systematically mandate facts about what we are entitled to imagine about what we are seeing (indirectly) in the fiction. It is an ungrounded convention that makes it possible for simple and more complex forms of movie fictions to be constructed in the first place. Although the convention is fundamental, it is defeasible as well. Sometimes, as I noted earlier, a fictional source for the image-track *is* identified within the work—in movies that are fictionally documentaries, for example.[26] But

---

[26] Probably *This is Spinal Tap* (Rob Reiner, 1984) is the most frequently cited example, but there are many more. *Caché* (Michael Haneke, 2005) is an interesting and complicated case. Certain key stretches of the image-track seem fictionally to have been made by a security camera (or cameras) whose provenance is sought out by the main characters in the story. However, they never reach a definite answer to this mystery. In fact, I would argue that, by the end of the film, it is implicitly suggested that we don't know that all of the image-track has not been fictionally derived from mysterious security cameras that somehow seem to be effectively present everywhere. (See, for instance, the late scene that is apparently a flashback to a crucial,

there is nothing special about the characteristic ungroundedness of the fictionality of film narration in this regard. I suspect that the appeal to the utter indeterminacy of the transparent derivation of the shots in movies strikes many, on first reflection, as being artificial and *ad hoc*. However, similar indeterminacies are frequently found in the basic frameworks of many other forms of storytelling.

Go back to the example of radio plays considered earlier. In listening to such a program, we probably do imagine that the fictional sounds and speeches are somehow being conveyed to us over the radio from the relevant fictional locale, e.g., from the vicinity of the rain-swept church. And yet, what are we supposed to imagine about how the sounds from the spooky church have come to be transmitted over the radio? The proper response in this case also would be: "The question is silly. This is a mode of the fiction-making to which we simply give our tacit consent without there being any further rationale, provided in terms of the fiction, for doing so." If we know the basics of radio dramatization and radio broadcasting, then we know at least roughly how the actual sound effects have been produced and transmitted. We grasp this work-external explanation and rightly feel that there is no mystery about what and how we are hearing what we do. However, nothing in the work itself purports to explain anything about how we fictionally have auditory access to the imagined sounds from in and around the imaginary church.

Or consider once again the case of works of literary fiction. There are many English novels, narrated in English, which have a narrator from a non-Anglophone country and in which there is every reason to accept that the narrator has not learned English. Imagine that the narrator is a Russian peasant or even a Neanderthal. Readers may (or may not) notice the discrepancy involved, but they will cheerfully accept that the text renders the thoughts and perceptions of the narrator. They will not worry at all about how his recounting of his adventures came to appear in English in the pages of the volume they are reading. The central character who narrates Horace McCoy's novel, *They Shoot Horses Don't They*, manages to run through the contents of a 250-page account of his early life in the slice of time (a period of five minutes at most) during which a judge delivers a verdict of guilty upon him in his trial for murder. Admittedly, these are somewhat extreme examples, but even in more conventional works it is typically the case that it is fictional in the narration that the narrator has asserted a range of propositions about the world of the story, but asserted them in an indeterminate way.

Here is an example, chosen almost at random, from Herman Melville's *Pierre: or the Ambiguities*: "As Pierre drove through the silent village, beneath the vertical shadows of the noonday trees, the sweet chamber scene abandoned him, and the mystical face recurred to him, and kept with him. At last, arrived at home, he found his mother absent; so passing straight through the wide middle hall of the mansion, he descended

earlier part of the story, but is oddly shot from the distanced, unmoving perspective that is characteristic of the shots that earlier have been identified as coming from a security video.)

to the piazza, on the other side, and wandered away in reveries to the river bank" (Library of America edition, *Melville*, p. 50). But what if one were to wonder about the specific manner in which the relevant assertions were made? Did the narrator assert these things by writing them down? Or did he say the words out loud? Or did he make these judgments only in his mind? In the *Pierre* example and in innumerable similar cases, there simply is no answer to this sort of question, and it would be bizarre to imagine that there might be. The narrator fictionally reports Pierre's activity, but it is fictionally indeterminate how this reporting has been performed.

Or finally, consider a question that would be even more radically misconceived. Suppose that someone were to speculate about how the narrator's judgments were transcribed onto the pages of the published volume. Naturally, it isn't just that the reader doesn't know how this has taken place. On the one hand, she understands enough about how fictional narrations are created by their authors and enough about how these works normally get published and distributed. On the other hand, nothing in the work will make it fictional that the narrator's report came to be published in such and such a way. Once again, there is no work-internal explanation of this point. The sort of challenge to the Mediated Version of the Imagined Seeing Thesis that many critics are happy to endorse would create pointless havoc for other types of works of fiction as well. I emphasized in "*Le Grand Imagier* Steps Out" (Chapter 2) that many of the conventions that ground a major mode of fiction-making flirt dangerously on the edge of paradox. Nevertheless, they usually avoid the conceptual collapse that might seem to threaten them. So it is with audio-visual narration in fiction films, or so I have maintained.

In concluding this section, I would like to correct for an oversimplification that the earlier discussion may have inadvertently encouraged. The audio-visual narration of a movie story clearly involves more than just the fictional presentation of narrative sights and sounds. Although the recounting of a narrative on film is continuously anchored in the fictional showing and the fictional presentation of fictive sound, the content of the former significantly outruns the restricted content of the latter. For instance, consider how editing may function in even the simplest modes of cinematic narration. Shot A may fictionally show us a character that is starting to run up the stairs. Shot B may show her arriving at the top. The juxtaposition of A and B will fictionally *indicate* that she has climbed the stairs. Shot A★ may show us in close-up the emotion expressed in a character's countenance, and shot B★ may show a dead body lying at his feet. The juxtaposition of the two shots may fictionally indicate that the character's emotion represents his reaction to his discovery of the body. Or again, a suitable montage may fictionally indicate that a great deal of story time has passed—a time that included, say, the collapse of the stock market and the start of a world war.[27]

---

[27] In fact, the shots, given what they fictionally show, or the sequences, given what fictionally they indicate about the plot, may go beyond these narrowly plot-driven moments and imply or suggest commentary or some other kind of meta-reflection on parts of the story. Such a commentary may go well

These elementary and commonplace examples are meant to remind us that the fictional recounting (the narration) of a movie story incorporates these and other more sophisticated instances of fictionally establishing information about how the diegetic action is unfolding. And, of course, editing is only one tool—albeit a central one—for fictionally presenting a variety of narrative relations. Almost all the familiar devices of cinematic technique are regularly deployed in the mechanics of generation to indicate facts about how the movie story is to be construed. Intertitles, voice-overs, and non-diegetic music are all regular components of an integrated fictional exposition of the narrative in question. They all figure, in other words, as components of the audio-visual narration of the film. This observation is entirely unsurprising, but its objective is to underscore the fact that storytelling in a movie consists in the complex construction of what we imagine seeing and hearing into a web of temporal relations, causal relations, and other kinds of explanatory, expressive, and symbolic connections.

Indeed, what gets 'perceptually presented' in a shot and what gets 'indicated' about story in the narrational context of the shot are deeply interconnected. Obviously, the content of a sequence that is fictionally implied depends upon the visual information that is fictionally recorded in the shots. But, on the other side of the equation, the fact that a particular shot prompts viewers to imagine seeing a specific action *from* a certain position within the fictional space presupposes the fact that continuity editing and related strategies have already constructed the configuration of the fictional space in the first place. The complexity of the structuring of film narration is not likely to be challenged, but the idea that narration in movies is seriously analogous to the *fictional* telling of a story in literature is challenged regularly. In assessing the nature and extent of the potential analogy, it is important to keep the considerable internal complexity of the fictional recounting in movies in mind. Audio-visual narration in a film involves a great deal more than the fictional showing of visible diegesis and the fictional register-ing of diegetic sound, at least when these notions are narrowly understood. The narration is the systematic *articulation* of the movie's 'sights' and 'sounds' into higher-level unities that represent the unfolding of narrative developments.

These observations return us to one of the questions that received a certain amount of consideration in Chapters 1 and 2: does the audio-visual narration of some or all movies presuppose the implicit existence of an audio-visual narrator who fictionally is the agent of the cinematic storytelling? This has been an enormous topic in the recent narratology of film theory, but I have come to think that it is a seriously ill-defined

---

beyond what is required to establish basic levels of narrative intelligibility. In literary cases, we will want to count this commentary on the characters and their drama as also constituting a part of the narration. Narration is certainly not restricted simply to the bare recounting of a tale. The same is true of audio-visual narration in movies as well. Earlier I mentioned briefly the use of non-diegetic visual (or audio) qualities for purposes of expressing or metaphorically stating some aspect of a commentary on the plot. Conceptualizing the uses of non-diegetic items and properties within cinematic narration that is used to comment upon and to express feelings and attitudes about the story would be a dauntingly enormous task. Here I merely want to acknowledge that such a task exists.

question. Further, I also think that it is a relatively unimportant question in this context. Or, in any case, its importance derives mostly from all the perplexity that it has caused. But, I discuss the matter further, reaching these deflationary conclusions, especially two chapters hence—in Chapter 6. In Chapter 5, I chiefly examine the idea of the narrator in literary fiction where I focus, especially, on the idea of the effaced literary narrator. The subject is of considerable interest on its own, but its importance in the present argumentative setting depends on the following.

If movies have intrinsic audio-visual narrators at all, these dim figures have at best a kind of 'subliminal' presence in the normal movie viewer's mind. Therefore it is tempting to compare cinematic narrators to effaced narrators in novels and short stories. But a number of recent writers have expressed deep and systematic skepticism about the existence of the effaced variety even in literature, and they are perfectly willing to argue against the (normal) existence of effaced narrators in either movies or literature. That skeptical position has come as a surprise to me, but the skeptical authors raise some good questions. Therefore, I answer them in Chapter 5. I return to the case concerning audio-visual narrators in movies, particularly in Chapter 6.

PART III

Narrators: In Literature and Film

5

Elusive Narrators in Literature

In literary works of narrative fiction, the story or *narrative* consists of a sequence of fictional or fictionalized characters, objects, situations, and events. The *narration* (in the most familiar sense) consists in the fictional presentation of those narrative constituents, and the presentation, in these literary instances, is a mode of a linguistic recounting. The critical point for present purposes is that such works have at least two dimensions of fictionality: there is the fictional narrative and there is the fictional narration that presents as actual the relevant narrative events. It is generally accepted that many and even most works of literary fiction involve both a fictional narrative and narration in this way, but, as we will see shortly, there continues to be a dispute about whether *every* work of literary fiction involves narration *qua* fictional recounting of the narrative events. Moreover, if there are narrative fictions that do not involve an implicit activity of narration, then correspondingly, these works do not presuppose the existence of a work-internal narrating agent, i.e., they do not presuppose the existence of a literary *narrator*.

In the case of the narrative cinema, there is no comparable consensus that films generally involve an analogue of this sort of two-tiered fictionality. In fact, as we have seen, it has been highly controversial whether a film that presents a fictional narrative normally involves a fictional audio-visual narration of the story, i.e., a *fictional* presentation of the sights and sounds of the narrative world. For those like me who are inclined to give an affirmative answer in this debate, the general claim will be that

(FSH) It is fictional in a movie that its shots are transparently derived, from a certain determinate visual perspective, from selected objects and occurrences located in the narrative world (while simultaneously the sound-track is fictionally derived from various of the associated diegetic sounds).

This is (a 'Mediated' version of) what I earlier called 'the Fictional Showing Hypothesis.' Several notable writers have simply denied that fiction films characteristically incorporate a fictive audio-visual narration in this sense. These skeptical theorists claim that it is enough to allow that the actual film-makers, in a given case, construct a sound- and image-track that consists of a sequence of on-screen sensory manifolds that audio-visually represent the evolving series of fictional narrative circumstances. There is, they maintain, no reason to posit that the sound- and image-tracks implicitly represent a more 'direct' audio-visual narration of those narrative circumstances—a make-believe depiction in which the story situations have somehow been set before the viewers' eyes and ears.

However, other writers have insisted that it is a distinctive aspect of the viewers' customary reception of and engagement with a fiction film that they are meant to *imagine* themselves as actually watching the segments of the fictional world portrayed in the movie.[1] Moreover, it is argued that there must be some basis in the film presentation itself that serves to ground this ubiquitous mode of imagined seeing, and that this basis must amount to some sort of fictional 'showing' (to a prospective audience) of the depicted narrative situations and events. Defenders of imagined seeing and fictional showing in fiction films have not had an easy time explaining how the postulated imagined seeing is more concretely to be conceived and, correlatively, what the nature of the movie's fictional showing of its story is supposed to be. In the last three chapters, I have tried to improve the conceptual situation. Thus, in those chapters, I proposed that it *is* fictional in our imaginative engagement with classical narrative films that they consist of 'motion picture-like shots' that have been derived, in a manner that is left fictionally indeterminate, from the circumstances in the fictional world that they themselves depict. Viewers imagine themselves as seeing the fictional circumstances through imaginatively seeing the on-screen transparent record of the relevant narrative world.[2] Other suggestions about the nature of imagined seeing and fictional showing in the movies have been put forward, but none of these conceptions has avoided challenging criticisms that we have considered.[3]

In the context of these disputes, there is a related but secondary question that arises. Do fiction films have implicit audio-visual *narrators*? If one is skeptical about the very existence of fictional audio-visual narration in film, then naturally one will find no reason to recognize the general existence of an implicit agency that fictionally executes such narration—no reason to posit an implicit audio-visual narrator. Non-skeptics, however, face a more delicate issue. They will be inclined to grant, as a conceptual point perhaps, that fiction films presuppose the existence of some kind of minimal agency—an agency that fictionally carries out the intrinsic audio-visual narration of the film. Still, proponents of this limited idea may also feel that the agency in question is different enough from literary cases that it is wrong or misleading to think of this 'narrating agency' as constituting a genuine filmic narrator at all.

---

[1] Among the writers defending various versions of this Imagined Seeing Thesis are Kendall Walton, Jerrold Levinson, and myself. References to relevant works are given below. (Up to this point, I have been careful to state the debate in terms that acknowledge that movies generally involve the presentation of both sights and sounds, but in the rest of the chapter I will talk mostly about 'showing' and 'visual presentation' in the cinema. My aim, in doing so, is to keep the formulations in the text from becoming even more complicated than they are. I hope that the qualifications that would be required to accommodate the dimension of sound in films are reasonably clear.)

[2] I somewhat tentatively defend this position in Chapter 2. I will return very briefly to this view at the end of the next chapter.

[3] For a useful overview of a number of the theoretical options here, see Gaut (2004).

It is worth rehearsing these questions somewhat more carefully. I take it that (FSH) above formulates the Fictional Showing Hypothesis. It claims, in effect, that the shots of a movie constitute a work-internal fictional activity of audio-visual narration. As discussed earlier, it is closely related to 'the Imagined Seeing Thesis', which (for present purposes) that

(IST) In viewing classical narrative movies, viewers imagine seeing (in the image-track) and hearing (in the sound-track) the objects and events depicted in the movie's dramatic action.

Indeed, the latter is normally taken as the basis for accepting the former. Now, does it follow from the Fictional Showing Hypothesis that, in classical movies, a fictional or fictionalized *narrator* is implicitly represented? The question has to be handled with care. Seymour Chatman and others have argued, in effect, that whenever we have the narration of a fictional story, then the existence of that activity of narration definitely presupposes the existence of an agency that performs the narration.[4] This would be the 'narrator' of the given work. But, as I and others have pointed out before, Chatman's argument is confused. In one sense of the word, the actual author of a work of literary fiction *narrates* (or at least *tells*) the fictional story in question. That is, the author, in writing the text, makes it fictional that various situations and events take place in and thereby constitute the story. However, in many such works, it is fictional that someone is recounting as actual the situations and events that the author has created by his or her actual telling. According to well-precedented usage, the fictional or fictionalized being who fictionally narrates the story is said to be 'the narrator' of the tale, and, in standard cases, the narrator is to be distinguished from the author or the actual creator of the work. Thus, Daniel Defoe wrote the novel *Moll Flanders*, but the character, Moll Flanders, narrates her own history. Therefore, the mere fact that a work W relates a fictional story does not imply that W implicitly depicts some fictional showing or telling of that story, and, *a fortiori*, it does not imply or presuppose that W involves a narrator. For instance, a standard comic strip visually narrates a fictional episode, but it doesn't, in addition, depict some fictional showing of the episode portrayed, and, of course, no fictional narrator is to be imagined as visually presenting the episode as if it actually occurred. This is an early observation in Chapter 2. Chatman relies on an oversimplified version of the idea that there is an analytic connection between the concept of 'narration' and the concept of a 'narrator' who carries it out.

Nevertheless, it is not obvious that a slightly modified version of an analytic connection thesis doesn't hold.

(WAC) If, in a given work, an activity of fictional narration is implicitly represented, then it is fictional in the work that there is an agent (the narrator) who does the narrating.

Call this 'the weakened version of the analytic connection thesis.' I'm doubtful that even this weakened version is correct. We will briefly return to that question in a bit.

---

[4] See various essays in Chatman (1990).

But, let us suppose for a moment that the occurrence of fictional narration does imply the existence of an agent who performs the narration. Is any such narrating agency tantamount to the existence of a narrator, as that notion is intuitively understood? Here the issues get pretty cloudy, the cloudiness corresponding to the dimness of our general idea of a fictional narrator.

In standard cases, we think of a narrator as a fictional or fictionalized *character* who is narrating the story as actual. Most of our interest in narrators in literary fiction and in the question of their relationship to the story they tell depends importantly on our sense of them as being genuine characters whose attributes of personality, intelligence, and sensibility are implicitly expressed in the narration. But how much *is* required for a genuine narrator *qua* character to be created? Obviously, it is not to be expected that there will be answers here that will be both relatively sharp and uncontroversial. It is clear, as many have emphasized, that a narrator *qua* character doesn't have to be a human being. In *Black Beauty*, the narrator is a horse. I'm sure that there are science fiction stories in which the narrator is a computer, and there could be a children's story in which it is fictional that a babbling brook is babbling out the story. But, in all of these instances, the narrating horse, computer, and babbling brook will have been developed as characters—characters who have been anthropomorphized to a significant degree. On the other hand, it seems to me that the mere existence of a minimal narrating agency is not sufficient to sustain our sense of the implicit existence of a narrator who is presented to us, however dimly, as a personified character, even one whose psychological and other traits remain by and large effaced. So, if you accept the weakened version of the analytic connection argument and wonder whether, when it is applied to various works, it yields the existence of a genuine narrator, then you need to draw a further distinction. Do you mean 'narrator as minimal narrating agency' or do you mean something more: do you mean, as I will sometimes put it, 'narrator as narrative recounting character'?

So, do I believe that all works of *literary* fiction have narrators in the weaker sense? Do I believe that narrators as minimal narrating agents are ubiquitous in works of literary fiction? No! First, I think that there are some fairly rare instances in which a fictional narrative gets told but there is, in the work, no fictional narrating of the narrative in question—hence, here there is no minimal narrating agency. There are certain novels of Ivy Compton Burnett, e.g., *The Present and the Past* (1953), which consist almost exclusively of a sequence of pure dialogue exchanges and are potential examples, in my opinion. However, I do believe that minimal fictional agency is *more ubiquitous* than many other notable theorists suppose.

Second, I think that there are lots of works of fiction in which there is a fictional narrating of the narrative history but where nothing more than a minimal narrating agency is presupposed. In these works, there is no narrator-as-character who fictionally tells the tale. This is generally the situation in connection with movies. I am inclined to accept the Fictional Showing Hypothesis but deny that movies have cinematic narrators when "narrator" in that debate means 'narrator *qua* discernible character.' On the other hand, I think that movies commonly have narrators when only minimal narrating agency is at stake.[5]

Many important commentators, however, simply reject the Fictional Showing Hypothesis in any form. Both Andrew Kania and Berys Gaut have raised considerations against this idea, and Noël Carroll, I believe, agrees with both of them and for reasons similar to theirs.[6] These writers are the implacable enemies of implicit audio-visual narrators in film. More recently, Kania, Gaut, and Carroll have even turned their nihilistic rancor on the effaced narrators in *literary* fiction, thereby attacking among the most timid and helpless of the creatures in all of literature. I am appalled at this attack! How much courage does it take to impugn the existence of creatures whose whole mode of being, after all, is self-effacement? That is, these theorists deny that we should posit even minimal narrating agency in literary fictional narratives in which the narration is in the third-person, epistemically unrestricted, impersonal, and otherwise recessive.[7] In this chapter, for reasons of length, I will focus primarily on the supposed case against merely implicit radically effaced narrators in literature, and I will speak up for the members of that almost silent constituency, defending them from their detractors. In my opinion, the questions that arise concerning elusive narrators in literature and in film are structurally quite similar. However, detailed discussion of the substance of the pertinent issues in the case of film will have to be reserved for the following chapter.

Andrew Kania is skeptical about merely implicit fictional narrators in literary fictions, and he gives the example of Graham Greene's *The Heart of the Matter* as a clear instance of the kind of work he has in mind. In these instances, Kania thinks that it is false that there is someone who fictionally recounts the events of the story. More specifically, he thinks that there is no fictional recounting implicit in the text. There is only the actual telling of the fictional story, and that is an activity that was performed by the actual author of the work. For instance, he says, "However, I would argue that there are also clear cases where there is *no* fictional telling" (Kania 2005: 50). He goes on to cite the Greene novel as an example. Later he claims again, " . . . sometimes we have no reason to suppose that there is a fictional telling of the story we read or see. Graham Greene spins a good yarn, but there is no reason to posit an overarching

---

[5] Although even this, in a conceptually prissy mood, can be denied. There can be activity—even a teleologically structured activity—that is not guided by a goal-driven agent. The progress of a hurricane or the activity of the stock market may be examples. Still, this is not a concern that I will pursue.

[6] Kania (2005). Gaut (2004), 241–248. Carroll (2006), 175–184.

[7] In fact, the general class of literary narrations for which any of these theorists deny a narrator is significantly unclear. Kania is even uneasy about making the claim about the Hemingway stories that are often portrayed as having no narrator. This lack of clarity will not affect the discussion that follows. However, Kania's objection to effaced narrators is interesting. Many writers on the topic seem to grant that works whose narration is substantially effaced do contain genuine implicit narration and seem also to allow that this may presuppose the existence of a minimal narrating agency. However, they maintain that this effaced agency is too 'minimal' to merit invoking a substantial concept of 'narrator.' Disputes of this ilk, in my opinion, tend to be pretty empty. In contrast, Kania stops at the first step: he denies that the works in question involve fictional narration at all.

fictional telling within it or co-extensive with it" (Kania 2005: 52). For Kania, the actual author then is, in that special sense, the narrator. In writing *The Heart of the Matter*, Graham Greene told as fictional the story in question, just as Boswell told as actual the events in *The Life of Johnson*. So both Greene and Boswell are *author/narrators* of their respective narratives. But, in the more specialized sense of 'narrator,' as it applies to works of fiction, there is no narrator—no fictional or fictionalized narrator—of *The Heart of the Matter*, according to Kania. Since he holds that the novel involves no fictional recounting of the events of the story, he also holds that it is not fictional in that work that someone is thus recounting them.

In stating his position from the outset, Kania says that his opponents hold that, if a work of narrative fiction has a narrator, then that narrator must be "...on the same ontological level as its characters and events" (Kania 2005: 47). In his terminology, the narrator must have the status of '*fictionality*.' But there is serious potential for confusion in stating the issues in this way. To see why this is so, we need to focus on the following observations. First, we should remember the familiar fact that actual people can appear as characters in works of fiction, e.g., Cardinal Richelieu in *The Three Musketeers*. Second, and more directly relevant, an actual person can appear as the narrator of a work of fiction, e.g., Nixon is the narrator in Robert Coover's *The Public Burning*. That is, it is fictional in *The Public Burning* that Nixon recounts as actual the events of the story (which feature him). No doubt the narrator of this novel is a fictionalized version of Nixon, but it is Nixon himself who fictionally performs the narration. Third, the actual author of a work of literary fiction can appear explicitly as the narrator of the story that he or she (the author) has constructed. This certainly can happen in postmodern meta-fiction, but examples are not restricted to such cases. There is an obscure novella by Alexander Dumas, *One Thousand and One Ghosts* (*Le mille et un fantomes*), in which this strategy is deployed, and Dumas is hardly a postmodern narratological novelist. It is fictional in *One Thousand and One Ghosts* that Alexander Dumas (the author himself) recounts as actual the events of the story (which also feature him). In *One Thousand and One Ghosts* it is stated, fictionally but quite explicitly, by the narrator that he himself is the famous novelist and playwright, Alexander Dumas. However, to make the point, we hardly have to resort to recherché examples of this sort. Dante is both the actual author and the fictionalized narrator of *The Divine Comedy*.[8] Now, are Nixon, Dumas, and Dante serving as narrators in the relevant works, on 'the same ontological level' as, say, the purely fictional characters in these same works? What are we to say? Unlike the *purely* fictional characters, these narrators are people in the actual world.[9] But, like their purely fictional counterparts, it is

---

[8] Kania mentions John Fowles's *The French Lieutenant's Woman* as a possible but decidedly unclear instance. I agree that the question of whether the narrator is to be identified with Fowles is simply too tough to call.

[9] Of course, it is possible for someone to hold that the actual Nixon is not the narrator of *The Public Burning*, but rather that the narrator is a purely fictional character, derived from the actual Nixon, and called by the same name in the novel. I am no more sympathetic to this kind of counterpart theory in connection

fictional in the relevant works that they perform various activities. In particular, they fictionally perform the telling of the story in question. It is this complex property that makes them narrators of the relevant work. The notion of sameness and difference of 'ontological level' simply has to be refined.

Kania's example of *The Heart of the Matter* occupies an interesting middle ground. In contrast with the Dumas example, *The Heart of the Matter* provides readers with no *explicit* identification of its narrator (if it has one) with the actual author. Nevertheless, it may be that there are features of the novel and facts about Graham Greene, his life, and his overall *oeuvre* that implicitly make it reasonable to posit an identification of the narrator (if there is one) with the actual author. A similar and more familiar question arises in connection with the novels of Jane Austen, e.g., *Emma*. Many of Jane Austen's readers find it natural to imagine that it is Jane Austen herself who is fictionally telling about the events in Fairfield. And they find it especially natural to imagine that it is Jane Austen who intermittently breaks in and fictionally comments 'in her own voice' on the significance of certain key developments of plot. In *Emma*, the narrator never speaks of herself in the first person and certainly does not identify herself as the author, Jane Austen. At the same time, nothing in the work seems to preclude us from making that imaginative identification either, and such identification seems natural enough. On this line of thought, *The Heart of the Matter* and *Emma* each has a narrator who fictionally recounts the fictional events, and the narrator in each case is *implicitly* but 'plausibly' understood to be the actual author of the work. I'm not inclined to insist on this perspective, but the line of thought, usually ignored, strikes me as natural and reasonably attractive.[10] In any case, it should be stressed that the suggestion is different from Kania's. Here it is granted that a work like *The Heart of the Matter* involves a fictional recounting (as actual) of the narrative events, and that it is fictional that this recounting is performed by the actual author of the work. The first of these claims is the thesis that Kania and others crucially deny.

Hence, Kania maintains that it is not fictional in the work that the events of the story are being recounted or otherwise reported as actual. Now, fictional recounting, when it exists, is the product of individual fictional speech acts (or fictional thoughts) performed at specific junctures in the narration, and the characteristic type of fictional speech or thought act is assertion. So, Kania's claim is tantamount to the claim, e.g., that

It is not fictional in the novel at juncture *j* that it is being asserted that such and such took place.

---

with fiction than I am in connection with the theory of modality. For that matter, neither is Kania. See page 52 of his article. Nevertheless I don't see a quick way in which the potential dispute is going to get resolved.

[10] It may be that it is most reasonable to suppose, in these implicit cases, that it is fictional in normal, legitimate games of make-believe, performed while reading the novels in question, that the actual author is recounting the narrative events but strictly speaking false that this is fictional in the works themselves. In fact, this is the position that seems most plausible to me, but I won't try to adjudicate the aptness of this refinement.

For instance, consider the characteristic line from *The Heart of the Matter* that Kania quotes. "Wilson sat on the balcony of the Bedford Hotel with his bald pink knees thrust against the ironwork." Kania denies that, when this line occurs, it is thereby made fictional that it is being asserted that Wilson sat on the balcony etc. It is this claim that strikes me as so extraordinarily unintuitive. Still, Kania has things to say in its favor.

First, Kania gives the example of a father telling his child a made-up bedtime story. He thinks that this is a case in which the father is simply telling as fictional the story he makes up. In the actual telling, there is no implicit fictional telling as actual by the father or anyone else. In the telling, no one fictionally asserts anything. Kania thinks that the narration of *The Heart of the Matter* should be understood on this model. But Kania's characterization of this example is controversial at least. I'm inclined to think that in this sort of example there is a storytelling game of make-believe that the father and child are mutually playing between themselves.[11] In their game of make-believe, it is fictional that the father *is* recounting as actual the events of the made-up story, and the child is fully aware that his father's recounting as actual is only fictional or make-believe in their game. (In fact, there is an interesting variety of possible cases in which fictional stories are told out loud to an actual audience.) If this is right, then the father, who is also the author of the actual story, is also the fictional narrator of the story in the context of their shared game. Kania believes that our understanding of the narration in *The Heart of the Matter* should be modeled after his understanding of this sort of example. But, in my opinion, the upshot of the thought experiment is inconclusive. This same example inclines me to prefer the hypothesis that, in our imaginative engagement with his work, Graham Greene fictionally recounts as actual the depicted events of *The Heart of the Matter*.

This simple observation that actual people, including actual authors, can fictionally recount a story suggests why I find Jerrold Levinson's 'ontological gap' argument difficult to construe.[12] Adapted to the case of literature, the argument seems to run as follows. In standard, authorized games of make-believe in which literary fictions are the props, it is fictional in that game that the reader is coming to know, by reading, about facts in the fictional world of the story. This entails that the reader is fictionally being informed about those facts by someone who has epistemic access to them. But the actual author who is, in one sense, telling and thereby creating the story does not have the right kind of access to those fictional facts. Hence, there must be a teller who is 'on the same ontological level' as the fictional facts that he recounts. Therefore, we must posit that it is fictional in the work that there is someone (who cannot be the author) who has such access and is reporting the history to us. This fictional teller is the narrator. But now, take the case where Nixon or Dumas or (maybe) Greene is the narrator of the fictional work in question. Are Nixon, Dumas, and Greene all 'on the same ontological level' as the world of the fiction? As I said before, the answer

---

[11]   See Walton (1990).

[12]   Levinson (1996), 251. Kania (2005) discusses this argument at some length.

here is equivocal. In one sense, the answer is "No"—they are not merely fictional constructions created by the work. But, in another sense, "Yes"—it is fictional in the work that these actual people are reporting the narrative events. If the conclusion of the 'ontological gap' argument is that, in the work, there must be an implicit agent recounting the story who is *merely* a fictional construct of the work, then the argument is unsound and the conclusion false.

But, there is another way of looking at the considerations that Levinson provides. In the reading of a work of narrative fiction, it is fictional in the reader's game of make-believe (and in the work itself) that the narrator asserted that P, and it is fictional in the reader's *game* that the reader, in reading, learns that the narrator has asserted that P. Finally it is fictional in this game that the reader thereby learns, by a defeasible inference, that P is true. So, it is in this way that the reader 'gains access' to the facts that belong to the fictional work, but, of course, it is only a *fictional* mode of gaining access. It is fictional in the reader's game of make-believe that he thereby comes to know the story facts. Clearly, it makes no difference to the account whether the narrator here is a fictionalized version of an actual person or is merely a fictional character created by the text. Now, perhaps Levinson is simply arguing (a) that this is the most natural, reasonable account of what it is for a reader to gain access to the fictional world of a literary work, and (b) that this preferred account directly presupposes the existence of a fictional or fictionalized narrator. His idea would be that we cannot make coherent sense of a reader's epistemic access to the fictional facts without assuming that it is fictional in the work that some narrator asserts that these facts obtain. Now the force of this argument depends centrally on the truth of (a), and it is plain that Kania, Carroll, and other skeptics about the existence of effaced narrators will reject this assumption that the account sketched above is either obligatory or optimal. They will want to offer an alternative to it. Nevertheless, (a) and (b) together may be all that Levinson intended to establish in his 'ontological gap' argument. If so, then I agree with him about both of these theses, and the dispute between the two parties concerning (a) turns chiefly on what constitutes the preferred description of the phenomenology of our imaginative engagement with novels and kindred fictions. Unfortunately, it is not obvious how a dispute of this sort is to going to get resolved.

However, let's return to Kania's objection. As noted above, it seems to be his position that Graham Greene has actually 'told as fictional' the depicted story of *The Heart of the Matter*, but he also thinks that it is not fictional in the novel that Graham Greene or anyone else is telling the story in this fictional mode. Telling as fictional then seems to be an illocutionary activity different in kind from the activity of telling something as actual. And yet, what can this 'telling as fictional' amount to? In a certain broad sense, *any* author of a fictional narrative is telling the story as fictional. That is, the author, in composing the work, aims to make it fictional, in the story she is creating, that various interconnected states of affairs obtain. However, in this broad sense, Herman Melville told the story of *Moby Dick*, with Ishmael as its undisputed narrator, just as much Graham Greene told the story he concocted in writing *The Heart of the*

Matter. So, presumably this cannot be the kind of 'telling as fictional' that Kania has in mind.[13]

Later in his article, Kania proposes that in *The Heart of the Matter* Graham Greene is a *storytelling* narrator, but one that is radically effaced. He also maintains that Thackeray is the storytelling narrator of *Vanity Fair* but that Thackeray's narrating presence is dramatically vivid throughout. So Kania maintains that both *Vanity Fair* and *The Heart of the Matter* each have storytelling narrators, differing chiefly in the dramatic salience of their fictional voices. However, this can't be right. In the sense of 'storytelling narrator' that Kendall Walton originally introduced, Greene is *not* a storytelling narrator in *The Heart of the Matter*.[14] A literary work of fiction W has a storytelling narrator just in case it is fictional in W that the narrator is thereby telling a story which he has invented or made up as a fiction. Thus, Walton says, "In some cases it is fictional that the narrator speaks or writes nonfictionally, but in others [the ones with storytelling narrators] it is fictional that he creates a fiction" (Walton 1990: 368). Uncle Remus, telling his tall tales in the relevant works of Joel Chandler Harris, is a paradigmatic storytelling narrator. If we imagine versions of the Harris works in which the frame stories about Uncle Remus and the situation of his storytelling were eliminated, then, in these hypothetical versions, Uncle Remus would be both the *primary* narrator of the work and a storytelling narrator as well.[15]

Walton offered the example of *Vanity Fair* as his chief example of a literary fiction that contains a storytelling narrator. At least intermittently throughout the narration, the narrator makes it clear that the story he is telling is a fiction that he himself is in the process of constructing. Kania adds to this the thought that Thackeray himself is the *non-effaced* narrator of the work, and I am prepared to countenance this further claim. In the novel, the narrator is never explicitly identified with the actual author, Thackeray, but much of what the narrator says about himself makes such an identification pretty natural. In my opinion, this work can probably be treated along the lines that I mentioned in connection with *Emma* and *The Heart of the Matter*. It is reasonable in all of these cases to imagine the narrator of the story to be the actual author, although only in *Vanity Fair* is it fictional that the author/narrator is telling the story as a fiction.[16] Certainly, there is nothing in the narration of *The Heart of the Matter* that

---

[13] Of course, it is possible for me to tell you (to report to you) that it is fictional in *The Heart of the Matter* that P and Q and so on. In one sense then, I'm explicitly telling you the story of *The Heart of the Matter* as fictional. But, this certainly is not the sense in which Kania thinks that Greene told the story as fictional. In writing the text, he was making it fictional in his novel that P and Q and not asserting that these propositions are fictional in the story.

[14] Walton (1990), 368–372.

[15] I'm assuming here that the hypothetically altered versions of the Uncle Remus stories will leave it clear that Uncle Remus is fictionally inventing his fables for an audience of children.

[16] In fact, the concept of 'storytelling narrators' merits more careful scrutiny. Suppose we grant that Thackeray is the fictionalized narrator of *Vanity Fair*. It is possible that the narration should be described in the following way. In most of the narration, the narrator fictionally recounts as actual the history of Becky Sharp and her adventures. However, in certain passages, Thackeray actually asserts certain claims about his role as author and about his adjacent activity of fictionally recounting the narrative events. He switches, so to speak,

makes it fictional in that work that the recounted narrative is something that is thereby being created as a fiction. And yet, this is the crucial necessary condition for a work to have a storytelling narrator in Walton's sense. Thus, for Kania, *Vanity Fair* and *The Heart of the Matter* both have storytelling narrators. In the latter, but not the former, the storytelling is radically effaced.

Here is a somewhat different way in which Kania's proposal might be stated. He denies, as we have seen, about *The Heart of the Matter* that it incorporates any fictional telling of the story as actual (or, for that matter, as fictional). As I indicated above, this seems to tantamount to denying that

(1)   In W at juncture *j* it is fictional that it is *being* asserted that P.

Well, one might deny *this*, while insisting that

(2)   In W at juncture *j* it is fictional that the proposition that P is expressed (and it is actual as well).

Moreover, given that the reader knows that the author of W intended to be constructing a straightforward, reliable narration, the reader is entitled to infer that

(3)   In W at juncture *j*, it is thereby made fictional that P.

The idea here is that no fictional *act* of asserting is implicitly represented, and none is presupposed in the reader's legitimate inference to (3). I think that Kania does endorse this idea (see especially p. 50) and it is the strategy apparently proposed by Noël Carroll in the following passage. He says,

> If signaling that such-and-such is fictional instructs the audience to imagine it as true, why isn't the fictive intention of the author (that we imagine such-and-such) adequate to warrant supposing that such-and-such is true in the fictional world? Maybe it will be said that if such-and-such is asserted, there must be an agency doing the asserting. But is "that Katie loves Hubble" [in *The Way We Were*] a genuine assertion? "It is true in the fiction that 'Katie loves Hubble'" is a genuine assertion, but is "that Katie loves Hubble" really an assertion, or merely a propositional content? (Carroll 2006: 176)

But, the proposal, stated so briefly in these terms, is somewhat hard to follow.

Suppose, for simplicity of formulation, that the narration of the novel, *The Way We Were*, contains the sentence, "Katie loves Hubble." Naturally, that sentence expresses the propositional content that Katie loves Hubble, and Carroll is opposing the idea that this propositional content is fictionally offered as an assertion. His counter-suggestion is that readers of the novel, knowing that they are reading a work of fiction, simply take the propositional content as something that they are to imagine as part of the story.

---

from fictional to actual assertion. If this is correct, why shouldn't it be the case that the author/narrator of *Vanity Fair* intermittently includes actual statements about what he is doing in fictionally telling his made-up story?

But, on the face of the matter, the readers will normally take this propositional content as something that they are prescribed (defeasibly) to imagine as a part of the story only if they suppose that it is presented in the narration as having some kind of assertive force—only if it is fictional that the propositional content is fictionally put forward as true. Notice that in fictional narration instances of fictional assertion may predominate, but in the course of the narration, various 'propositional contents' may be presented in a range of different modes. The propositional content 'Katie loves Hubble' may occur as merely something that some character in the novel said or thought. Some propositional contents may be presented as having the force of a supposition, something that is merely to be entertained as possible at the pertinent juncture in the narration. Or a propositional content may be presented as something whose truth value is being questioned. (The hypothetical occurrence of the sentence 'Katie loves Hubble,' could be followed in the narration by, "Many people thought so, but was it really true?") Therefore, at a minimum, we are going to have to draw some distinctions between the kinds of illocutionary force that fictionally attach to the propositional contents expressed in the narration. We will need to distinguish at least between

(4)   In W, at juncture j it is fictional that it is asserted that P,

i.e., it is fictional that P is expressed as having the force of an assertion, and

(5)   In W, at juncture k, it is fictional that it is supposed that P

and

(6)   In W, at juncture l, it is fictionally asked whether P,

and so on. Nevertheless, I suppose that one could still insist that (4) or (5) or (6) may be true, although no fictional *acts* of asserting, supposing, and questioning are represented in the narration. Hence, it still remains that no fictional activity of recounting is involved in the narration, and no agent of such a fictional recounting needs to be assumed. Let me offer this as a friendly amendment to the Carroll proposal.

Having offered the amendment let me proceed to vote against it. Perhaps some line of thought like this can be maintained, but it strikes me as extremely strained and artificial. For one thing, in the course of the narration, all these fictional assertions, suppositions, questionings, and whatever are intertwined in the unfolding discourse. It seems to me that it is most natural to imagine all this as the interconnected fictional *activity* of reporting and commenting upon the evolving narrative—the activity of an at least minimal narrating agency. Moreover, it seems to me that we are usually intended to imagine the narration along these lines. Again, I'm sure this can be resisted, but I'm dubious about the reasons for doing so. As a description of what readers normally imagine and are supposed to imagine, this seems to me to be most natural and accurate. So, this is the chief reason that I have for accepting minimal narrating agency in the cases where Kania and Carroll find none. I don't think that there is some kind of analytic argument (based, say, on the thesis (WAC) above) to show that narrators are always present in these cases, and I don't accept an argument that depends upon a supposed 'ontological gap' between readers and the fictional worlds they contemplate. In the end, my arguments rest on putative facts about what we imagine and are supposed to imagine in our normal games of make-believe with works of literary fiction. As I said earlier, these considerations rest finally on claims about the phenomenology of our imaginative engagement with novels and kindred works of literary fiction. Unfortunately, it is not clear to me how these disputes can be definitively resolved. No purely *a priori* or conceptual reflections are likely to establish whatever facts might be in question here. But, the issues are not going to get settled by the reader's introspection of her experience in reading fictions either, and I do not see how some kind of non-question-begging experimental strategy is going to elicit compelling evidence one way or another in the debate. In the end, I find the methodological status of the *basic* issues here quite puzzling, and this is a question that deserves further investigation.

Berys Gaut, seconded also by Noël Carroll, has developed a different argument against positing merely implicit, '*omniscient*' narrators. He says,

It may be true that when we imagine something on our own without fictional guidance, we are not always required to imagine the implications of our imaginings . . . But when we appreciate fictions, we are generally required to imagine a wide range of implications of what is explicitly fictional. Comparatively little of a fictional world is made explicit, and we are required to imagine many other states of affairs to interpret correctly what is explicitly fictional. (Gaut 2004: 245)

Moreover, a little earlier in his discussion, Gaut remarks, "But we can note as a general heuristic principle that when we interpret fictional worlds we should attempt, *other things being equal* [my italics], to render them as like the real world as we can" (Gaut 2004: 245).[17] Adopting Carroll's terminology, let us refer to this as 'the Realistic Heuristic.' This consideration is applied to literary instances of implicit omniscient narration in the following passage:

But a similar argument would, it seems, yield the same result for literature. For consider the case of purported omniscient narrators, such as that in George Eliot's *Middlemarch*. The omniscient narrator is presumably a human being (the fictional teller is not usually an extraterrestrial or God). How could a mere human being gain access to all this knowledge, often the most intimate thoughts of people, which they don't tell anyone else? (Gaut 2004: 247)[18]

---

[17] Gaut seems to have in mind something like Walton's Principle of Reality and/or the Principle of Mutual Belief as the basis of these inferences. See Walton (1990), 144–169.

[18] *Middlemarch* may be another case in which it is reasonable to take the narrator to be the actual author, George Eliot, despite the fact that the narration does not explicitly say that this is so. If we do accept this identification, then it is fictional in the work that George Eliot has improbably extensive knowledge of her characters and their story world. But then, it is clearly silly to wonder about how fictionally it has come to be that George Eliot acquired her more than human knowledge.

The argument, I take it, runs as follows.

(A)   If there is a narrator in such a case of 'omniscience,' then it is fictional in the work that the story is told by a human being who has an extensive knowledge of the world of the story, impossible or improbable for any human being.

By the Realistic Heuristic it seems to follow that

(B)   If there is a narrator in such a case of 'omniscience,' then it is fictional in the work that there is *some way* in which the human narrator has *come to have access* ('gained access') to this improbably extensive knowledge.

But

(C)   It is not fictional in such works that there is some way in which the human narrator has come to have access to this improbably extensive knowledge.

Therefore

(D)   It is not true that there is a narrator in such works.

The problem with the argument lies in the notion that the transition from (A) to (B) constitutes an acceptable application of the Realistic Heuristic. As Gaut's rough formulation of the heuristic indicates (see the phrase that I italicized), the Realistic Heuristic is a defeasible principle. It can be defeated when it conflicts with apparent facts about what is fictional in the work that are so fundamental that they can't be overturned by whatever local lack of realism this conflict engenders. I think that this is precisely what happens in the cases of omniscient narration that Gaut considers.

   There are at least two kinds of 'omniscient' narration, although it is the second type that figures in Gaut's argument. *First*, if the narrator is situated in the world of the story—if it is indicated or implied that he somehow learned of the events of the story—then it does make sense to wonder how it was that he came to learn omnisciently of those events. Now, even in this 'heterodiegetic' case where the question makes sense and the application of the Realistic Heuristic seems at least initially reasonable, it may be that the work will leave it more or less completely indeterminate as to how he came to learn these things. The work just doesn't give us enough to go on to enable the reader to fill out an answer in any substantial way. Whether this indeterminacy will trouble us depends on further considerations. If there are clear storytelling or stylistic reasons why it wasn't worth bothering to spell the matter out or why it was best to keep it a mystery, we are unlikely to be bothered. But, this is not the type of case that Gaut envisages, since here the narrator is not merely implicit in the work.

   Second, in the standard 'omniscient' case, it may well be fictional that the narrators know the facts that they relate, but it is determinately not fictional that they came to *learn* of those facts in any way. It is a more or less basic prescription for establishing fictional truths in this kind of narrative fiction that, if the narrator fictionally asserts that P, then it is fictional in the story that P, unless that presumption is specifically defeated or otherwise cast in doubt. Call this "the basic prescription of 'stipulated' omni-science," and let us say that the narration of a work W is wholly reliable under 'the basic prescription' just in case the work is properly understood to be governed by the prescription throughout—the default condition it contains is never triggered. In addition, let us say that, if W is wholly reliable in this way and, in W, the narrator asserts that P, then we presuppose that it is fictional in W that the narrator *believes* and even *knows* that P. It is easy enough to explain why this presumption is natural. Thus, if W is wholly reliable under 'the basic prescription' then, for any proposition P, if it is fictional in W that the narrator asserts that P, then it is fictional in W that the narrator knows that P. Hence, if P is something that the narrator fictionally asserts, then, by implicit stipulation, it is fictional that he knows that P. But, when the narrator's fictional knowledge arises by stipulation in this way, there is no requirement or expectation that there should be in the fiction some narrative (story-internal) explana-tion of how it is that he has come to have the knowledge that he has. And generally it will be a silly question to ask for such an explanation of his knowledge. We understand the basic prescription of stipulated omniscience well enough, and we understand what story generating functions it serves. In this sort of case, we are actually blocked from asking, "How fictionally did the putative narrator learn all these things?" because it is not fictional in the work that the narrator somehow *learned* of these things at all. So here there is a direct clash between the consequences in the work of the Realistic Heuristic and 'the basic prescription,' and here the latter decisively trumps the former.

Here is a related type of case adapted from Walton's 'Othello' example in *Mimesis and Make Believe*.[19] Suppose that a narrative work is written in a series of beautifully contrived sestinas. The work has a narrator who is a military man who tells the tale of various great battles in which he participated. And, in the work it is clear that he is a simple professional soldier with little or no training in the literary arts. It may even be well known that the sestina, as a poetic form, did not exist during his lifetime.[20] Now it is fictional in the work (more specifically fictional in the narration) that the narrator tells his story in elegant sestinas. By the Realistic Heuristic it should follow that it is fictional that the narrator has somehow mastered the literary skills required for producing such a work. So there is some way in which he came to have the needed skills. But, at best it is fictionally indeterminate what that way might be, and, at worst, it is false in the fiction that there is a way in which he could have acquired them. But surely the reasonable conclusion here is that the default condition on the Realistic Heuristic should be activated. What is plainly established as fictionally true in the narration ("that it is written in rhymed sestinas") again trumps any conflicting applica-tion of the supposed Heuristic. In this case, the facts about what is fictional in the work arise fairly directly from facts about the form that the narration patently embeds. In the previous case, the facts about what is fictional in the work arise, somewhat less directly,

---

[19] Walton (1990), 174–175.　　[20] Ibid.

from facts about 'the machinery of generation' (the basic machinery for generating what is fictional in the work) that operate within the 'omniscient' narrative in question. In both cases, however, the fictional facts that I have highlighted will yield silly consequences through ill-considered applications of the Realistic Heuristic. Nevertheless, these fictional facts are so patent in the pertinent works and so fundamental to them that the reasonable conclusion is that the Heuristic should be tactfully withdrawn from operation in these regions.

In his marvelous new book on film, Berys Gaut has a rather extensive critique of the remarks I have made above.[21] Gaut says, "Wilson's basic principle of stipulated omniscience does not solve the problem of [omniscient] narrational knowledge,"[22] and he gives a pair of related reasons for thinking so. He thinks that I take the basic principle to be

(1)   If the narrator fictionally asserts that P, then ... it is fictional that P,

where this conditional is true, when it is, because there is a tacit understanding between authors and their readers that the narrator's assertions are to be regularly and reliably connected to fictional truth in the story. I claim that, in the work, the narrator is so universally reliable about matters in the fictional world just because of the reader's tacit acceptance of the stipulation. The stipulation makes 'omniscience' automatic and precludes any work-internal explanation of what makes the narrator so trustworthy. The ellipsis in (1) indicates that a minimally adequate statement of (1) would incorporate some further qualifying conditions, but Gaut and I agree that these conditions, important as they may be for other issues, are not critical to the present disagreement.

If (1) purports to state schematically the basic principle of stipulated omniscience, it exhibits a glaring ambiguity that affects the plausibility of the supposed stipulation in a critical way. The locus of the ambiguity lies in the antecedent of (1)—the fictionality operator could take either wide or narrow scope. That is, the antecedent could be read either as

(A1)   The narrator is such that *it is fictional that* he asserts that P,

or as

(A2)   *It is fictional that* the narrator asserts that P.

Now Gaut insists that (1) cannot be read as having the antecedent (A1), since having the reference of 'the narrator' outside the fictionality operator would entail that the narrator actually exists. Since the narrator is normally an artifact of the fiction, this result cannot be right.

It is worth having a brief discussion of why Gaut insists so unequivocally that the narrator does not exist. After all, the narrator of, say, *Middlemarch* surely does *exist in that*

---

[21] Gaut (2010).   [22] Ibid., 215.

work. Now, it is clear enough that Gaut, in his discussion, means that we can regularly expect that the narrator of a work of fiction does not *actually* exist. True enough, but it isn't simply obvious how that point should bear on the correctness of 'the basic stipulation' under scrutiny. Let's agree that the antecedent of that stipulation—given in (1)—should indeed be (A2). However, Gaut will pounce again, and claim the content of (1), so construed, cannot be true in virtue of a convention or a 'stipulation' between authors and their readers concerning these matters. As Gaut explains the question, if the narrator is himself a member of the fictional world that he 'describes,' then the narrator is in no position to 'stipulate' the range of (fictional) facts that constitute that world. Only the author of the work who creates that world could do that.

Nevertheless, I think that Gaut is ignoring an aspect of the case under consideration, and correlatively misses a distinction that this special case makes salient. That is, the 'basic stipulation' has potential application in cases of prose narration in which the narrator is heterodiegetic (doesn't belong to the world of the story) and is, in some sense, putatively omniscient about the world of the story. In such heterodiegetic narrations, we clearly need to distinguish between the question of whether something is 'fictional in the work' and the narrower question about whether something is 'fictional in the story.' In general, the writing of the work will make it the case that there are things true about the narrator—things true in the narration as it were—that are *not* true in the story that the narrator tells. On the other hand, everything that is fictional in the story will be fictional in the broader work as well. Thus, *Vanity Fair* includes the elements of the story of Becky Sharp, Rawdon Crawley, Amelia Sedley, and the rest, but it also establishes truths about its witty and highly self-conscious narrator. Nevertheless these are not truths that belong to the story. In the light of these considerations, I would envision the basic stipulation as saying something like

(2)   If *it is fictional in the work that* the narrator asserts that P, then . . . *it is fictional in the story that* P.[23]

Now (2) does not imply that the narrator exists in actuality and it does not even imply that he exists in the story. It may imply that he exists within the overall work, but I see nothing questionable in this. In addition, I can see no reason why there cannot be an implicit understanding between the author and the readers of the work that (2) will hold uniformly and reliably throughout the telling of the tale. In fact, I think that such a convention is very commonly picked up by ordinary readers, and, when this is so, the narrator is thereby made omniscient by the tacit stipulation in question. This is pretty much what I had in mind originally.[24]

---

[23] Among other things, the ellipsis here would have to stipulate that the narrator's assertion must concern elements in the story.

[24] Gaut also discusses my hypothetical case of the work of literary fiction that has as its narrator an unlearned old military man whose narration is conducted in elegant sestinas whose prosodic strategy he could not have mastered. Gaut is right that this is not a case in which the narrator is omniscient and, more to the point, merely 'implicit' in the narration. However, I wanted this example to show that applications of the Realist Heuristic to considerations about the narrator and his/her activity of narration that lead to out-and-out absurdity, do not always lead properly to the conclusion that there is no such narrator in the work.

6

Elusive Narrators in Film

In this chapter, I will take up a final time the question that has recurred so frequently throughout this book. Do movies—sometimes or always—involve the implicit presence of an audio-visual (cinematic) narrator? Probably this is *the* question that has figured most extensively in the literature on the nature and function of narration in fiction film. However, I think that this focus has been seriously misconceived. For reasons I will explain shortly, it is my opinion that issues about cinematic 'narrators,' when these issues have been suitably separated from various basic issues about cinematic 'narration,' are actually of relatively minor interest. Of course, there are a number of different problems about narrators in film that have been posed and investigated by various writers, but in my opinion, it has been easy for separate issues to become conflated. Worse yet, many of these issues are individually murky enough to make it very hard to be sure about how they can be fruitfully examined, even when the more dire conflations have been avoided. Finally, the ultimate theoretical worth of worrying about narrators in movies has not been adequately scrutinized. Why should one care very much about whether such narrators should be acknowledged or posited or whether they should not? In the end, I cannot see that a great deal turns on this question. As I have argued at great length, there are several central issues about the foundations of narration in film that need to be clarified and, where possible, resolved. Once these issues have been resolved (either along the lines I favor or others), there will remain some lingering problems about the nature and the extent (if any) of the agency that drives cinematic narration. Nevertheless, as I will try to explain in this chapter, these left-over problems will be of decidedly lesser import; some of them are treacherously confused; and many of them are little more than terminological.

So why not just cut the cackle about narrators altogether? Most ordinary moviegoers have the strong 'intuition' that movie stories are *not* presented by cinematic narrators of any kind. Why not respect the intuitive convictions here, and let the whole topic of 'effaced' audio-visual narrators lapse? This proposal will appeal to many, but I think that the subject cannot be so easily deflated. Influenced by Edward Branigan,[1] I will argue later that our 'intuitions' about narrators in movies are conflicted and not very

---

[1] Branigan (2006).

reliable. So I do not think that most of the familiar disagreements about such 'narrators' will simply disappear.

In fact, I think that these disagreements should be divided into two parts, and these parts correspond to the two parts of the discussion in the previous chapter about narrators in literature. A cluster of questions defines each part. The first cluster consists of questions about whether there are cinematic narrators *qua minimal* narrating agents. In the second part of the 'narrator' debate, there is a related cluster of questions about whether there are cinematic narrators in some *richer* and more *robust* sense. Minimally narrating agents are prone to be pretty minimal after all; their presence can be highly recessive in every way. Do we have any substantial reasons for going beyond a minimal account, e.g., reasons for recognizing narrators that are present in the work as genuine *characters*, characters that fictionally are performing the activity of narrating the pertinent story? 'Strongly robust narrators,' as I will use the phrase, require some identifiable *personification* of the narrating agency. For reasons that will emerge, it is useful to distinguish strongly robust narrators in the movies (if they exist at all) from narrators who are only modestly robust—modestly expressive and intrusive. That is, it is arguable that there are cases of audio-visual narration that express a rich range of thoughts, feelings, and attitudes that are imagined as work-internal responses to the narrative material, even though this range of commentary and expression in the narration does not systematically add up to the portrayal of a recognizable, narrating *character*. I take up these different levels of expressive narration one by one.

At the heart of the first cluster are questions about the truth of the Fictional Showing Hypothesis. To repeat, this is the thesis that it is fictional for competent viewers of movies that they are genuinely being shown items and events in the fictional world of the film.[2] Question one is this: Is there plausible *prima facie* evidence in favor of the hypothesis of the Fictional Showing Hypothesis? Question two asks: Is the *prima facie* evidence that exists on this score ultimately defeated by considerations drawn from putatively basic principles of interpretation, e.g., the Realistic Heuristic mentioned toward the end of the previous chapter? Question three is: assuming affirmative answers to the first two questions, does this give us adequate grounds for accepting the existence of cinematic narrators *qua minimal narrating agents*?

One of the chief aims in some of the earlier chapters of this book has been to argue that the Fictional Showing Hypothesis is true. Indeed, I have argued more narrowly for a Mediated Version of the Fictional Showing Hypothesis. In the end, the basic case for Fictional Showing has rested rather directly on the Imagined Seeing Hypothesis,[3] i.e.,

(IST) In viewing classical narrative movies, viewers imagine seeing (in the image-track) the objects and events depicted in the movie's dramatic action.

---

[2] Again, this brief statement needs to be amplified, but the reader can consult earlier discussions, e.g., in Chapter 4.

[3] For a brief discussion of the connection between the two, see pages 111–112 of the previous chapter.

Naturally this is a fundamental claim that I strongly endorse. On the other hand, it is pretty plain that authors like Carroll, Kania, and Currie do not accept it. There are various reasons that they have given or might give, but one such reason parallels a suggestion, aimed against (IST), that Carroll and Kania put forward in the case of literature. It is a suggestion I discussed and rejected in the previous chapter.

The proposal *for the case of movies* is this: there is no need to assume that movie viewers imagine seeing or are meant to imagine seeing events and situations depicted in the story. It is enough that we assume that they are prompted and prescribed by what they actually see on screen to imagine (as genuinely occurring) just the narrative events and narrative circumstances themselves.[4] Thus, for instance, suppose that the viewer sees a shot that represents an alien spacecraft hovering above the prison. Given that the viewer knows that she is watching a movie (a work of cinematic fiction), isn't the existence of such a shot in the movie *sufficient* to justify her imagining that it is fictional in the story that a spacecraft was hovering over the prison? The answer, of course, is "No! It patently is not sufficient."

In the larger context of the shot it might be clear that the hovering of the spacecraft is only something that a certain character in the movie hallucinated or that one character incorrectly reported to another.[5] Or it might turn out that the hovering of the spacecraft was an event that belonged to some merely *possible* future story development—a development that never comes to pass. It could be, as it were, a false 'flash-forward' to something that *might* have happened in the world of the narrative but never did. The shot, in the setting of the narration that includes it, will play a role in making something fictional, e.g., that the protagonist hallucinated that a spacecraft hovered over the prison or that someone reported that a spacecraft came and hovered over the prison, or whatever qualified content is suitable, but it will not make it fictional in the story that such a spacecraft hovering actually took place. The shot will make the latter content fictional in the story only if viewers are supposed to imagine the shot in question as a visual recording of an incident that really took place in the fictional world of the story. Some of the complexity of contextual factors in helping to assign appropriate contents to a given shot or sequence is explored at some length in the following chapter. The problem here is an analogue of the one that defeated the idea that the mere occurrence of a complete declarative sentence, e.g., "Katie loves Hubble," in the course of a stretch of fictional narration in a novel, is sufficient to mandate the reader's accepting that in the story Katie loved Hubble. In both cases, considerations about the contextualizing narration may serve to embed the simpler and

---

[4] The proposal in the case of literary works was: there is no need to assume that readers imagine that the propositional contents literally expressed by sentences in the narrative text are asserted or otherwise the subject of an appropriate illocutionary action. It is sufficient simply to imagine those propositional contents as realized in the story. See the previous chapter. My point is that the objections to the two proposals are essentially the same.

[5] The example is derived from *The Man Who Wasn't There* (Coen brothers, 2001).

salient propositional content inside a qualifying phrase or operator, where it will only be the qualified content that is meant to be imagined as belonging to the story.

What is more, I would also argue that the evidence that supports the Fictional Showing Hypothesis (whether in its Mediated Version or not) is not defeated by any reasonable version of the Realistic Heuristic or by any comparable principle for assigning fictional truth or falsity to a given work. Since the arguments I would give on this point would parallel the arguments I gave in Chapter 5—arguments concerning a similar point that I supported in the discussion of effaced literary narrators—I will not run through those considerations again. Based on this line of argument, is it reasonable to propose that movie viewers imagine and are meant to imagine that their engage-ment with a movie is guided by a minimal narrating agent—a goal-directed agency who has the aim of displaying to the audience emerging segments of the diegesis? As a rule, I believe that this is so, and I therefore accept that minimal narrating agents in fiction films are ubiquitous, or, as I put it earlier, *almost* ubiquitous. For me, the narration of movies and of literary fiction are isomorphic at least in this regard. Instances of both artistic forms almost always presuppose the existence of minimal narrating agents. By contrast, strongly robust narrators, i.e., robustly personified narra-tors, are common enough in literature, but I will urge that they are rare or non-existent in the cinema. So novels and movies are *not* isomorphic with respect to 'narrators' construed in this more restricted way. No wonder the whole debate about cinematic narrators has often been contentious and bewildering. This claim about strongly robust narrators in film calls on us to take up the second cluster of questions.

This second cluster concerns, in effect, whether the Fictional Showing Hypothesis (or any other kindred consideration) helps to support the thought that movies have more or less *robust* audio-visual narrators, e.g., strongly robust narrators who make their appearances in a cinematic work as identifiable narrating *characters*. If movies are fictionally recounted *only* by some *merely minimal* narrating agency, then it is unclear whether we still would be inclined and entitled to think of such a severely undrama-tized narrating agency as a figure that genuinely presents the movie narrative to us. Such a case, in connection with fiction films, would contrast sharply with the case of literature. In literary fiction, narrators, appearing frequently as characters of various types and degrees of complexity, unquestionably abound. A related puzzle is that it is unclear what explanatory role could be played by the postulation of a storytelling agency that supposedly recurs from movie to movie but is merely minimal, i.e., generally invisible and inaudible to the spectator, uniformly effaced, and characteristi-cally inexpressive.

Surely a part of the interest of noticing that a novel has an effaced narrator lies in the fact that the strategy of effacement represents a significant artistic *choice* about how the narrative is best conveyed. If it were true that only merely minimal narrators are implicated in the audio-visual narration of movies, then the importance of the allegedly hidden presence of such agents to the appreciation and understanding of the narrative cinema would be significantly in doubt. However, cinematic narrators can be minimal without being merely minimal but without being strongly robust either. These are (roughly) the modestly expressive narrators, and movies that involve them constitute a fairly distinct and important category, as we will see. In any case, we can ask what more one might require in order for strongly or modestly robust audio-visual narrators to make a noteworthy appearance on the narrational scene. For example, I have stressed above that we are stipulating that, for a strongly robust narrator to exist, there must be some notable 'personification' or 'positive characterization' of the individuality of the otherwise minimal narrating agency. Fine! The idea surely has some content, but how much or how little can reasonably be built into such an added constraint of 'personification'? There seem to be an almost countless range of qualifications that one might try. These questions are perplexing, and, in my experience, the perplexity is not easily dissipated. However, the task of resolving this kind of perplexity is, perhaps, of limited importance.

One key aspect of the trouble we meet in the overall debate about narrators lies in the fact that even some of the basic intuitions that we have concerning these matters are conflicted, confused, and pretty deeply equivocal. When spectators who are uncontaminated by prior narratological theory are asked about the plausibility of postulating audio-visual narrators in movies, their response is usually downright negative or skeptical at best. The putative existence of such narrators seems not to answer to anything that most moviegoers have readily discerned as a part of their experience of the narrative cinema. So, isn't this a basic intuition about what we do and don't imagine in watching movies? And shouldn't it be respected? Shouldn't this widespread intuition count pretty definitively against the hypothesis of 'robust' cinematic narrators? With proper qualifications (to be introduced shortly), I am inclined to think that this is right. Robust 'character-like' narrators are very common in literary fictions, but they are either non-existent in movies or they are so elusive as to be positively exotic. This point, if accepted, counts as a major structural disanalogy between literary and cinematic fictions. However, although I have already recognized and affirmed this disanalogy, I also think that one needs to be careful about how it ought to be construed.

First, despite the fact that most people have the negative intuitions about 'audio-visual narrators' that I have just outlined, I believe that the force and status of these intuitions are more complicated and equivocal than I have tended to recognize. Many other authors on this subject seem to have been equally blind to these complications. When certain of the relevant complications concerning these intuitions are brought to light, it isn't so clear that we do *not* implicitly recognize 'more' work-internal dramatization of an agency involved in some movie narration than one might initially have supposed. We will take up some of these complexities in a moment. Second, we should be careful about how much or how little we are prepared to read into various instances of more than minimal film narration. I accept that the dramatization of narrating agency need not give rise to 'strongly robust' narrators, imagined as identifiable characters in the work, but the conscious or subliminal presence of such dramatization in our imaginative experience of a film's narration should somehow get registered in our overall theory. I attempt to recognize the extent and import of this phenomenon under the heading of 'modestly expressive narration.' Certainly, in some manner or another, an account of movie narration should make sure that the expressive phenomena in movie narration are neither overlooked nor suppressed.

One source of some confusion in our intuitions about cinematic narrators may be terminological. As Seymour Chatman pointed out a long time ago, the word 'narrator' tends to carry the connotation, 'someone who recounts a narrative *verbally*' or something of this ilk. It is difficult to remove the influence of this linguistic connotation from our 'intuitions' about the existence of work internal audio-visual narrators, and for this reason Chatman preferred 'show-er' (or possibly 'audio-visual presenter') to state the position that he favors (Chatman, 1990). No doubt Chatman is right about the potentially misleading impact of the relevant connotation on our intuitions, but I doubt that the impact is a decisive factor in our intuitive judgments.

Another source of confusion seems to me to be of greater consequence, and it causes trouble for reasons that are a good deal more interesting. It raises hard questions about the epistemic value of our 'intuitions' about narrators in movies. Edward Branigan, in his recent book, *Projecting a Camera*, does a lot to summarize the complications of the case. He describes a range of intriguing and relevant features of the way in which we tend to think about narration in fiction films.[6] That is, he points out that spectators and critics often describe the activity of 'the camera' in presenting a certain shot or sequence in ways that cannot coherently be taken literally. The remarks about 'the camera' that he singles out for attention simply cannot be construed as making reference to whatever physical camera was involved in the shooting. Really, this is just an instance of a crucial point stated by Bernard Williams—a point that I have cited at length in the introduction to this book. That is, in a movie, we see the fictional contents of a shot at a given time, and, at any such time, we see the fictional scene from a 'point of view' established by the movie. It is a determinate visual perspective that we know to be created by the physical vantage point of the actual camera—the camera that took the shot. But *knowing* that this point of view has been established by a camera in the actual setting of the dramatized 'scene,' we nevertheless *imagine* the situation in quite different terms. We imagine that the point of view is, as I have called it, 'an unoccupied point of view.' It is a visual perspective that normally does not fictionally belong to anyone or anything—a conception not altogether easy to grasp. Worse yet (from a conceptual angle), the movement of this unoccupied point of view may serve to express complicated thoughts, attitudes, and emotions about the fictional objects that it surveys. Moreover, these may be thoughts, attitudes, and emotions that cannot, in general, be attributed with confidence to the actual film-makers, considered either individually or collectively.[7]

[6] Again, see Branigan (2006).
[7] That is, the viewer cannot, in general, suppose that these are states of mind that the relevant film-makers *actually* had. The importance of this qualification will emerge a little later.

For instance, a viewer might well say, "The camera knows that the barmaid is about to scream, and it shifts position to capture her anticipated response." Or, in a more elaborate vein, the viewer might report, "The camera moved across the bar-room in order to focus on the barmaid's horrified response with sympathy and tact." And yet, in the movie's narrative fiction, there will have been no camera present in the bar-room, and the actual camera used to shoot the scene surely had no knowledge about or empathetic reactions to the barmaid or to anyone else. One often sees claims about what '*the* camera' has visually conveyed in the course of several successive shots even though it may be plain enough that several cameras must have been employed. Branigan offers a host of more complicated examples of this same ilk, but here is one brief and especially telling illustration of his point. Branigan cites a comment by Raymond Durgnat concerning the action of 'the camera' in a film by René Clair: "[the camera] . . . moved along the outside walls of apartment houses, often in *company* with some bitter-sweet tune, *peeping in* through windows and *sidling round* chimney stacks, *glancing in* at little vignettes of human privacy and loneliness, and *smiling ironically* before moving on to the next, like a 'God's eye view' of urban man" (the italics are Branigan's).[8]

Perhaps the Durgnat passage is a little extravagant in its metaphorical treatment of what 'the camera' is doing, but the kind of metaphors that Durgnat deploys are not at all of unusual sorts in this connection. There is the notion that 'the camera' seems to be metaphorically 'present' in the narrative space, that it 'sees' various aspects of the dramatic action from there, and that it 'experiences' psychological reactions to aspects of what it 'sees.' For me, a perfectly wonderful instance of empathetic commentary on a character and his impending fate is provided in the final scene of *Au Hasard Balthassar* (Bresson, 1966) the scene in which Balthassar lies beside a flock of sheep on a hillside and quietly waits to die (see figures 13 and 14). But it would be possible to offer a host of powerful examples, equally to the point, from other stretches of the narration in Bresson. Although Bresson's films are exemplary for me in this regard, his expressive use of the camera for commentary on the action is by no means unique.

In fact, Branigan, in this same volume, goes on to delineate still more complicated strands in our talk about 'the movie camera,' and, on the basis of these, he maintains that a host of different but related concepts are expressed in this discourse about the camera and its achievements. I won't try to unweave the intricacies of Branigan's exposition of these matters,[9] but at least the following thought is salient in his discussion. We sometimes speak of 'the camera' in a way that apparently makes figurative reference to a personified source of the fictional showing—a source of the visual perspective on display in the image, situated at its imagined vantage point. Speaking roughly but bluntly, when we talk about 'the camera' along these lines, we

---

[8] Branigan (2006), 37–38.
[9] But any future discussion of audio-visual narration in movies will need to consider Branigan's contribution very carefully.

Figure 13 Balthassar wanders among the sheep

Figure 14 Balthassar lies down beside the sheep to die

seem to mean something like: 'the audio-visual narrator of the narrative action.' Thus, as I observed above, our intuitions about this matter are conflicted. If we ask most people about the existence of audio-visual narrators in movies, then they are likely to be nonplussed or dismissive. But these same people may easily turn around and apparently conceive of 'the camera' in a particular film as if it were something akin to a personified visual narrator of the tale. Of course, these considerations do not establish that film theory ought to endorse such confusing intuitions—intuitions of a strong narrating agency that is both reflective and expressive in reaction to items and features of the movie's fictional world. Nevertheless, these remarks remind us of the fact that this intuitive conception is less foreign to our thinking about seeing fictions in film than one might, at first blush, be disposed to think.

In fact, as I asserted at the beginning of this chapter, I am inclined to support the view that the presence of fictional recounting in a movie presupposes the existence of a minimal narrating agency—an implicit agency that performs the pertinent recounting. But, how minimal is this agency? Is it reasonable to think of this kind of agency, in its merely minimal exemplifications, as comparable to the more or less radically effaced narrators of literary fiction? I have already insisted emphatically on the overall elusiveness of these questions. Stated in this manner, one hardly expects the questions to have a sharp answer. Nevertheless, the considerations derived from Branigan demonstrate that the implicit agency that shapes the narration in various films is fairly often more than just a merely minimal registration of the 'bare visual facts' of the movie story. So, are these reflections sufficient to justify the notion that movies frequently do feature more than minimal narrators? I think they are. But, more specifically, do they make room for an imaginatively salient, coherent, and full-blooded figure of narration? Do they validate strongly robust narrators? I doubt it. I think that strongly robust cinematic narrators, comparable to the dramatized narrators in literature, are rare at best, but the existence of more than minimal narrators that are modestly robust or expressive is neither uncommon nor mysterious. Why insist that in these cases it is better to recognize modest robustness over strong robustness? The question is distinctly too broad to admit of any quick, definite, and illuminating answer, but my impressions are the following.

Compare the case of movies with the case of comic strips.[10] It is not at all unusual for the style and strategies of depiction involved in the telling of a story in a comic strip to express judgments and feelings about the story in a fairly rich and complicated way. Nevertheless, even when the visual narration of the strip is 'modestly expressive' in this fashion, I think that readers have little temptation to imagine some *character*, explicit or implicit in the work, that is creating and presiding over that narration. The narration is not 'strongly robust' in this way, and it is not easy even to grasp how a work-internal 'visual narrator' could get constructed and effectively conveyed in comic strips. As I see it, this is the situation we also face in considering the possibilities of cinematic narration and our possible experiences as viewers of the mediated narrative.

It is worth noting in addition that there is a problematic assumption that is almost universally embraced in discussions of audio-visual narrators in movies. This is the thought that, if a movie has an audio-visual narrator, then the narrator must be a

---

[10] I made some use of this comparison in Chapter 2 on p. 34.

fictional (or make believe) character that has been created as part of the cinematic construction.[11] In the previous chapter, I questioned this assumption in connection with works of literary fiction, and it seems to me that it ought to be questioned in the case of movies as well. I noted that it is rare that the narrator of a work of literary fiction is explicitly identified as being the actual author of the work, but it may not be unusual that readers imagine, quite reasonably, that it is the author who fictionally reports the events of the story. When no fictional character has been explicitly created as the narrator of the tale, it may even be a natural fallback assumption that it is the author who fictionally describes the action that constitutes the narrative. I gave several examples of this possibility before, and here is still another.

In most of Victor Hugo's *Notre Dame de Paris*, the narrator fictionally recounts the strange story of Quasimodo and Esmeralda. However, in writing the novel, Hugo was concerned to give an accurate account of the layout of medieval Paris and its architecture, and he intended the reading audience to recognize that this was his enterprise. So, it seems to me that we can rightly take it that, in the 'non-fiction' passages, the narrator, Hugo himself, is actually asserting that, e.g., certain regions and structures in Paris had such and such a character. And yet, the 'non-fiction' and 'fiction' passages are thoroughly intermingled and the transitions between them are seamless. It is wholly natural to assume that the same person *qua* narrator *actually asserts* the propositions in the historical disquisitions and *fictionally asserts* the propositions that specify the fantastic and melodramatic plot. That person—the narrator of *Notre Dame de Paris*—will be Victor Hugo. Naturally this example has special features that facilitate the imaginative identification of the narrator with the author, and I am increasingly inclined to believe that similar imaginative identifications may be relatively widespread. But I also grant that the whole issue here is obscure and fraught with uncertainty.[12]

However, if it is correct that the actual author can be the narrator in a literary fiction, then why shouldn't the *actual* film-maker (or, for that matter, the actual film-makers)[13]

---

[11] See Kania (forthcoming). In this article Kania makes it quite explicit that he believes that his philosophical opponents all hold that narrators of works of literary fiction are always literary characters. Since I am one of the chief targets of his criticisms it is worth stressing the present point. I maintain that the actual author may be the narrator of a literary fiction. When this is so, it is fictional in the work that the actual author is recounting the events of the story. Where we differ is over the following point: he holds that there are instances of narration in literary fiction that do not involve any activity of fictional recounting at all, and I deny this.

[12] See the more extensive discussion of this point in the previous chapter.

[13] In the case of literature, it is hard to think of a work that is fictionally narrated by a group of agents working in collaboration. (Of course, a story told by a sequence of narrators, e.g., *The Sound and the Fury*, is common enough.) It is not hard to imagine, however, a version of, say, *Snow White and the Seven Dwarfs* in which the seven dwarfs collaboratively narrate, in a mix of voices, their adventures with Snow White. When the linguistic telling of a fictional or non-fictional tale is in question, we are most familiar with situations in which a single person has somehow constructed a narrative for his/her audience. In dealing with literary fictions, this is the model of the 'narrating agent' and the 'narrating situation' on which we characteristically rely. However, it is doubtful that this model must carry over to the telling of a fictional story on film. Even moviegoers who are largely ignorant of how movies are actually made have some dim awareness that the making of films is normally the result of collaborative activity, and it will be natural for both untutored and

do the audio-visual narrating in movies as well? This will mean roughly that the actual film-maker(s) fictionally recount the made-up series of narrative events. In fact, one can give an argument based on considerations similar to those about the mixed narrational register in *Notre Dame de Paris*. Certainly this type of mixed register occurs in many movies. To choose just one example from many that would serve, take *Deux ou trois choses que je sais d'elle* (*Two or Three Things I Know about Her*) (Jean Luc Godard, 1967). This movie is a striking mixture of a documentary about aspects of late twentieth-century Paris and a fragmented fictional story about the female character, Juliette Jeanson (Marina Vlady). In the documentary parts we can rightly say that Godard (and/or his collaborators) actually shows us real parts and features of Paris in the early 1960s. When the movie turns to episodes in Juliette's made-up story, it is only fictional that we are shown Juliette's actions and their circumstances. Nevertheless, it is utterly natural to have the impression that a single agency—perhaps a collaborative agency anchored in Godard— both *actually recounts* the facts about Paris and its operations *and fictionally recounts* the events about the fictive characters of the movie like Juliette. In this case and in others, it is reasonable to imagine the actual film-maker (or the actual film-makers) as serving throughout as the (possibly collective) narrator of the pertinent fiction. As I stated in the last chapter, I merely regard this as a reasonable perspective on the film's narration. Adopting such a perspective will rarely if ever be mandatory.

This line of thought suggests one further observation. In discussions of cinematic narrators in film we are regularly warned not to confuse what might be legitimately supposed concerning a putative 'audio-visual narrator' of the movie and an 'implied author' or an 'implied film-maker' embodied in the cinematic work.[14] Usually, such warnings seem to presuppose that the second of this pair of concepts is, all in all, the clearer and more basic of the two. I have no desire to wade many steps deeper into this particular narratological swamp except to add the following. If my last remarks can be fleshed out and their plausibility defended, then the distinction between 'narrator' and 'implied film-maker' is in danger of collapsing, at least over a significant range of cases. That is, if it is fictional for us that Alfred Hitchcock somehow relates the dramatic action of *Vertigo* to the audience (functions fictionally as narrator), then he is both the agent of the story's narration, and, in carrying out that task, he depicts an implicit version of himself in the crafting of the film. He thereby defines himself also as the 'implied film-maker' of *Vertigo*.

---

more sophisticated movie consumers to model the typical 'narrating situation' based on this piece of common knowledge. That is, it will be natural for viewers to imagine that some kind of pooled, multi-agent effort has produced the fictional recounting of the movie story. No doubt such imaginings about the narration in fiction film are likely to be hazy—indeterminate about what collaborators might be involved and about what exactly their various contributions to the recounting might have been, but the character of a fictional narration in literature may be hazy as well.

I don't know whether these speculations about how viewers might 'model' the nature of film narration are right, but, if they are, they lead to further interesting consequences that I don't have the space to pursue here.

[14] I issued such a warning many years ago in *Narration in Light*.

In most conventional fiction films, the range of personal traits that get expressed in the fictional recounting will be limited, and consequently any implicit narrating agency, collective or otherwise, that we might apprehend will strike us as effectively effaced. But, I have already rejected the view that internally expressive narration is *always* drastically circumscribed in this way. Attributes of idiosyncratic intelligence, sensibility, and personality registered in the narrating agency of a specific movie are not always so rigorously concealed. If severe effacement *were* omnipresent in cinematic fictions, then it seems to me that the concept of 'the narrating agency' of a movie would be of little or no critical interest. The narrating agents would be 'merely minimal' across the board. However, I want to emphasize that this is not so. Film criticism needs to recognize a range of movies with modestly robust narrators (under some terminology), and it may turn out not to be unreasonable to recognize at least some strongly robust narrators as well. I will give some possible examples in a moment. Certainly I do not accept for a moment that there are never (or almost never) any aesthetically interesting contrasts to be drawn between audio-visual narrators from one movie to another. They are not all totally minimal and they are not totally eclipsed, and this is a matter that good interpretation of movies should get right, at least film by film.

In richer, somewhat more personalized movies, traits of intelligence, sensibility, and personality *are* rather extensively manifested by details of the manner in which the fictional story and its denizens have been presented. Severely minimal narrating agency may be the norm in commercial movies, but narrators that are more expressive in various styles and to various degrees are not at all out of the ordinary. To explore this topic adequately, one would need to investigate various key concepts of storytelling manner and strategy—crucial facets of narration that have played very little role in the discussions developed in this book. I have in mind concepts like 'point of view,' 'style,' and 'tone' as they are instantiated in the audio-visual storytelling of particular movies.[15]

Point of view in film narration registers a systematic approach to the way in which information about the narrative is regulated and deployed, and it sometimes marks a personalized slant upon how the viewer's imagined seeing is to be conducted. Correlatively, it is in the style and tone of the presentation of the dramatic action that the viewer's impression of the personal traits of the narrating agency can often come to be filled in. A particular shot or sequence frequently shows the story segment it depicts with the aim of showing the segment in a richly expressive manner. Thus, there may be an attempt to portray the narrative action bluntly or intrusively, or, alternatively, it may be rendered with a certain noteworthy restraint and discretion. The narrative meaning of the action may be approached directly or obliquely, and it may be handled with a sustained sense of troubling candor or with a sense of irony and distance. Parts of the shot or sequence may seem to 'react' to occurrences in the fictional world, reacting, for

---

[15] Of course, there is an enormous literature on these subjects. For especially insightful recent discussions, see Gibbs (2006) and Pye (2007).

example, with sympathy, shock, indignation, curiosity, or puzzlement. Such reactive attitudes and responses presuppose the fictive reality of the situation that has thereby been presented and, hence, it will only be fictional in the work that these attitudes and responses are attributable to an agent who is showing us that situation in that reactive way.

The style and tone of the showing may bring an extensive range of human qualities to bear upon how the narrative action is to be apprehended, and various structures of point of view will work to a similar effect. Surely these are aspects of movies that carry a great deal of interpretative interest for critics and aesthetic theorists but also for ordinary movie viewers who have come to be seriously engaged by particular films. However, even in the richer examples of style, tone, and point of view, the audiences of these works probably will not be particularly inclined to assign the whole constellation of the human qualities that get expressed to some *unified* narrator who is imagined to have constructed the narration on his own. That is, in the standard film case, it is unlikely that audiences will discern in the narration the kind of single, vivid, dramatized narrating agency that is familiar to them from the case of literature. This is to repeat my general repudiation of strongly robust narrators. On the whole, I embrace this claim, and yet, there are potential exceptions to even this guarded thesis.

There are some movies in which the personification of a thoroughly coherent narrating agency does seem to inform the audio-visual narration from beginning to end. These involve paradigms of what I have called strongly robust narrators. For me, a scattering of such examples from the late/middle period of classical narrative film would include: *The Rules of the Game* (Jean Renoir, 1939), *Scarlet Street* (Fritz Lang, 1946), *The Earrings of Madame de . . .* (Max Ophuls, 1952), *The Searchers* (John Ford, 1956), *Vertigo* (Alfred Hitchcock, 1958), and *L'Avventura* (Michaelangelo Antonioni, 1960). In movies that are as consistently crafted and as analytically and evocatively 'told' as these, it is tempting to think of them as if they have a consistent audio-visual narrator, a narrator who is responding systematically to attributes of the fictional world. It is in these kinds of cases that it is especially tempting to imagine the director as the personified agent of the audio-visual narration. So maybe in these and related cases we *should* be prepared to acknowledge the existence of a strongly robust narrator. However, if this is so, are the strongly robust narrators to be identified with the actual director in each case? And, if this identification is admitted, are there strongly robust narrators in movies where such identification fails? I am more than happy to leave these and similar issues hanging in the void without an answer.

In conclusion, I would like to return to the quotation from early Christian Metz with which I began Chapter 2. I repeat the passage here: "The spectator [of a narrative film] perceives images which have been obviously selected (they could have been other images) and arranged (their order could have been different). In a sense, he is leafing through an album of predetermined pictures, and it is not he who is turning the pages but some 'master of ceremonies,' some 'grand image-maker' . . . situated somewhere behind the film, and representing the basis that makes the film possible."[16] If the Mediated Version of the Fictional Showing Hypothesis is correct, then viewers do not imagine that the implied film-makers have photographed the fictional situations presented in the shots. This consideration may explain why Metz speaks in this passage of the images as being 'pre-determined.' I am supposing that he means here that the image is pre-determined, not just for the spectator, but also for the agency 'behind the film,' the agency that created the narrative construction. 'Pre-determined,' on this construal, means here that it is indeterminate how those images came to be and how, in some fashion, they pre-existed the specific construction of the work.

Metz asserts also that the *le grand imagier* has *selected* the images that register the fictional world and has *assembled* them into a narration that articulates a coherent story. Although it goes a bit beyond what Metz says, it would be in the spirit of the passage to allow that *le imagier* may have also manipulated and modified the images that he/she has in hand for purposes of amplifying the storytelling in the first place, and sometimes for the purposes of personal expression, analysis, or broader commentary as well. Of course, I have lately been intimating that it could be more appropriate here to speak of '*les grands imagiers*,' allowing for 'joint agency' in our implicit conception of how the cinematic narration of fictional works is conducted, but this is a peripheral matter. Nevertheless, taken as a brief and metaphorical synopsis of the kind of narrational agency that I have been defending in these essays, the famous Metzian passage, with the amendments I have proposed along the way, still serves that summarizing function pretty well.

In the next chapter I will take up an enormous subject that I have essentially left in abeyance up to now. When we examine the Imagined Seeing Hypothesis,[17] there is a very broad issue about what the *scope* of the thesis is supposed to be. Does the thesis claim only that movie viewers, *when they are watching impersonal or inter-subjective shots,* imagine themselves seeing the on-screen items within the narrative space? Or do viewers engage in some mode of imagined seeing throughout the film, whenever they are watching one type of subjective shot or sequence or another? For instance, if viewers watch dream sequences, do they imagine that they are thereby seeing the contents of the dreaming character's depicted dream? This is a large and complex topic, and we will only make a first stab at comprehending the various ramifications it involves.

---

[16] Metz (1974), 20–21.

[17] Or, alternatively, when the Fictional Showing Hypothesis is under scrutiny.

PART IV

Some Strategies of Film Narration: Point of View

7

Transparency and Twist in Narrative Fiction Film

I. Transparency in narration

One of the characteristic marks of classical narrative films is that their audio/visual narration is, in a certain sense, transparent. Very roughly, this means that (1) most of the shots in these movies are understood as providing the audience with 'objective' or inter-subjectively accessible views of the fictional characters, actions, and situations depicted in the film and that (2) where the shots or sequences are not to be construed as objective, there is a reasonably clear marking of the fact that they are, in one of several different ways, 'subjective.' Of course, 'subjective shots and sequences' come in various modes. For instance, some shots and sequences depict the perceptual field of a particular character. Others depict a character's visual imaginings, memories, dreams, or hallucinations. Still others render in visual terms the content of something that some character is verbally reporting or describing. This short list of possibilities is obviously not exhaustive, and the individual 'subjective' modes deserve lengthier discussion. Nevertheless, let us say that (1) and (2) give us, as a crude first approximation, a specification of the norm of 'the transparency of *narration*' in classical narrative film. Although the conception that these conditions jointly express has a recognizable intuitive import, it is not easy to elaborate the conception more sharply. The concept of an objective shot or sequence in fiction films is problematic and, correlatively, so are the various concepts of subjective depiction. Moreover, the nature and functioning of the factors that contextually mark the epistemic status of a movie segment (that is, a shot or edited sequence) can be surprisingly elusive. These are among the issues I will address in this chapter.

However, my investigation is not simply motivated by an untrammeled analytic impulse. I have been struck by the fact that there are a number of fairly recent mainstream, commercial films—films that present an elaborate, detailed, and more or less coherent narrative—that depend on surprising, systematic violations of narrational transparency. The narration in the films I have in mind is significantly unreliable in particular ways, and its unreliability depends precisely on the audience's confounded expectation that the norm of narrational transparency will have been in place. These movies have come to be known as 'twist movies,' where the 'twist' in question is predominately epistemological. *The Cabinet of Dr. Caligari* (Robert Wiene, 1919) is a celebrated early example of the strategy, and there have been scattered instances throughout the history of film. But lately we have enjoyed (or deplored) a positive explosion of epistemically twisted movies.

The films I am thinking of come in at least two broad kinds. First, there are movies in which the cinematic narration, as the audience eventually comes to realize, represents the narrative action through the subjective perspective of a particular character, although, in general, that action has not been represented from the perceptual point of view of the character in question. That is, the narration stands outside the 'focalizing' character, regularly presenting him or her within the frame. Still, at the same time, the narration reflects the problematic way in which the character imagines the relevant fictional history to have transpired. *Jacob's Ladder* (Adriane Lyne, 1990) is one example of this strategy, appearing early in the recent cycle. David Fincher's *Fight Club* (1999) and the framed core story of *Secret Window* (David Koepp, 2004) are paradigmatic instances of global non-transparency, and David Cronenberg's *Spider* (2002) constitutes an interesting variant on the strategy. *Vanilla Sky* (Cameron Crowe, 2001) and, arguably, David Lynch's *Mulholland Drive* (2001) fall within the category as well.

In a different but related category, there are films in which it emerges that the fictional world contains special (typically, supernatural) beings that can be perceived only by conscious agents with non-standard perceptual powers and not by means of normal human vision. In the course of these films, it is revealed that the central character or characters are themselves among the 'humanly invisible' special beings, although the film's viewers have been seeing them throughout. *The Sixth Sense* (M. Night Shyamalan, 1999) and *The Others* (Alejandro Amenabar, 2001) are epistemological twist movies of this second variety.

My chief example of an epistemological twist movie will be *Fight Club*, although I will comment briefly on *The Others* as well. The films in question are of varying complexity and merit, and all of them, it seems to me, have defects of conception and execution. Still, the questions about them that interest me most concern the matter of how their narrational strategies can be coherently described, and this requires one to confront problems about how certain sorts of subjectivity are represented, and identified as such, within the setting of the films. These movies all pose hard problems about how spectators are to imagine or otherwise comprehend what they are seeing as they watch the unfolding image-tracks before them. Of course, it is hardly news that the history of the cinema includes a multitude of movies whose narration fails to conform to the norm of transparency. It is a recurrent feature of certain kinds of art films that their instances repudiate the familiar classical norm. *Last Year at Marienbad* (Alain Resnais, 1961), *8½* (Federico Fellini, 1963), *Belle de Jour* (Luis Buñuel, 1966), and *Persona* (Ingmar Bergman, 1966) are some obvious examples. Naturally, it is not my goal to examine all the ambiguous interplay of objectivity and subjectivity in film. For starters, that topic is unmanageably vast. I will begin with some simple subjective segments and build to higher levels of narrational sophistication—the narration of *Fight Club*, for instance.

In the history of film theory, there has been a range of worthwhile discussions of subjectivity in film. For instance, Jean Mitry addressed the subject in an extended section of *The Aesthetics and Psychology of the Cinema.*[1] In the 1970s, Bruce Kawin published the book *Mindscreen*, an ambitious and helpful contribution to the topic.[2] A few years later, Edward Branigan developed an elaborate, detailed theory of cinematic subjectivity in his *Point of View in the Cinema*, especially in Chapters 6 and 7 of that volume.[3] These constitute only a small selection from a rather extensive literature. As suggestive as these and other works are, they seem to me to suffer from various misconceptions, confusions, and lacunae, although I will not engage here in an explicit critical discussion of them. On the other hand, film theorists who write from the perspective of analytic philosophy and cognitive psychology have not thus far investigated subjectivity in the cinema to any considerable extent. However, as I will try to demonstrate, there certainly are problems in the area—some of them exemplified by the twist movies—that are worthy of more careful analytic attention. In particular, certain types of subjective cinematic representation raise tricky issues for the phenomenology of film viewing or, as I would put it, for a general account of what it is that spectators *imagine themselves seeing* in a narrative fiction film.[4]

Some analytic philosophers of film have maintained that film spectators imagine seeing and are meant to imagine seeing whatever fragment of the movie's fictional world is presented in the relevant shot or sequence. I have called this 'the Imagined Seeing Thesis' as it applies to fiction film. As noted earlier, the thesis has been principally elaborated by Kendall Walton and endorsed by Jerrold Levinson and myself.[5] In opposition, Gregory Currie and Berys Gaut have argued, for instance, that the thesis is mistaken,[6] and I have tried in previous chapters to respond to some of their specific, key objections. However those specific issues are eventually to be resolved, I think it is fair to say that there are further questions about the thesis that none of the debaters has adequately investigated. These questions include the following: First, what is the *scope* of the Imagined Seeing Thesis for film? Is the thesis supposed to apply only to the objective or impersonal shots and sequences in a film? Or, is the thesis supposed to apply in some fashion to various categories of subjective shots and

[1] Mitry (1977).   [2] Kawin (1978).   [3] Branigan (1984).

[4] Here and elsewhere in the chapter, I speak of the subjectivity of the visuals in a film and of what it is that viewers imagine seeing in a visual segment. But, as Michael Renov stressed to me, this is a serious oversimplification, perhaps even a significant distortion. The representation of cinematic subjectivity is often a crucial dimension of segments of the sound-track, and related issues arise concerning what film viewers imagine hearing in the sound-track. I stick to my oversimplified statement of the issues only to avoid recurrent qualifications and complexities of formulation that are likely to impede the reader's comprehension.

[5] See Walton (1990), especially section 8, "Depictive Representation," and also Walton (1997); Levinson (1996); and, for my views, Chapter 2 of this volume.

[6] See Currie (1995), 170–179; Gaut (2004).

sequences as well? Second, if it is contended that we do imagine ourselves seeing something in a subjective segment of such-and-such a type, then how does the specific subjective character of the segment affect or qualify the content of what we imagine ourselves seeing in the scene? Finally, what difference, if any, does it make to what the viewer imagines seeing in a subjective segment when it is not immediately identified as such in its broader narrational context? For reasons that will emerge in time, answering these last two questions, for certain types of subjective segments, is a delicate matter. In the ensuing discussion, I am going to assume provisionally that the Imagined Seeing Thesis is true in the case of objective segments, and I will go on to investigate how the thesis is likely to fare when it is extended to different kinds of subjective shots and sequences.

However, let me say once more something to explain and motivate, at least minimally, the assumption I am here adopting. The phrase 'to imagine seeing' has various readings and, in the present context, its employment is potentially confusing. "Jones imagined seeing his mother" may mean that he formed an inner visualization of her. Or, it might mean that Jones had a false visual impression of seeing her where that impression was crucially triggered by his imagination. Neither use is in question here. In watching a film, we regularly speak of 'seeing' the fictional characters and situations depicted in the work. But what it is to see such fictional items in a movie is significantly different from what it is to see (as film viewers also do) the actors, the acting, and the configurations of *mise-en-scène* that portray those fictions. In newsreel footage of the Yalta conference, there may be a segment that shows Stalin waving, and I can say correctly that I see Stalin waving in that segment. Similarly, in a fictionalized movie reenactment of the conference, there may be a segment in which the actor playing Stalin gives a wave. In this case also, fully cognizant of the movie's artifice and fiction, I can also say that I see Stalin waving in the segment. The proposition that I principally intend to assert by my second utterance is different from the first. In the second case, I am manifestly describing some episode in my imaginative engagement with the fictionalized film and that fact conditions what I am rightly understood to be asserting. What I assert is that, in my imaginative engagement with the film, it is fictional for me that I see Stalin waving in the segment—or something of the sort. It is in this sense that I imagine seeing Stalin wave in a segment of the docudrama.

So, in this volume, I have followed Kendall Walton in saying that viewers *imagine seeing* the fictional contents in a fiction film. However, I use the phrase to designate whatever kind of imagination-conditioned seeing is involved in seeing fictional objects and events in movies, without, in general, relying on any specific account of this delicate phenomenon. In fact, I am sympathetic to key aspects of a Walton-style approach to the matter. A viewer imagines seeing a certain fictional situation in a segment S just in case, in watching S, it is make-believe for the viewer, from the inside, that he or she is thereby seeing that situation depicted in S. Without extended commentary, this characterization yields limited enlightenment at best, and alternative approaches are feasible as well. I think that, at least in the course of this chapter, I can afford to be neutral concerning the details of a plausible explication, but I have wanted to signal the special character of the use that I will employ—a use in which it figures, to some degree, as a convenient term of art.[7]

Viewers know an indeterminate host of things about what is fictionally the case in a given movie, but they come to know different fictional film truths in very different ways. It is difficult to make sense of basic differences in the nature of their knowledge of what is fictional in a film story unless some version of the imagined seeing thesis is accepted. This is a point that I elaborated at length in Chapter 3. For instance, viewers of *The Searchers* (John Ford, 1956) know that it is fictional in the movie both that Scar's (Henry Brandon) tribe of Comanches is slaughtered by the cavalry and that later Ethan (John Wayne) disrupts a marriage ceremony. However, they know that in *The Searchers*, the cavalry slaughters the Comanches because they make a correct inference from what they see and hear in a central, rather elliptical section of the movie. On the other hand, they know that fictionally Ethan disrupts Laurie's (Vera Miles) wedding because they imagine seeing him do just that. Certainly, this is the easiest and most natural way of distinguishing between instances of perceived and inferential knowledge of what is fictional in a movie, and it is unclear what better way of distinguishing them might be drawn. Perhaps, one is inclined to protest that the viewers simply see Ethan disrupt the wedding—no qualification by 'imagined' is required. However, in watching the very same scene, viewers also see John Wayne stride onto a Hollywood set and act out the pertinent prescriptions of the script. And yet, surely, viewers do not 'see' both the behavior of the actor John Wayne and the actions of the character Ethan in the same way, although it is also not credible that 'see' is lexically ambiguous across the two assertions. The difference, I am assuming, should be explained in this way: viewers actually see John Wayne and his behavior, and it is make-believe for the viewers that they see Ethan and what fictionally he does, that is, the viewers *imagine* seeing those constituents of the fiction.

II. Point-of-view shots and subjective inflection and saturation

I will begin by introducing some reflections on the concept of a 'subjective' shot and about some of the important subdivisions within the category. These considerations will be pretty rough and ready, since each category to be discussed involves considerable variation and complexity, but I will say enough to argue for two points. First, subjective segments of the sorts that I will examine involve at least two different notions of 'the subjective.' Second, subjective segments, of these different kinds, do not pose a serious problem for the Imagined Seeing Thesis, if the thesis is suitably

---

[7] For a much fuller explanation of 'imagined seeing' in movies as I understand it, the viewer should review the discussion of the pertinent concept in Chapter 3.

formulated. Finally, it will be crucial for us to have at least a schematic overview of a number of the main kinds of subjective shots. Later, I will distinguish, from the more familiar kinds, one special type of subjective shot—what I will call 'impersonal but subjectively inflected shots.' This category does not seem to be adequately delineated in the literature, and I will highlight its interest later in the discussion. I will start out by considering segments whose 'subjective' character is more or less clearly indicated in their immediate context. In the last part of the chapter, I will turn to some issues that are raised by segments whose 'subjective' status has not been marked immediately in this fashion—segments of non-transparent narration, in other words.

Among the shots commonly deemed to be 'subjective,' one naturally thinks first of veridical point-of-view (POV) shots. These are shots that represent (at least approximately) the visual perspective, anchored in an implicit visual vantage point, of a designated character at a given time. Although this is the simplest case, it is not really clear why veridical POV shots are regularly counted as 'subjective.' It is often said that viewers are meant to imagine that they are seeing the relevant fictional items and events 'through the eyes' of the relevant character. In some sense, this is no doubt true, but the sense in question is not so easy to pin down. In my opinion, what film viewers imagine seeing in a veridical POV shot are the fictional circumstances that the character perceives, and viewers imagine that they are seeing the depicted fictional material from a visual perspective that coincides more or less with the visual perspective of the observing character in the film. Nevertheless, certain tempting misconceptions need to be avoided. As Kendall Walton and I have argued elsewhere, film viewers, in so imagining, do not imagine either that they are, at that moment, identical with the movie character or even that they occupy the implied vantage point of the character within the movie's fictional space. Rather, it is to be imagined that the visual perspective offered on the screen arises from the same vantage point as the vantage point that fictionally the character is occupying at the time of his or her viewing.[8]

So, in what sense *is* a veridical POV shot subjective? After all, if what viewers imagine seeing in the shot is, in the first instance, the objective circumstances in the fictional world that fall within the character's gaze, then the depicted content of the shot is not subjective. Both the film viewers and the viewing character are being supplied with inter-subjective information about these observable circumstances. In this respect at least, the information that is fictionally presented in the shot is just as 'objective' as the information in shots whose visual perspective is not identified with that of any character.[9] Of course, the veridical POV shot simultaneously makes it fictional that the character is seeing the circumstances before his or her eyes and seeing them from the vantage point implicit in the shot. And yet, a non-POV shot that showed the same character gazing at the same fictional circumstances (for example, in an over-the-shoulder shot of those circumstances) would generate more or less the

---

[8] Walton (1997) argues this thesis and I argue it in Chapter 2.
[9] See Smith (1995), 158–160 for this point.

same fictional truths about the character's seeing and what it is he or she sees. However, such a shot would not normally be deemed subjective. If we were to suppose that the visual contents of the POV shot are to be imagined as representing the private field of vision of the perceiving character, then that putative fact would yield an obvious sense in which POV shots are 'subjective.' Nevertheless, it is doubtful that this is a part of what viewers normally imagine or are meant to imagine when they watch veridical POV shots. Hence, it is correspondingly doubtful that this explanation of POV subjectivity should be endorsed.

The subjectivity of veridical POV shots may well consist in nothing more than the coincidence of vantage point between the onscreen imagery and the character's visual perspective. Or, alternatively, it may be that POV shots are thought of as subjective because the occupation of their vantage points by a fictional perceiver always raises the question, at least potentially, of whether the shots in question are fictionally veridical. By contrast, given the strong but defeasible expectation of transparency, non-POV shots are tacitly and almost automatically construed as offering film viewers inter-subjectively accessible information about the objective scene in view. I will leave this question about the general nature of the subjectivity of POV shots unresolved, but I want to stress the fact that the sense in which veridical POV shots are subjective is really pretty weak.

On the other hand, there *are* POV shots and sequences in which a viewer *is* expected to imagine something about the phenomenal qualities or contents of a character's field of vision. We are all familiar with POV shots that are, as I will say, *subjectively inflected*. That is, a range of the visual properties of the shot are supposed to represent subjective enhancements and distortions of the character's field of vision at the time. For instance, when the character is drunk, dizzy, or otherwise perceptually disoriented, then special effects of focus, lighting, filtering, or camera movement may be employed to depict the way these psychological conditions have affected the character's visual experience. Similarly, consider a POV shot in which a character is seeing items in his or her immediate environment, but the character's field of vision also includes some halluci-natory objects or events. For example, in a POV shot, some character may be represented as looking into his or her garage and hallucinating a pink aardvark on the car. Of course, partially hallucinated perceptual structure shots of this type occur in many films.

Robert Altman's *Images* (1972), which is itself a kind of epistemological twist film, features many partially hallucinatory POV shots from the heroine's (Susannah York) perspective, and the psychological drama of the movie is centrally built up around them. In any case, I am stipulating that these partially hallucinated POV shots are to count as subjectively inflected as well. Since certain internal properties of a character's perceptual state are represented in such shots, they are understood to be 'subjective' in a straightforward sense. Normally, the objective and subjective aspects of the image and the way the two are related are specified clearly enough in the immediate film context. Let us say that these aspects and the relations between them constitute 'the epistemic structure' of the pertinent shot or sequence. That is, in standard segments of this type, it is plainly indicated by the context that the character is actually seeing a certain fictional situation before his or her eyes and that he or she is also seeing the situation from a certain visual perspective that is subjectively inflected in a certain way—the way that is depicted on the screen. Correspondingly, film viewers imagine seeing the same fictional objects and events as the character does, and they imagine seeing them from the very same inflected visual perspective.

On one extreme of the subjectively inflected mode, the subjective inflection of the visual perspective may be *total*. That is, movie spectators are to imagine that the character's visual perspective is completely determined by his or her present state of dreaming, hallucination, or inner visualization of one sort or another and to imagine themselves seeing those private visual contents. I will call such shots 'subjectively saturated.' In this sort of case, spectators are mandated not to imagine that they are being provided with information about whatever fictional environment lies outside the character's mind. So, is it correct to say that spectators imagine seeing *anything* in such cases of total subjective saturation? Well, should we say that people who are subject to total hallucinations are seeing something? In one sense, "yes," and in another sense, perhaps "no." "No" because they are blinded to their environment by their total hallucination. "Yes" because they 'see' the things that they hallucinate. In the case of film spectatorship, if the viewed segment is contextually marked to indicate that it depicts, for example, what a character is dreaming, then spectators do imagine seeing something, but it is 'seeing' in the more inclusive sense. What they imagine 'seeing' is what they recognize to be the visual contents of the character's dream.

However, none of this implies that the film viewers imagine themselves dreaming that very dream. More generally, it seems to me that visually subjective shots (whether the shots are subjectively inflected or saturated) never call on spectators to imagine that they are identical with the visualizing character nor that they are actually having the fictional visualizer's visual experiences. Film spectators merely imagine that the visual perspective presented onscreen coincides in its important, salient respects with the phenomenal qualities and contents of the character's visual experience, but not that those subjective visual experiences are their own. (This generalizes a point I mentioned earlier.) However, is the imagined seeing by one person of the private visual experiences of another really coherent? It depends, I believe, on how deep we expect the coherence of what viewers imagine in such a case to be.

The following is one way we might imagine seeing the visual contents of someone else's dream. We can imagine that neuroscientists have discovered in exhaustive detail the physical basis of dreaming. Implementing their discoveries in video technology, they come to have the capacity to introduce sensitive probes into a dreamer's brain and record the dream-relevant electrochemical activity that is taking place. Suitably transforming that recorded information, they are able to project a phenomenologically accurate visual representation of the dreamer's dream imagery on a large monitor above the dreamer's head. Thus, anyone suitably placed before the monitor is able to see the contents and phenomenal qualities of the projected dream.[10] If we can imagine this scenario, then we can imagine seeing (as observers) the contents of someone else's dream, and we can imagine this without imagining that we are having the dream experiences ourselves. In a similar way, when viewers watch a dream sequence in film, they imagine themselves seeing the contents of the fictional dream, but they do not imagine themselves to be experiencing that very dream.

I am claiming that we can imagine dreams to have a kind of public visual accessibility, but I do not claim that what we imagine is philosophically or scientifically coherent in any substantial detail. Almost surely it is not. (The superficial coherence may well depend on our tendency to imagine our dreams as if they were movies in our heads.) After all, a fair amount of what we imagine to ourselves is only superficially coherent in just this way. Also, I am not supposing that when we imagine seeing someone's dream in the movies that we imagine this by imagining that some agency of dream engineering has projected the dreamer's experience on the movie screen in front of us. On the contrary, we simply do not imagine much of anything in particular about how the dreamer's visual perspective has been presented to our view. It is imaginatively indeterminate how this has come to be, but this indeterminacy is nothing special. In the same way, we imagine almost nothing about the means or mechanisms by which the movie's impersonal views of objective circumstances in the story have come to be fictionally visible to us.[11]

One further observation is in order. In general, it will be significantly indeterminate as to how close the detailed match of movie images and fictional private experience is supposed to be. For instance, we presumably are supposed to imagine that we share our visual perspective on the dream with the dreamer's own perspective, but the film segment may offer a slight and rather unconvincing basis for imagining this. In particular, the screen imagery will establish fairly definite fictional vantage points from which the various visual perspectives arise, but these are implicit vantage points within the constructed and often shifting spaces of the dream. As film viewers, we do not imagine that the dreamers actually occupy those vantage points. The dreamers are fictionally located wherever it is that they are sleeping. Perhaps we imagine that they dream that they occupy (usually in a highly indeterminate fashion) those vantage points. This sometimes is so but, more often, what we imagine on this score is probably even more thoroughly indeterminate. For example, dreamers in movies frequently make an appearance within their own dreams. So, is it fictional for the viewer that the dreamers dream that they occupy two different places at the same time? Of course, we know that dreams can be like that—featuring the bizarre and even the absurd. And yet

[10] It is not simply that this scenario is something we can imagine. It is a scenario that is actually depicted in an episode of the television series *The Prisoner*. "A, B, & C," *The Prisoner*, directed by Pat Jackson and written by Anthony Skene, ITV1 (UK), Oct. 15, 1967. I owe this reference to Steve Reber and Geoff Georgi.

[11] The thought experiment and the argument based on it that I give here parallels a similar thought experiment and argument in Chapter 2.

the dreamers' visible presence in the shot does not normally strike us as paradoxical or even especially odd.

I suspect that, in general, the question of the dreamers' vantage points on the scenes of their dreams is supposed to be passed over in the spectator's imagination. Perspectival implausibility here is accepted as the consequence of a standard and convenient practice in showing dreams in movies. It is easy to disregard the question in movies because, in real dreams, the matter of vantage point is normally vague as well. Hence, there is no presumption in 'dream sequences' that the vantage points of the film shots and of the fictional dreaming are meant to correspond in any sharply determinate way. This has the consequence that the thought that we imagine seeing the contents of the dream (or hallucination or whatever) from the subject's point of view has to be understood as having a significant looseness of fit. It follows from this fact that such shots are not POV shots in a strict and unqualified sense. At the same time, there is an important sense in which subjectively saturated shots are not impersonal shots either. The visual perspective of these film shots does provide us with the visual perspective defined by the character's private sensory manifolds. For this reason, I do not take the concept of a POV shot to be strictly coextensive with the concept of a shot whose visual perspective is personal.

III. Impersonal subjectively inflected shots

Let us now consider an important way in which the epistemic structure of a segment may be even more complicated. All the types of subjective shot that I have described are to be contrasted with another kind of subjective shot. It is a type that is not as frequently deployed as, say, POV shots, but it is common enough in conventional narrative films. These are non-POV shots (more broadly, impersonal shots) that are subjectively inflected but do not share their vantage point with the visual perspective of any character in the film. Here is one simple and fairly well-known example: in *Murder, My Sweet* (Edward Dmytryk, 1944), Philip Marlowe (Dick Powell) has been knocked out and drugged. When he eventually comes to, we see him (that is, we imagine seeing him) stagger around the room. However, these shots of him are, in a certain respect, clearly subjective. In voice-over, Marlowe describes his clouded perceptual experience, and the shots with which we are presented look as though they had been filtered through smoke and spider-webs. The look of the shots in this respect is obviously meant to correspond to key aspects of the way that things are looking to Marlowe in his drugged condition, but the screen image here does not purport to give us his actual visual perspective. As in an objective shot, we imagine seeing Marlowe as he wanders around the room, but, at the same time, we do not imagine that the room is filled with smoke and spider-webs. The look of smoke and spider-webs is imagined to represent certain phenomenal properties present in Marlowe's field of vision. In this example, we are prompted to the conclusion that these features of the image are subjective because Marlowe, in voice-over, tells us that this is what his drugged visual experience is like. So, we imagine seeing Marlowe and his actions from a visual perspective he does not and could not occupy. Moreover, it is a visual perspective that is not experienced by anyone else in the film. Still, we are keyed to suppose that the pertinent phenomenal properties included in the on-screen visual perspective reflect specific qualitative inflections with which we imagine the detective's visual perspective to be suffused. This constitutes a third kind of subjective shot, and I will call it 'an impersonal, subjectively inflected shot.' In this example, we imagine ourselves seeing Marlowe and his actions from an unoccupied visual perspective that is subjectively inflected in specific ways. As noted above, this kind of shot or sequence is not at all infrequent. They are not as common as veridical POV shots, but they are quite common even in 'classical' Hollywood films.

The concept of 'impersonal but subjectively inflected shots' should be understood strictly to entail that the phenomenal qualities or contents of a character's perceptual experience are mirrored in the shot. They should be distinguished from still another type of psychologically charged impersonal shot. Mitry and Branigan both point out that there are impersonal shots that pick out objects and events that have been shown to be perceived by a character and present them in a way that illuminates the psychological significance they have for the character. For instance, the clenched fist of one character, Jones, may be shot in a close-up that expresses the looming threat that Smith feels when he notices the clenching of Jones's hand. The hypothetical shot is a close-up, but Jones is standing at a considerable distance from Smith. The shot is therefore not literally a shot from Jones's visual perspective, although, in its narrative context, it may tell us a fair amount about Jones's reactive thoughts and emotions. This would be a good example of what Mitry refers to as a "semi-subjective shot." Nevertheless, since the shot does not show us anything about the *phenomenal* character of Jones's visual field, it is not a subjectively inflected impersonal shot, as I have introduced that concept. I have the impression that Mitry's category may include impersonal, subjectively inflected shots, although he never describes an instance of this narrower kind. The danger is that he effectively conflates them with other types of impersonal shots whose chief function is to *imply* something about a character's *cognitive* or *affective* states.[12]

Still, one might worry that my characterization of subjectively inflected impersonal shots verges on inconsistency. The characterization seems to ask us to suppose that film viewers imagine that they are visually presented with a subjectively inflected field of vision, but a field of vision that impossibly belongs to no one. Of course, if we assumed that the various non-POV shots in a transparent film depict, in the first instance, the perceptual experience of an invisible camera witness, then there would be no problem here. We could readily allow that subjectively inflected images

---

[12] Mitry (1997), 214–219. On page 216, Mitry gives an example from *Jezebel* (William Wyler, 1938) that is similar to but somewhat more complicated than the one I offer.

present the phenomenal contents and qualities of the field of vision of this implicit witness. However, the general identification of the camera with such an invisible spectator is, for well-canvassed reasons, quite implausible. It is equally implausible to posit that such a witness pops into fictional existence only to accommodate the subjectivity of these impersonal shots. As I have argued before, there really is no incoherence in the concept. The visual perspective of a shot is not to be identified with the field of vision of a character, explicit or implicit in the fiction, unless the film narration specifically establishes such an identity. We imagine the shots in *Murder, My Sweet* as showing us Marlowe's action from the visual perspective a person would have if he or she were viewing the action from a certain vantage point and if he or she were afflicted with the type of clouded vision that Marlowe is experiencing. This visual perspective is not fictionally identical with anyone's actual field of vision. The distinction between veridical POV shots and impersonal subjectively inflected shots underscores the treacherous ambiguity of the phrase 'point of view,' even when that phrase is constrained to apply to matters of strict visual experience. Shots of the latter kind show us the character's perceptual point of view in one sense (they delineate the qualitative nature of his or her perception) but not in the other (they do not present the vantage point from which he or she looks).

Impersonal subjectively inflected shots and sequences range from the trivial to the rich and intricate. A segment in which a character is shown pondering some decision while the character's visualized thoughts appear as if they were projected behind him or her is subjectively inflected in a trivial way. However, subjectively inflected shots can exhibit a nuanced epistemic structure. They offer the possibility of directly showing the audience inter-subjectively accessible information about a character and his or her behavior while, at the same time, presenting important facets of the character's private perceptual impressions. We can see the character and, to a significant degree, see with him or her at the same time. Such shots have the further potential of insinuating some outside comment from the film-maker about the relations between the characters' depicted states of sentience and the actions they produce.

It would be interesting to try to work out a comparison between impersonal shots that incorporate subjective inflection with stretches of literary narration that employ 'free indirect discourse.' Unfortunately, both narrational modes can be constructed in various ways, and some of these constructions can be quite complex in design and effect. It is the mark of indirect free discourse (in a work of fiction) that, although the words or thoughts of the discourse are fictionally the words or thoughts of the narrator predominantly, the words or thoughts or sentiments of some character other than the narrator are directly interpolated into the discourse, and the interpolation is not overtly marked as such. Very often the effect is the following. We get a stretch of narration in which various events and situations of the story are recounted, but the recounting is marked by eruptions from the thought or consciousness of some character who is not, on the whole, the agent of the recounting. The parallel with impersonal but subjectively inflected shots is striking, although, as noted above, it is not easy in either case to define either of these strategies with precision. Both of the narrational phenomena violate or at least complicate an audience's normal mode of access to the fictional narrative presented in the work, but, at the same time, they are not recherché devices. They are relatively familiar devices, familiar both to novel readers and to moviegoers. Indirect free discourse has been the subject of extensive investigation; impersonal but subjective inflection in films has been less studied. More balance should be restored.

We can invoke some sense of the more interesting possibilities of impersonal but subjectively inflected sequences if we remind ourselves of the famous shot from Hitchcock's *Vertigo* (1958) in which Scottie (James Stewart) kisses and embraces Judy (Kim Novak) just after she has remade herself as Madeleine.[13] The couple are in Judy's hotel room and, as they kiss, the camera (or so it seems) begins to track around them.[14] In the course of the shot, the hotel setting gradually fades into blackness and is replaced by a slightly dimmed view of the stable in San Juan Bautista—the place where Scottie had kissed Madeleine just before her apparent death. Still embracing Judy, he looks around him, appearing troubled and disoriented. The background view of the stable fades back to black, and the hotel room gradually reappears, bathed now in a ghostly green. This shot contains additional complications that I will ignore, but the effects of the features I have already mentioned are tricky to characterize accurately. I take it that this is a subjectively inflected shot, but the inflection is more elaborate than in the shot from *Murder, My Sweet*. Presumably, the circling 'camera' vantage point is meant to depict the nature of the overwhelming emotion Scottie feels at that moment, and it is an emotion that is here being linked to the film's recurrent motif of vertigo. The background shot of the stable represents a hallucinated memory image—an image that has flooded into Scottie's consciousness, superimposing itself on his view of the hotel room. Presumably, the experience is so unexpected and so vivid that it causes the bewilderment that is registered in Scottie's face. So, what is it that film viewers imagine seeing in this extended shot? They imagine seeing Scottie's and Judy's intense embrace in the Empire Hotel, and they imagine seeing the embrace from an impersonal moving vantage point that circles around the couple. Spectators also imagine that the circling visual perspective expresses the vertiginous sensations that Scottie is experiencing at the time. When the view of the stable appears, they imagine seeing Scottie hallucinating as he holds Judy/Madeleine to him and the content of what he is then hallucinating. What is more, the dynamics of this non-POV shot suggest a narrational comment on the narrative situation. For example, they hint at the entrapment of both characters in their private obsessions and the uncanny nature of the circumstances that these obsessions have led them to create. I say that this subjectively inflected shot is impersonal, but this

---

[13] The aptness of this shot for my purposes was suggested by Deborah Thomas's sensitive discussion, Thomas (2001), 102–105. Our conclusions concerning the shot are somewhat different, however.

[14] Despite appearances, the shot was not made with a tracking camera. See Auiller (1998), 119. This is cited in Thomas (2001).

application of the term should not mislead. The vantage point is impersonal—it is not occupied by anyone in the fiction—but what the shot expresses about the characters is not emotionally impersonal. It is engaged and sympathetic, expressing the film-maker's attitudes toward the scene.

IV. Subjective inflection whose status is unmarked

In the example from *Vertigo*, the structure of objective and subjective elements of the shot is elaborate, but its structure and import are reasonably clear. Viewers may differ about interpretative details, but it is apparent that we are seeing Judy and Scottie embrace in the hotel room as Scottie flashes back in memory to the earlier incident in the stable. The epistemic structures of the segments in my earlier examples are simpler and, correspondingly, the structures are even more plainly delineated in their immediate narrative contexts. So, these are shots and sequences in which the norm of narrational transparency has been locally preserved.

However, there are numerous exceptions to the practice of immediate transparency. Even in classical narrative films, there are many cases in which the epistemic structure of a segment is not specified straight away when the segment occurs. In fact, there are many instances in which there is some deliberate delay in identifying a significant aspect of the segment's epistemic structure. Indeed, in a number of these examples, the specification of structure is long postponed, sometimes for almost the whole length of the film. In these instances, the nature of the epistemic structure of particular earlier segments is eventually settled at narrative closure. Epistemological twist films are defined by the fact that global aspects of the epistemic structure of their narration are clarified, in a surprising way, only toward the end of the movie.

Hitchcock's *Stage Fright* (1950) opens with a notorious 'lying' flashback. One character (Richard Todd) verbally tells another (Jane Wyman) about what happened when a murder took place and, as he narrates his story, there is a long visual sequence that seems to be a flashback to the events that he is recounting. It is only at the film's conclusion that we learn that this character has been lying and that the relevant sequence has to be reconstrued as merely a visual illustration of the content of the liar's false assertions. Of course, this segment narration is 'subjective' in still a different sense—it is the rendering of what a character has verbally reported. In this instance, the report is false and, for present purposes, what is important is that the movie suppresses the fact that it is false until the story's end approaches.

In Fritz Lang's *The Woman in the Window* (1944), we discover near the conclusion that the whole story of Professor Wanley's (Edward G. Robinson) involvement with a treacherous *femme fatale* (Joan Bennett)—an involvement that leads him to murder her lover—has been a nightmare that the professor has been dreaming. Almost nothing in the style of the film's visual narration prompts us to suppose that what we are seeing is a dream. That disclosure is simply announced by showing Wanley as he finally wakes up in a chair in his club (see figures 15 and 16). In both these cases and others like them, the movies wind up revealing an epistemological twist, but the twist, as it is handled here, can seem arbitrary and artificial. Viewers often feel cheated by the tricks. Be this as it may, suppose that long-delayed and suppressed issues of epistemic structure are eventually settled in a given film. Should we say that the movie satisfies the norm of narrational transparency? Must epistemic structure be clear more or less continuously throughout the film? I do not think it matters much what stipulation we adopt, but the twist movies certainly violate at least the classical implementations of transparency.

Returning to *The Woman in the Window* for a moment, there is a question about what viewers who already know about the dream twist imagine seeing in the scenes that relate the contents of the dream. As one first watches the relevant segments, one imagines seeing, for example, the professor murder his romantic rival. However, after it has been revealed that Wanley has been dreaming all along, do viewers still imagine themselves as having seen the murder? Or, alternatively, when viewers see the movie a second time and know that Wanley dreams his adventures, then, as they re-watch the murder scene, do they still imagine seeing the professor commit the crime? Or, at this juncture, do they merely imagine seeing the contents of his dream? My own strong inclination is to say the following. Both the first time and the second time that viewers watch the scene, they do imagine seeing Professor Wanley kill his rival. The murder is, as it were, visually present on the screen. However, on the first viewing, while implicitly accepting the assumption of transparency, viewers suppose that the murder actually takes place (in the overall world of the story). Seeing the same scene again, they have learned that this supposition about the status of what they have imagined seeing is false. Thus, on a second viewing, they continue to imagine seeing Wanley perform the murder, but this time they imagine, that is, they suppose, that the murder is merely

Figure 15 Professor Wanley is dying of poison

Figure 16 Professor Wanley awakens in his club

something that the professor fictionally has dreamed. Hence, we need to draw a distinction between what viewers imagine seeing in a stretch of film and the imaginative suppositions that they adopt about the epistemic and ontological standing of the things and events that they imagine seeing. The 'core' contents of what viewers imagine seeing remains roughly the same from viewing to viewing. It is what the film viewers imagine (suppose) about the epistemological status of what they imagine seeing that alters so sharply.

Compare this with a case in which there is a notable change of dramatic aspect for the viewer between two viewings of the same scene. Watching a close-up of Octave in *The Rules of the Game* (Jean Renoir, 1939), the viewer might, the first time through, imagine seeing Octave's (Jean Renoir) face as expressing one set of emotions, but imagine seeing, the next time around, a different mix of feeling and motivation in Octave's countenance. Here, I am inclined to say that there has been a change in the 'core' content of what the viewer has imagined seeing from one showing to another. The very look of Octave's face, as the viewer imagines it each time, has changed. In my opinion, this contrasts with the situation of the viewer before and after the disclosure of a systematic epistemological twist.

Jacob's Ladder, *Vanilla Sky*, and *Mulholland Drive* are twisted like *The Woman in the Window*.[15] The greater part of the narration turns out to be a rendering of a character's dreams, and this is a fact that is disclosed only late in the movie. In these cases, the

---

[15] For an interpretation of *Mulholland Drive* with which I am in broad agreement, see McGowan (2004). In particular, McGowan interprets the first two-thirds of the movie as the dream or fantasy of the character Diane (Naomi Watts) as she emerges in the last third of the movie. This line of interpretation has been suggested by many, but McGowan works it out in an especially careful way.

strategy is handled in a much more elaborate fashion than it is in Lang's film. On the other hand, *Fight Club* and *Secret Window* portray the hallucinated experiences of their main characters, although the drastic subjective inflection that predominates in the film narration is, for the most part, impersonally represented. Large sections of the cinematic narration are partially inflected by the hallucinations experienced by the chief character in each film and depicted from a vantage point the characters do not occupy.

Let me explain this claim by focusing specifically on *Fight Club*. First, here is the barest skeleton of its plot. An unnamed character played by Edward Norton—I will call him "Jack"[16]—meets an intense, charismatic young soap salesman, Tyler Durden (Brad Pitt). Jack and Tyler form a close friendship, live together in a house on Paper Street, and become founders of a series of underground fight clubs—clubs in which marginalized young men meet together and pound each other into pulp in arranged fights. Jack has a tentative, sour friendship with a woman Marla (Helena Bonham Carter), but it is Tyler and Marla who come to have an explosive sexual affair. The fight clubs evolve into Project Mayhem, a quasi-fascistic organization of urban guerrillas who aim to destroy the credit-based foundations of the contemporary economic system. Tyler is the moving force behind Project Mayhem, while Jack is apparently a more passive fellow traveler in that enterprise. What we discover, as the narrative concludes, is that Tyler is the hallucinated ideal projection of Jack's volatile and distorted psyche. Jack imagines seeing Tyler in his company and he imagines that they regularly talk and interact. Nevertheless, Tyler is a creation of Jack's imagination. We also find out, late in the movie, that Jack has sometimes adopted the Tyler persona and acted under that fantasized identity. For instance, he travels around the country promoting the fight clubs and expanding Project Mayhem. Apparently, Jack has no memory of what he does as Tyler and it is only in the scene of revelation that we are directly shown a moment in which Jack assumes the role of Tyler. However, we are repeatedly shown scenes in which Jack and Tyler appear together—conversing, fighting, engaging in horseplay, and so on. These are the scenes that most straightforwardly raise the question of the overall coherence of the film's narration. After all, Tyler really does not exist, so how do we construe his repeated appearances in the film's narration?

Take, for example, all the scenes in which we imagine seeing Jack and Tyler together in their house on Paper Street (see figure 17). It simply does not make sense to suppose that nothing of what we imagine seeing in this setting actually took place. Many of the events portrayed in these inflected scenes have causal consequences that turn out to be real in the ultimate fiction of the film. The chemical burn that Tyler inflicts on the back of Jack's hand is just one rather emblematic illustration of the point. What we have to imagine, when we consider the film in retrospect, is that Jack does utter most of the things we hear him say and performs most of the actions that we observe. We are also meant to imagine that, on these occasions, Jack is simultaneously

---

[16] It has become standard, in the literature on *Fight Club*, to refer to this character as "Jack," for reasons that are easily enough inferred from the movie.

Figure 17 Jack and Tyler Durden at home on Paper Street

hallucinating Tyler's presence, his deeds, and speeches, and that Jack is responding to these fantasized occurrences. Characteristically, the two characters are presented together in the frame and shot from an impersonal vantage point. However, in light of the culminating disclosure, we are forced to look back and reconstrue these sequences as perspectivally impersonal but subjectively inflected. They are inflected to represent in a single shot both Jack's actual behavior and the content of his concurrent delirious experience. That these segments are to be understood as inflected versions of an otherwise objective situation is implied by the following considerations. There are scenes in which Jack and Tyler are together in the kitchen, scenes that are either preceded or followed by Marla's entrance into that room. When she is there, Tyler is always absent. The scenes between Jack and Marla would seem to be patently objective, and the continuity of the space between these scenes and the adjacent sequences with Tyler indicates that Jack remains objectively present in the kitchen throughout. But when Tyler also seems to be present, Jack is actually by himself and talking to a hallucinated figure.

Near the end of the movie, as the truth begins to dawn on Jack, we are given several short shots that show Jack acting by himself in situations where earlier we had seen Jack and Tyler acting together. These later shots model for us what we are now to imagine about the real circumstances after we have discounted for the subjective inflection. When Tyler finally explains the psychological state of affairs to Jack, he says: "Sometimes you're still you—sometimes you imagine yourself watching me." At this juncture, there is a shot of Jack lecturing the members of the fight club, echoing an earlier shot in which Tyler delivered the lecture. The late shot establishes that it was Jack who had spoken these words, imagining himself as Tyler. However, in the earlier counterpart scene, we were also given brief glimpses of Jack standing in the crowd and gazing at Tyler. So, presumably, Jack both hallucinates being Tyler and being himself (*qua* Jack) watching Tyler perform. In any case, given the ultimate perspective of the film, we are asked to reimagine earlier critical scenes either in these kinds of terms or in minor variants thereof. The sequences with Jack and Tyler constitute the most extensive and daring uses of impersonal subjective inflection that I know. They are particularly audacious because the massive subjective inflection is left unspecified until so late in the movie.

The global narrational structure of the film is cleverly designed. Jack is the intermittent voice-over narrator of the film, and the film's narration is probably best understood as an audio/visual rendering of the narrative that he is verbally recounting. The film narration includes many segments (most of the ones in which Tyler does not appear) that are, even with hindsight, genuinely objective. However, as we will see in a moment, it also interpolates some shorter sequences that are marked in the immediate context as subjective depictions of Jack's fantasies. So the narration, in an apparently conventional manner, moves between depiction of the objective world of the fiction and the private perceptions and fantasies of the main character. The twist, of course, is the fact that the full extent of the inflection of the narration of Jack's consciousness has been systematically obscured.

The objective presentation of the story, then, is troubled from the outset by odd, seemingly unmotivated incursions from the contents of Jack's mind. At the beginning of the movie, we are given a POV shot from Jack's perspective as he looks out the window of an office building, but his view out the window morphs seamlessly into a dizzying traveling shot that careens down through the building and into the underground parking garage below. This highly dynamic subjective shot encapsulates in a flash Jack's memory of the bomb that Project Mayhem has planted in a van that is sitting in the garage. Also, on two occasions, we see Jack's surreal daydream of wandering through an icy cavern. The first time he is accompanied by a playful penguin, the second time he discovers Marla there. Or, taking a business flight, Jack wishes in voice-over for a plane crash and hallucinates the disaster in grim detail. This hallucination immediately precedes his meeting Tyler, who is sitting next to him in the airplane. All these segments are subjectively saturated, but there are also short instances of subjective inflection, plainly identifiable as such. Thus, Jack sits on the toilet reading a home decoration catalog, and the movie cuts to a tracking shot that explores his fantasy of his apartment fully furnished with Ikea-like products, each item still labeled by its blurb in the catalogue. Subsequently, we see Jack, having risen from the toilet, still in his underwear, amble through the blurbed apartment and go to the refrigerator. Or, prior to the point at which Tyler has made his entrance as a definite character in the film, various 'objective' shots of sundry circumstances incorporate brief, usually subliminal, images of him. It is as if the narration were already haunted by Tyler-laced eruptions from Jack's volatile sub-consciousness (see figure 18). I do not believe that we can understand the overall film narration as a representation from the inside, as it were, of Jack's actual hallucinated memories of his history with Tyler, but, as these last examples illustrate, the narration is repeatedly ruptured by outcroppings from Jack's

Figure 18 Tyler erupts into Jack's subliminal consciousness

imagination and memory. In this fashion, the movie's narration subtly hints at the larger strategy of non-transparency that it so cunningly constructs.

The Others is a kind of epistemological twist-of-the-screw movie, but the twist it takes raises an interesting question about the characterization of film narrational transparency with which we started. For most of its duration, the film seems to tell a rather traditional type of ghost story. A young woman, Grace (Nicole Kidman), and her two children (Alakina Mann and James Bentley) live in an isolated house on the Isle of Jersey, where they are joined by a trio of creepy servants. The house appears to be haunted and the family is regularly troubled by spectral sounds and other weird disturbances. The ghosts, it seems, are invisible, although Grace's young daughter has intimations, including sketchy visual intimations, of them and their doings. In the culminating twist, it turns out that it is actually Grace's family and the servants who are dead and that they are actually the ghosts. The source of the disturbances is a family of living human beings who are trying to move into the house, and the genuine ghosts, about whom members of the living family have their own intimations, are completely invisible to them. And yet, Grace and her children and servants have been visible to the audience throughout the movie, normally in impersonal 'objective' shots. This is the basis of the narration's problematic transparency. It is natural to explain an 'objective' shot or sequence as one that represents the inter-subjectively accessible visual appearances of the situation it depicts, and it is natural to take 'inter-subjectively accessible' to refer to the powers of normal human perceivers. Accepting the narrative's implicit assumption that ghosts and ghostly behavior are not accessible to human vision, and presupposing the transparency of this film's narration, audience members unreflectively take it for granted that Grace and her children couldn't be ghosts. But the audience has just been fooled. In retrospect, what film viewers have been watching in the film is a certain course of narrative action as only the sentient dead could perceive it. The viewer's imagined seeing has been systematically linked to what fictionally 'the others' might see. In most other twist movies, we are encouraged to construe certain shots and sequences as objective that in fact are inflected (partially or totally) by the subjectivity of one of the characters. In *The Others*, we construe the visual objectivity of the film narration with reference to human perception. We fail to notice that there is an alternative standard of perceptual objectivity that the film has tacitly invoked and then quite systematically exploited.

It would be interesting to inquire why cinematic assaults on the norm of narrational transparency have become so common around the turn of the century.[17] I do not know the answer, and I am not sure how such an inquiry, responsibly conducted, should proceed. No doubt a certain amount of copycatting has gone on, and perhaps some kind of postmodern skepticism about the duplicity of reality and the photographic image has drifted over Hollywood. In any event, my present aim has been to say something fairly systematic about what some of these subversions of cinematic transparency amount to. Much earlier in the chapter, I raised a related but more general question about the thesis of imagined seeing as it applies to film. I asked whether the thesis can be sustained, in some form, when various types of subjective segments are examined, particular segments that are non-transparently subjective. The answer, implicit in the foregoing discussion, is "yes," although it has emerged that an adequate formulation of the general thesis will necessarily be multifaceted.

There are two broad points that I would like to emphasize. I have reaffirmed the claim that when viewers watch a POV shot that is from the visual perspective of a character C, it does not follow either that the viewers thereby imagine that they are identical with C or that they imagine themselves located at the implicit vantage point from which C is looking. In this chapter, I have argued for a similar stricture concerning POV shots that are totally subjective. If, in such a case, viewers imagine themselves seeing the visual contents of C's private visual experience, then again it does not follow either that they thereby imagine that they are identical with C or that they imagine that they are experiencing C's own visual sensations. These negative strictures and the basis for them are important. If the strictures are not observed, then the Imagined Seeing Thesis will wrongly seem to be committed to disastrous absurdities. But really, the Imagined Seeing Thesis, properly stated, engenders no such commitments.

Second, if viewers imagine seeing an item X perform or undergo Φ (for example, they imagine seeing Professor Wanley drive off) from a certain visual perspective P, then the content of what they imagine seeing in this way is not on its own sufficient to determine how they are to understand the epistemic structure of the shot or sequence they are watching. That is, the fact that they imagine seeing X Φ in the segment does not determine for them whether X's Φing constitutes an objective situation in the

---

[17] Murray Smith reminds me that transparency was also assaulted with significant regularity in Hollywood films during the 1940s.

world of the fiction or whether it is merely a content of the visual experience of some character in the film. Or, somewhat more subtly, it does not determine whether certain aspects of the visual perspective P are to be imagined as inter-subjectively accessible properties of the observed circumstances or as phenomenal qualities of the manner in which some character is perceiving the depicted situation. The possibilities of epistemic structure, as I have explained, can get pretty complicated. How viewers understand or imagine the epistemic structure of a given segment turns both on what they imagine seeing in the segment and what they take the wider context to prescribe about the epistemic status of the contents of their imagined seeing. Moreover, sometimes viewers imagine, when they view a segment, that its epistemic structure is such-and-such, discovering only later that what they earlier imagined about that structure was mistaken and that the segment needs to be differently construed. So, at least two types of imagining are characteristically involved in our basic comprehension of a shot, a sequence, and, sometimes, a film's cinematic narration overall. Spectators imagine seeing various items and situations as the film is shown, and they imagine that these items and situations have one or another epistemic standing within the larger contexts of the narrative and its narration.

This point is implicit in some of Walton's remarks on the theme of subjective shots. He says: "We imagine seeing things from a certain point of view, noticing certain aspects of them, and so forth. And we *understand* [emphasis added] that what we imagine seeing is what fictionally the character sees; we *imagine* [emphasis added] that that is what the character sees. The film thus *shows* what the character's experience is like."[18] In this passage, Walton is concerned only with POV shots, but notice that, even to analyze the basics of that simple case, he invokes a contrast between "what we imagine seeing" and "what we understand about it," for example, that it constitutes the content of what a certain character is experiencing.

Notice also that the understanding to which he here refers is immediately equated, in the next sentence, with a kind of suppositional 'imagining'—the viewer understands or supposes or (in that sense) imagines that so-and-so. Walton is right to suggest that both the concept of 'imagining seeing' and the concept of 'suppositional imagining' need to be introduced if we are to be in a position to articulate properly our intuitions concerning the visual contents of a shot or sequence. The pertinent suppositional imaginings one brings to the viewing of a segment will affect what one imagines seeing in the segment, and further suppositional imaginings will influence the way one parses the epistemic and dramatic structure of what one imagines seeing. Acknowledging this point and its importance leaves one with a considerable and difficult project. How should we conceive of the interrelations between imagined seeing and suppositional imaginings in a manner that is adequate to describe the rich varieties of visual content in film shots and longer sequences? Walton's brief comments on one simple, albeit

---

[18] Walton (1997), 63.

paradigmatic, type of subjective shot do not begin to cover the wealth of varieties that are in question here. It has been my ambition in this chapter to sketch some of the intricacy of the broader topic of transparent and non-transparent subjective segments in movies and to elaborate some of the considerable conceptual complexity that the topic potentially subsumes.

8

Transfiguration and Self-Conscious Narration: On Von Sternberg's Last Films with Dietrich

I. Introduction

The question of originality considered as a criterion of value has vexed assessments of the artistic merits of classical Hollywood cinema almost from the outset of critical discussion of studio-produced movies. Since it was a characteristic mark of most of these films that they relied on standardized formulas of storytelling and on the familiar 'personae' of well-known stars and character actors, and that they generally were framed within fairly conventional forms of narrative exposition, it was only in rare cases that a startling novelty of style or substance was among the obvious chief virtues of the works. What is more, the question of merit becomes peculiarly pressing when the movies are instances of one or another of the more hackneyed genres; instances where the plot, dialogue, and characterizations seem humdrum and even tacky, at least when judged by prevailing standards of taste. Such movies strike many viewers, whether they find them enjoyable or not, as woodenly predictable or downright silly. In cases of this sort, it is likely to seem absurd to suppose that any major form of artistic creativity lends special value to the work.

This sort of critical issue has arisen again and again concerning the films of many genre film-makers such as Josef von Sternberg, Douglas Sirk, Nicholas Ray, and later Fritz Lang. The movies in question here include over-the-top melodramas (*Blonde Venus*, *Written on the Wind*), fantastic swamp flicks (*Wind Across the Everglades*), and perversely opaque Westerns (*Johnny Guitar*, *Rancho Notorious*). These are all works in which the literary merits of their scripts or the power of their acting, conventionally assessed, are limited and would not redeem them. Often it is possible to argue that these films contain worthwhile moments or elements, but, even when this is possible, it remains incredible that such rigidly contrived works might have been structured throughout by global aesthetic strategies that reconfigure their significance in a drastic way.

The idea that superficially unpromising genre movies may contain a subtle manifestation of the film-maker's personal perspective is usually associated with auteurist defenses of Hollywood directors. These defenses have sought to demonstrate that directors sometimes *did* have enough degrees of freedom in the making of their movies to institute a level of sophisticated artistic creativity, even in projects whose narrative parameters were to a great extent pre-established. However, the issue of the range and character of creative expression in these movies should not be tied too closely to the stronger, characteristic theses of auteurism. There is no reason why whatever creativity has been exercised in such a film should not have been the product of collaboration among several of the participants in the construction of the work. Sometimes the director *will* have been the central figure responsible for the imaginative inventiveness; sometimes cooperative efforts will have been primarily responsible. Occasionally, I imagine, an intriguing and original framework may fall into place largely through fortunate happenstance. In any case, in this chapter I am concerned with the possibility of rich, extensive artistic significance in outwardly problematic Hollywood movies, and not with the question of who gets credit for whatever hidden meaning might be present.[1]

Dubious as this claim of recessive large-scale signification might appear, I think that it can be sustained in a range of instances, including a number of the examples cited above. A particular instance of the claim is sustained when it can be shown, in detail, how suitable signifying strategies are present in the given film and how the strategies guide (potentially) a viewer's comprehension of it. And yet, in mounting such a defense—that is, in constructing a suitable close interpretation of the film—one is forced to think through matters that often are ignored, or at least are not adequately considered. Thus, one may discover that certain seemingly questionable facets of the narrative exposition or of the *mise-en-scène* have been methodically fashioned for interesting and intelligible ends. Or one may learn that various customary forms and practices of genre film-making have been heightened, extended, and exaggerated to serve some novel function—to provide implicit 'authorial' expression or commentary, for example. In other words, the central, distinctive creativity in such movies may depend precisely upon the systematic exploitation of their familiar narrative and narrational constraints—the very constraints that do the most to lend a formulaic character to their style and content. These matters will figure importantly in what follows. In these instances, it will often be an original framework that guides and informs the audiovisual narration that shapes the enterprise.

Although, as I have noted, these questions have arisen repeatedly in discussions of Hollywood genre films, it is not easy to generalize about how the pertinent issues play out from one case to another. Therefore, in this chapter, I want to achieve a certain sharpness of focus by investigating at some length one notorious case in which the

---

[1] However, in the case I will be considering in this chapter—that of von Sternberg's final three movies with Dietrich—I believe it was the director who was the central creative force. The evidence for this claim lies in the nature of the complicated design of these films, which I will be discussing in the bulk of this chapter, and in everything we know about von Sternberg's quite stringent control of his soundstage.

issues surface pretty insistently—the last films that Josef von Sternberg made with Marlene Dietrich. Although this is a unique and singular instance, the movies in question paradigmatically raise the problems about heavily stereotypical Hollywood movies I have been trying to sketch, and the upshot of my examination of them will illustrate several of the general points I have just described.

In fact, the case of the Dietrich/von Sternberg movies is especially instructive. On the one hand, these are films that have seemed to epitomize much of what has been most deplorable in the products of the Hollywood 'culture industry.' For many critics, they exemplify a sleekly customized brand of kitsch, a brand that traffics, not so much in the sentimental or the moralistic, but in a highly aestheticized, mildly perverse depiction of the erotic. A widely influential legacy in the criticism of mass art has set this sort of voyeuristic kitsch (and other sorts as well) in stark opposition to the challenging creations of 'high art.' In particular, repetitive, undemanding genre pieces like these films are contrasted adversely with the abstract, experimental works of the modernist avant-garde.[2] But I will argue that these films, properly understood, actually show that the stark opposition is misconceived; or, at any rate, it is a mistake to assume that a pair of mutually exclusive categories has been clearly identified. Whether we allow that the culminating films von Sternberg made with Dietrich are 'modernist' or 'experimental' is unimportant, as long as we grasp that they bear remarkable affinities, in their objectives and achievements, with works that are squarely within modernist or avant-garde traditions. As I will try to show, the films in question here invent an acutely *self-conscious* mode of cinematic narration and, correlatively, deploy tactics of *self-reflexive* inquiry into the nature of their own fabrication. They investigate aspects of the medium of fiction film-making and the conventions and practices in terms of which their own identity, as instances of a certain genre, has been established. On my view, it is these properties of the Dietrich/von Sternberg movies that establish their notable kinship to modernism in its more familiar guises. Actually, I will argue later in this chapter that we need to draw a rough division between at least two categories of self-conscious narration. There are movies that fail to be consistently 'transparent' in the sense defined in the previous chapter. However, there are also movies in which the ontological integrity of their cinematic world is recurrently ruptured. I will explain shortly how this second notion is to be construed and why the von Sternberg/Dietrich films provide apt examples of this more unusual narrational category.

Earlier writers have attempted to explicate the peculiar originality of von Sternberg's later films with Dietrich, and some of these have glimpsed the radical character of the enterprise. Probably, most accounts have appealed primarily to the conspicuous visual beauty of the motion-picture photography in the films. That beauty is unquestionable, but, if there is nothing more to add, their loveliness is not enough to lift the movies out

---

[2] I am thinking, of course, of the critique whose most famous instance is Adorno and Horkheimer (1990) and has been repeated, with variations, by hundreds of others. See also Adorno (1991) and Greenberg (1986). For a helpful overview and critical discussion of these and related critics of mass culture, see Carroll (1998).

of the realm of amusing, decorative camp. Some other more daring attempts have floundered, I believe, because they purport to locate the source of the movies' originality in an unprecedented semiotics (almost a metaphysics) of photography that their filming distinctively exemplifies. It is symptomatic of the confusion here that these bolder analyses tend to contain puzzling explosions of overheated philosophical prose. For instance, in *Signs and Meaning in the Cinema*, Peter Wollen says: "Von Sternberg was virulently opposed to any kind of Realism. He sought, as far as possible, to disown and destroy the existential bond between the natural world and the film image. But this did not mean that he turned to the symbolic . . . It was the iconic aspect of the sign which von Sternberg stressed, detached from the indexical in order to conjure up a world, a heterocosm."[3]

Wollen's remark is outstripped in semiotic ambition and sheer conceptual exuberance by the following assertions from Gaylyn Studlar's book on the director: "While symbolism might be a part of that [von Sternberg's] aesthetic, it is a metaphorical symbolism grounded on iconic signs, not formed out of arbitrary units . . . Von Sternberg's film world creates a syntax that is analogical-topological and grounded in iconic representation."[4] In both of these quotations, the authors seem to suppose that the significant but peculiar aesthetic qualities of von Sternberg's films (with Dietrich) derive centrally from a distinctive representational relation between the film image he creates and the objects and events that they depict—between his segmented image-tracks and their photographic subject matters.

But these proposals are hard to grasp. The photography in these movies is certainly scintillating, and the editing is often elaborate and colorful. Nevertheless, neither the photography nor the editing establishes some unprecedented 'iconic' link to the movies' photographed material. Wollen tells us that these films are fashioned from photographic images that are 'iconic' but not 'indexical.' For him, this seems to mean that von Sternberg created images in which the natural 'realism' of photography—its causal dependence on the visible world?—has been sundered. Studlar agrees that the films are 'grounded in' iconic images, and, for her, the ground-level image-track exhibits an exotic syntax and supports the expression of 'metaphorical symbolism.' In fact, I do not really understand what either of those achievements would amount to. And besides, as I have suggested above, it seems wrong to try to define the central attributes of von Sternberg's overall cinematic style by focusing so narrowly on the formal and representational properties of the visual narration.

No doubt the style of the photography and editing plays a significant role in establishing the idiosyncratic character of the late von Sternberg/Dietrich films, but the systematic stylization of *the acting*, *the setting*, and *the staging* of the narrative action is

---

[3] Wollen (1969), 136–137.

[4] Studlar (1988), 90. Although the quoted formation and some others like it in the book seem confused to me, I think there is significant overlap between my conception of what von Sternberg has wrought in his Dietrich films and the conception that Studlar develops.

at least equally important. And, of course, many critics have discussed the intricacies and oddities of these facets of von Sternberg's work as well. However, it is not obvious how adding a consideration of von Sternberg's arch handling of *mise-en-scène*, for instance, will reveal the level of fundamental artistic accomplishment that Wollen and Studlar envisage. Naturally, one might simply judge that their views about the originality and value of von Sternberg's films should be dismissed as baseless, but in my opinion that would also be a serious mistake. While I think that the formulations quoted above are badly confused, I share the overarching critical conviction of both writers that the von Sternberg/Dietrich films (their last three films especially) *are* distinctive and ambitious in their fiction-making. More specifically, I agree with their implicit suggestion that these movies somehow initiate an interesting self-referential project in the cinematic narration itself which von Sternberg and Dietrich use to explore aspects of the problematic ontological status of the fictions that they make.

Nevertheless, as indicated above, Wollen and Studlar are badly off the mark when they try to identify the foundations of von Sternberg's 'self-conscious' cinematic narration. They fail to delineate the specific filmic materials and the expositional strategies that constitute that framework. Still, the issues here are tricky. If the challenge to do better is to be met in the present case, then there is a pair of tasks that need to be carried out in tandem. First, a certain amount of philosophical ground-clearing is required to elucidate a conceptual apparatus in terms of which the special character of the self-conscious narration in these movies can be framed more adequately. The quotes from Wollen and Studlar do more to muddy the waters than to clarify. Second, these improved claims, both interpretative and theoretical, need to be given detailed, articulated support by paying close attention to the films themselves.

Here, I will begin by focusing on one striking narrational strategy that runs through all of the final three von Sternberg/Dietrich films. Having delineated this characteristic strategy in a fairly abstract way, I will offer some proposals about how the strategy can be construed as functioning within the broader narrative context of these movies. In dealing with *Blonde Venus* (1932) and *The Devil Is a Woman* (1935), I will be relatively brief. My discussion of these two films seeks mostly to specify the narrational strategy in question and to sketch the general type of function it appears, in both instances to serve. In the last section of the chapter, I will describe in more detail an occurrence of the same strategy in *The Scarlet Empress* (1934), and will offer a more extended analysis of how the segment is structured and how it works within the total film. This strategy represents an especially clear example of the way in which von Sternberg plays with conventional narrative forms to establish a certain degree of self-consciousness in his cinematic expositions, and it is illuminating to notice from the outset that it constitutes a strategy to which he recurs.

The course of this discussion will lead us to explore, at least briefly, some fairly general issues about 'standard' modes of cinematic narration in classical film and to make some comparisons with the less standard counterpart modes in these von Sternberg movies.

However, this inquiry will not ask us to speculate upon the relations of von Sternberg's image-tracks to the 'iconic,' the 'indexical,' or the 'symbolic,' and it will not encourage us to discern some special form of cinematic syntax in his work. Still, I think it will allow us to distinguish at least two important types of self-consciousness in film narration and to single out one of these as operative in von Sternberg's later movies. Finally, this approach will help provide a novel account of the remarkable 'irrealism' that permeates the fictional worlds of these films.

II. A recurrent narrative strategy

Let us start with a famous sequence from *Blonde Venus* in which the Marlene Dietrich character really hits rock bottom. Helen Jones, the character in question, has lost her husband, her lover, and her son. The loss of the husband is perhaps not such a big deal. He is, after all, played by a stifling Herbert Marshall, and, worse yet, he is the one who has vindictively taken her son away from her. But Cary Grant is the lover, and losing him is surely a calamity. Helen has sunk into poverty and prostitution, and she despises the little money she possesses because her husband has given it to her as a kind of payoff for the child. In the sequence I shall discuss, Helen is living in a miserable flophouse in New Orleans, and things couldn't get much worse. In fact, she announces to another denizen of the dead-end hotel that she is going to kill herself the following day. She staggers across the uncanny, smoke-filled lobby and pauses to pluck a card from a quartet of card players as she announces, "That's me! I'm the Queen of Hearts." Following those gnomic words, she arrives at the foot of a set of stairs. Here she turns and shouts back defiantly, "I'm leaving this dump. I'm going to find myself a better bed. Just watch!" The shot fades as she starts up the steps, and as Dietrich calls out, "Just watch!" we in the audience do watch while the camera tracks across the Atlantic Ocean, surveys in montage the Parisian skyline, and rediscovers Helen as the leading chanteuse in the whole of France. Now *that* is a steep rise in fortune! We should all have a career path like hers.

I have opened with this selection because it illustrates, in a fairly simple form, a local narrative manipulation that appears in all of von Sternberg's last three films with Dietrich—the type of strategy I want to emphasize in the present discussion. Such a segment is marked by the following attributes:

1. The narrative segment is strikingly *elliptical*, and the narrative, odd as it may have been up to the point of the ellipsis, becomes, at that juncture, especially opaque and even enigmatic.
2. The elliptical segment depicts a general *transfiguration* of the character Dietrich portrays, a transfiguration that remains, to a significant degree, unexplicated.
3. The arbitrary, puzzling character of the narrative development is foregrounded stylistically and, in fact, is rather flaunted. Usually, this is underscored by visual punning and by related cinematic figuration.

All three of these conditions are satisfied in the selection from *Blonde Venus*, and I will say that it constitutes a *segment of minimally motivated narrative transformation*. As noted, I will examine two other instances of minimally motivated narrative transformation in von Sternberg's later work, one from *The Devil Is a Woman* and the other from *The Scarlet Empress*. I will try to explicate the ways in which these highly charged transitional sequences serve related narrational objectives in the last two films as well.

The segment from *Blonde Venus* deserves an extended analysis I cannot offer here, but some of the broader functions that it performs are reasonably plain.[5] It establishes an especially wayward shift in a story trajectory that has already shown itself to be amply erratic. Second, in this manner, it advertises the artificial nature of its driving mechanisms of plot and character. While many of the earlier dramatic developments have been almost languorously retarded, Helen's radical reversal of fortune in this moment is compressed, foreshortened, and absurdly expedited. Moreover, it is as if this glitzy visual condensation occurs in response to Helen's own invitation to "Just watch!" as she starts to climb the stairway before her—the stairway to success, it seems. In any case, I will argue at some length that the minimally motivated segments from *The Devil Is a Woman* and *The Scarlet Empress* play a similar role: they flag crucial junctures in a nonstandard narrative and offer some comment about how the nonstandard functions of the exposition ought to be construed. These segments, with their puzzling condensation of the action, do not *demand* that the audience actively reconsider what they have just seen. It is easy enough to make some kind of *minimal* sense of the narrative developments and to proceed passively and without further hesitation from there. Nevertheless, they do *invite* reconsideration, and careful reconsideration can yield the indicated rewards.

It is my conviction that film scholars and critics have misunderstood von Sternberg's approach to *narrative* construction and, concomitantly, have misassessed the character of the filmic narration in his movies. These writers have a lively awareness of von Sternberg's well-attested indifference to the properties of standard narrative exposition. The plots of all of the von Sternberg/Dietrich films are pretty weird, and the acting in them is so strenuously stylized that the characterizations range from the merely oddball to the intensely zany. David Selznick once said contemptuously that von Sternberg's movies were about "... completely fake people in wholly fake situations."[6] Selznick was right about this, of course, but wrong to suppose that he had formulated the grounds for a negative assessment of the work. It is one thing to affirm correctly that von Sternberg repudiated various conventions and constraints of classical Hollywood storytelling. It is quite another matter to maintain that the detours and disruptions in his exposition of plot do nothing toward defining the 'meaning' that those narratives may bear. Certainly, it *is* tempting to dismiss all questions about the significance of these

---

[5] For an interesting discussion of the film and the history of its making, see Baxter (1994).

[6] I have been unable to locate a source for this quotation, but even if Selznick did not utter quite these words, they express bluntly the plain man's characteristic response to the Dietrich/von Sternberg movies.

bizarre, minimally motivated narrative episodes. After all, their most obvious immediate effect is to obscure the development of the characters and to muddle, at least briefly, the stories they enact. However, this is to assume that we know the kind of story it is the objective of the movies to be telling and to ignore the possibility that these minimally motivated segments may help to establish the evolving intelligibility of the films as a whole. So, first of all, this possibility *is* exactly what these segments *do* pull off, and I will explain this contention at some length, especially in connection with *The Scarlet Empress*.

Another important theorist and critic who, in my opinion, drastically underplays the importance of narrative structure is Laura Mulvey in her highly influential essay, "Visual Pleasure and Narrative Cinema."[7] She says, for instance,

Sternberg once said he would welcome his films being projected upside-down so that story and character involvment would not interfere with the spectator's undiluted appreciation of the screen image. This statement is revealing but ingenuous: ingenuous in that his films do demand that the figure of the woman . . . should be identifiable; but revealing in that it emphasizes the fact that for him the pictorial space enclosed by the frame is paramount, rather than narrative or identification processes.[8]

I also believe that the director's remark is ingenuous, but it is ingenuous precisely because 'narrative processes,' broadly construed, are much more important in these movies than Mulvey supposes. In the quoted passage, she seems to conceive of von Sternberg's movies as painterly in nature, reveling chiefly in the exquisite perversity of their formal visual design, a design constructed around the 'fetishized' figure of Marlene Dietrich. In the dynamics of the narration, the stories, such as they are, are punctuated by crucial episodes in which "The beauty of the woman as object and the screen space coalesce; she is no longer the bearer of [male] guilt but a perfect product, whose body stylized and fragmented by close-ups, is the content of the film and the direct recipient of the spectator's look."[9] Now, as we will see, there are important episodes that satisfy Mulvey's description here, and these are episodes in which narrative development can seem to be more or less on hold—the action virtually frozen. Nevertheless, I will argue (chiefly in connection with the example of *The Scarlet Empress*) that it is essential that even these episodes need to be scrutinized within their larger narrative context: these segments play a significant, if unusual, role in defining the emerging strategies of the peculiar tale that the movie tells.

I will also argue, in a related vein, that in all three of these movies, the stylization of the acting foregrounds the 'actorish' quality of the performances and inflects them with a certain wry, self-conscious absurdity. This strategy is given particular emphasis by Dietrich's especially showy posturing in our elliptical fragment from *Blonde Venus* and by the abrupt and arbitrary transfiguration of self that it presents. Similarly, in all of these films, the excessive and oppressive staging highlights the artifice of the narrative

[7] (Mulvey (1989), 14–26. [8] Ibid., 22. [9] Ibid.

development and underscores the fact that the dramatic action has been shaped and distorted by causes outside the fictional world altogether. Again, the caricatured intensity of the melodrama in the *Blonde Venus* segment and the startlingly sudden transition from rags to riches—from Skid Row den to Parisian nightclub—accentuate the capricious nature of the story construction.

More specifically, by foregrounding the acting, the settings, and the staging for the audience, von Sternberg's films give unusual prominence to an essential ambiguity in the photographic representation of mimetic fictions; that is, the motion picture shot is simultaneously a shot of an actual actor in an actual location performing some actual behavior, *and* it is a shot of a fictional character in a fictional site performing the fictional action which the behavior represents. This ambiguity of photographic content is exemplified in any fiction film, and classical movies have often traded upon the ambiguity in familiar, sometimes complicated, ways. For instance, although the movie audience is normally meant to see the on-screen human figures primarily as the characters portrayed, viewers are also implicitly aware of the presence of the stars themselves and the attributes of character and personality that they have come to convey. This secondary awareness of the stars and their 'personae' will usually be elicited with varying degrees of distinctness and intensity during the course of the drama. Von Sternberg is atypical only in the salience that this representational ambiguity takes on within his work and in the sorts of significance he builds upon it. I will argue later that the strategies of the odd narrative apparatus in his last two movies with Dietrich assign an almost thematic status to the ambiguity, and the minimally motivated transformations in the films instruct us in the issues and the feelings that these narrative strategies express. This will take us some distance toward specifying the conspicuously innovative nature of the narration in these films.

The Devil Is a Woman is probably the movie in which von Sternberg's reflexive, self-conscious strategies are most directly exhibited. Because I have discussed this film at considerable length in *Narration in Light*, I don't want to spend too much space going over old ground.[10] However, the central, minimally motivated transformation is so enlightening for the purposes of this chapter, I must examine it briefly.

In this film, Dietrich plays Concha, a Carmen-like *femme fatale* who entrances every man whom she encounters. The segment under consideration takes place in the upper room of a casino where she is with Antonio (played by Cesar Romero), a handsome young revolutionary with whom she is having her first assignation. The dramatic action occurs during a period of Carnival, so everyone is masked and in disguise. Antonio is keenly attracted to the glamorous Concha, but he is deeply leery of her as well. Another character, Don Pasqual, has earlier told him the tortuous story of his own long, frustrating infatuation with her. Don Pasqual will make his own appearance in the scene. The character is played by Lionel Atwill, and it is widely recognized that

---

[10] Wilson (1986), 145–165.

Atwill was made up to bear a striking resemblance to von Sternberg himself. In some sense—intriguing to work out—Don Pasqual is von Sternberg's surrogate within the fictional world of the film. Early in the transfiguring sequence, Concha offers to tell Antonio's fortune from the cards, and she identifies several of the movie's characters with figures on the face cards in her deck. In particular, she identifies herself with the Queen of Hearts. (Helen Jones, it will be remembered, makes the same identification in the segment from *Blonde Venus* previously discussed.)

The two are interrupted by a masked messenger who bears a letter from Don Pasqual declaring his abiding devotion. Antonio is angered by the hypocritical duplicity revealed in Don Pasqual's letter, and he kisses Concha passionately. As they embrace, however, the doors to the private room fly open and Don Pasqual is revealed (see figure 19). Angrily he challenges Antonio to a duel with pistols and, meaning to demonstrate his marksmanship, he picks up the Queen of Hearts, plants the card in a window, and shoots it—his bullet piercing one of the pictured hearts that signify its suit.

Just after the shooting, two striking consequences ensue. First, the governor and his police materialize to shut down Carnival altogether. The celebrants are forced to strip off their masks, and the great masquerade is at an end. Second, it soon emerges that Concha herself has been mysteriously transformed. Up to this point in the story, she has apparently been impervious to any affection and has been content to control and manipulate the passions she inspires. But, after Don Pasqual's shot, she seems to have fallen genuinely in love with Antonio, and it is *she* who begs *him* for his attention and

Figure 19 Lionel Atwill (surrogate for von Sternberg) bursts into the room

favor. In the first part of the movie, Don Pasqual has established the pattern of offering to free Concha from some form of social constraint, embarrassment, or oppression, but always with the transparent motive of thereby binding her to him—in marriage, for example. But now, after Carnival has been ended by a gunshot, Concha seeks out Antonio to plead that he take her with him out of Spain. As she makes the plea, she wears the bullet-pierced Queen of Hearts over her own heart.

Later after Antonio is put in prison for dueling with Don Pasqual, Concha is the one who goes on to bargain with the governor to have him set free. Oddly reprising Don Pasqual's earlier pattern, she has already struck a bargain with Antonio: she will intercede with the governor for his freedom only if she is allowed to accompany him to Paris. One has the sense that the transfiguration of her heart has somehow been caused by Don Pasqual's act of shooting the Queen of Hearts. The narrative reversal seems to be somehow the arcane consequence of the pistol shot in the casino.

But then, how, if at all, is this causation supposed to be comprehended? The fictional world of *The Devil Is a Woman* is strange, but nothing in it prepares us for a turn of events as metaphysically radical as this. I take it that Don Pasqual *is* von Sternberg, or, at least, he is his fictional delegate within the film. The story line, during the Casino scene, has reached a crux which is intolerable to Don Pasqual: Concha is about to leave him once more, and this time she will desert him for Antonio despite Don Pasqual's earlier rhetorical attempts, as the storyteller within the film, to block precisely that result. It is in Concha's infallible power to land a callow fish like Antonio, and she is on the verge of succeeding. Hence, I have purposed that Don Pasqual *qua* von Sternberg intervenes. He is implicitly the master of the fictional world, and it is therefore in his power to shape the remainder of the drama as he sees fit. And, this is what he does by literally shooting an image—in this instance an image of the Queen of Hearts—namely an image of Concha, by her own accounting. Concha's position in the game of love and seduction is thereby turned upside down. Because of the shot, she is now as helplessly in the thrall of Antonio as Don Pasqual has heretofore been in hers. And that is the revenge that Don Pasqual effects: now she is brought to suffer as dreadfully as she has made him suffer all along. The movie spins out of the peculiar, somewhat baffling, consequences of this reversal of her role.

In the famous Daffy Duck vehicle *Duck Amuck* (Chuck Jones, 1953), the animator's brush and pencil appear, so to speak, as active 'characters' within the cartoon fiction. To Daffy's utter confusion and consternation, the represented brush and pencil change him from one costume to another, switch his background settings, and, at one point, erase him entirely from the scene. Here the animated brush and pencil are the fictional agents that have been assigned the powers of Chuck Jones and his collaborators. In a similar fashion, I maintain, Don Pasqual is to be construed as the story-world surrogate for von Sternberg—the fictional agent in the film who assumes some of the director's actual powers to invent his own fate and the fates of his co-characters and to regulate the remaining course of the narrative. Neither *Duck Amuck* nor *The Devil Is a Woman* is a full-scale modernist counterpart of works by, say, Brecht, Beckett, or Pirandello,

I suppose; but in both the cartoon and the culminating von Sternberg/Dietrich collaboration we do have a self-conscious form of narration that intrudes upon the casual coherence of the narrative events and humorously destabilizes the ontological status of the characters. However, there are hosts of ways in which cinematic narration can be self-conscious, and one would like to specify the Sternbergian mode of narrational self-consciousness somewhat more narrowly.

I imagine that everyone who has seen these sequences from von Sternberg has the sense that their normal, natural relationship to the fictional world of the film has been disrupted in some way. Some fundamental norm of standard movie viewing has been abrogated, but it is not at all easy to say what the norm is. Consider, in this connection, the following passage from David Bordwell's *Narration in the Fiction Film*. Bordwell comes close to articulating the basic cinematic conventions that are put at risk in our examples, but he obscures a distinction that is important in the present context.

By virtue of its handling of space and time, classical narration makes the *fabula* world an internally consistent construct into which narration seems to step from the outside. Manipulation of *mise-en-scène* (figure, behavior, lighting, setting, costume) creates an independently existing pro-filmic event, which becomes the tangible story world framed and recorded *from without* [my italics]. The framing and recording tends to be taken as the narration itself, which can in turn be more or less 'intrusive' upon the posited homogeneity of the story. . . . the *fabula* seems not to be constructed: it appears to have pre-existed its narrational representation.[11]

Now it seems to me that these remarks, helpful as they are, run at least two distinguishable considerations together and thus efface the difference between two 'norms' of classical narration in Hollywood film. One of these *is* flouted in our von Sternberg movies, but the other one is not. It tells us something significant about the global narrational strategies in the von Sternberg movies to be clear about which is which.

On the one hand, Bordwell asserts that the characters, events, and situations of the diegetic world are presented in a classical narration as having an existence and internal integrity that does not depend *at all* upon the film-making process. We will return to this point shortly. One the other hand, he also states that it is a part of the total fiction that these independently existing (albeit fictional) items and occurrences have been "framed and recorded" by some means whose character is itself left fictionally unspecified. As Bordwell puts it, these items and events are recorded "from outside," and this means for him, 'from outside the world of the *fabula*.' That, however, is a second and more restricted point. Although viewers properly imagine themselves seeing sights and hearing sounds belonging to the fictional world, the way in which these sights and sounds have come to be registered on-screen is assigned no determinate status within the work at all. In fact, it is fictional in the film story that no such recording actually took place. Nevertheless, for the movie audience, the edited results of the actual framing and recording is experienced as an audio-visual narration of the events

---

[11] Bordwell (1985), 161.

portrayed, and the fictional constituents of the narrative are apprehended as the 'pro-filmic subjects' of this cinematic 'reportage.' To paraphrase the end of Bordwell's remarks: the fabula seems not to be constructed by the framing and recording: it appears to have pre-existed its *photographic* depiction. Call this 'the norm of the *photographic transparency* of the fictional world.'[12]

It does not follow from adherence to this second, significantly qualified norm that the transparently depicted world of the film will not have been presented as a manifestly fictional construction, internally acknowledged as such. The film's diegetic substance may not appear to be "independently existing" in Bordwell's full-blooded sense. Spectators can be asked to imagine that they are offered, by means of the image-track, fully *objective* views of a world that is perceived (and is meant to be perceived) as an artifact of the film-makers' construction through and through. Thus, what Bordwell calls "manipulation of *mise-en-scène*" may regularly leave foregrounded traces of the sensibility, intelligence, and personality that designed the style of the acting, the staging, and the lighting and *fabula* that they depict. In classical narrative film, it is ordinarily not self-consciously acknowledged, *within the fiction*, that the characters are fictions portrayed by actors, and it is not affirmed, directly or indirectly, that the dramatic situations are also fictions staged to advance the larger teleology of the tale. When this type of reflexive acknowledgment is absent, I will say that the narration satisfies "the norm of the *ontological self-subsistence* of the fictional world."

Of course, there are delicate questions in this connection about what counts as a film's genuine self-acknowledgment that its diegetic constituents are fictive. After all, a lot of musicals, wacky comedies, and films of fantasy exhibit, in different degrees, broad manipulation of *mise-en-scène* that arguably conveys at least some sly reflexive implications. *The Road to Rio* (Norman Z. McLeod, 1947), *The Pirate* (Vincente Minnelli, 1948), *Million Dollar Legs* (Edward Cline, 1932), *The Crimson Pirate* (Robert Siodmak, 1952), and *The 5000 Fingers of Dr. T* (Roy Rowland, 1953) are a few examples out of a large list of possibilities. It is probably unhelpful, in the present context, to try to establish a boundary in this region that firmly divides the late Dietrich/von Sternberg films, as I interpret them, from various brands of conceptually less ambitious fare. We *do* need to draw the general distinction between photographic transparency and ontological self-subsistence, since it is the latter form of self-consciousness, and not the former, that operates in our von Sternberg films. Perhaps we can afford to leave further refinements and finer discriminations of value for another occasion.[13]

Most classical narrative films predominantly conform to both of these norms, but the norms are different and come apart in special cases. For instance, films like *This Is Spinal*

---

[12] I offer a much longer discussion of photographic transparency (although not using this phrase) in Chapter 2.

[13] It would be a difficult and delicate task to provide a reasonable clarification of the character and the extent of the 'self-acknowledgment' involved in films that are *not* ontologically self-subsistent in the intended sense. For a bit more on this, see my remarks in the final section.

Tap (Rob Reiner, 1984) and *David Holtzman's Diary* (Jim McBride, 1967) discard photographic transparency but not ontological self-subsistence. The fictional worlds of these movies are presented as if they existed independently of the represented film-making activities, but it is a key of both movies' fictions that a camera was present at the narrative action and recorded, as a kind of documentary, the images presented on the screen.

As noted above, these same norms also come apart in a different way in the movies under study here. *Blonde Venus*, *The Devil Is a Woman*, and *The Scarlet Empress* all consistently accept the norm of photographic transparency. They operate within the fiction that the viewer is watching photographic (or better, photograph-like) shots of slices of their fictional world, although it is also fictional that no camera or other recording device was present in the fictional setting or registered the dramatic activity they contain. However, the ontological self-subsistence of their diegetical worlds *is* disturbed over and over again. The artifice of the narrative circumstances and the fabricated nature of the fictional agents and their actions are repeatedly (if only implicitly) asserted, diagrammed in the exposed machinery of von Sternberg's patently synthetic *mise-en-scène*.

In any event, Bordwell's remarks ignore the differences between these classical norms and therefore do not distinguish the two corresponding modes of reflexive self-consciousness in film narration. For many purposes, this does not matter much. However, if we miss the distinction, we may be tempted to assimilate a narrower question ("Is the movie's *photographic* representation of narrative self-conscious?") to a broader one ("Is the movie's portrayal of narrative self-conscious *at some level of representation*?"). I opened this discussion with quotations from Wollen and Studlar—quotations that are, in several ways, confusing and opaque. I have argued, on the one hand, that they are right to affirm that the von Sternberg movies make a drastic break with norms of representation in classical film. But they are wrong in trying to define the fractured norms as pertaining to the very nature of the photographic depiction the films employ. In other words, they seem to have fastened wrongly on the narrower possibility of transparency because they failed to grasp the pair of possibilities that the present distinction seeks to elucidate.

To clarify and elaborate my conception of von Sternberg's mature narrational strategies more concretely, I want to turn finally to a central sequence from *The Scarlet Empress*. So far, I have offered a rather schematic account of the role of the minimally motivated segments from *Blonde Venus* and *The Devil Is a Woman*. In doing so, I have wanted to stress the similarity between the two selections and to elucidate the reflexive, narrationally instructive roles that both selections play. However, in the present instance, I will examine the internal structure of the elliptical transformation in greater detail, arguing that it constitutes a key moment in a whole sequence of narrative transitions, a sequence that depends importantly for its overall meaning on the 'double level' of photographic content discussed earlier. That is, I will argue that *The Scarlet Empress* exploits, in a surprising, sophisticated way, the ambiguity of an image-track that simultaneously depicts Marlene Dietrich (with her well-known screen persona) *and* the equally notorious character from history, Catherine the Great, whom she therein enacts.

It is precisely in this respect that von Sternberg's regular incursions upon the ontological self-subsistence of his fictional worlds are so distinctive. It is not just that the *mise-en-scène* is blatantly constructed to serve various 'expressionistic' objectives. One might contend, whether rightly or wrongly, that the expressionistic world of, for example, *The Cabinet of Dr. Caligari* flouts the norm of ontological self-subsistence in this fashion.[14] But the method and aims of stylization in *The Scarlet Empress* are not primarily expressionistic, in the most common sense. The latter film foregrounds broad issues of make-believe and performance, and its acting, settings, and staging are designed to represent the historical episode of Catherine's political career through metaphors of fictionality and histrionic contrivance. *The Scarlet Empress* also works very differently from *The Devil Is a Woman*, but both films share a vital use of these related metaphors in defining their overall thematic concerns. Or so I will maintain.

III. *The Scarlet Empress*

The plot environment of the targeted segment can be minimally summarized as follows. Princess Sophia, played by Dietrich, has been brought to Russia to be married to the future czar—"the royal half-wit" Peter. By marrying Peter, the erstwhile Sophia becomes Catherine of Russia. In the first part of the movie, Dietrich portrays Sophia as an innocent virgin, shy and kittenish in demeanor. The performance in this stretch of the movie is fun and utterly preposterous. Dietrich seems to be more 'playing with her role' than playing it. She is conveyed to Russia by the incredibly handsome and utterly narcissistic Russian ambassador, Count Alexey, who, as he is portrayed by John Lodge, comes across as a kind of gorgeous male counterpart to Dietrich. It is wholly natural, therefore, that the Dietrich character falls for him like a ton of bricks. However, just prior to the action in our minimally motivated narrative segment, Catherine has discovered that Alexey, apparently like everyone else at the Russian court, has been sleeping with her mother-in-law. She regards this as very bad news and reacts crossly. In anger and distress, she throws a locket containing Alexey's portrait out of her bedroom window and then runs down to the palace garden to retrieve it. It is

---

[14] Here again, a longer discussion of the idea of "reflexive self-acknowledgment" is needed. In an expressionistic film, I am supposing, the acting, sets, and staging are meant to symbolize or, in any event, to express certain generalized psychological states or conditions or, alternatively, to represent a certain broad metaphysical conception of the world. In so doing, it is plausible that they *thereby* acknowledge (call attention to) the status of the film and the world it portrays as fictional constructions. But, in these cases, the acknowledgment is a by-product of and incidental to the primary symbolic or expressive enterprise. In *The Scarlet Empress* and *The Devil Is a Woman*, I am arguing, the fictive status of the characters, their actions, their circumstances, etc., is both foregrounded and made a part of the very subject of the film. So this suggests a narrower sense of "reflexive self-acknowledgment," but it is not a sense that is easy to spell out explicitly. A range of possible distinctions in this vein deserve to be explored.

nighttime as she searches, and as she finds the locket, she encounters a handsome young lieutenant of the guard in the dark. He, with no difficulty whatsoever, seduces her on the spot.

This opens an extraordinary sequence. As it proceeds, it is not always easy to say with real confidence just what is going on. The lieutenant announces at the very outset, "On a night like this, *anything* could happen." Given the various things that subsequently do happen or seem to happen, his remark comes across as a flagrant understatement. Catherine submits to the guard, and we see the token of her submission, the relaxation of her hands upon his back. That image then is dissolved into images, themselves intercut in dissolves, of huge bells ringing and mighty guns firing. At first sight, this appears to be a rather vulgar cinematic metaphor—an instance of the kind of ersatz Freudian symbolism that stands in for the act that cannot be shown in classical film.

And yet, wait a minute! Why is it that these shots and bells and cannons are gradually edited into shots of happy crowds out celebrating some momentous event? One has the brief impression that most of St. Petersburg is in a state of exaltation because Catherine has lost her virginity in the palace gardens. And yet, of course, that isn't right. As the sequence continues, it emerges at the conclusion of some exuberant montage that a considerable period of time has passed, and, in fact, the cheering crowds are celebrating the birth of a royal heir. But, even this realization is confusing. In the ensuing scene, it is the Dowager Empress Elizabeth who is shown in bed with a new baby, and she is the one who is receiving congratulations from a band of courtiers for *her* splendid achievement. It is, at this moment, as if Catherine's midnight indiscretion in the garden had caused her mother-in-law to conceive a child. (This is not the kind of causal connection one would like to see raised to the status of a universal law.)

Eventually, this gets straightened out as well. We realize that nine months have passed. Catherine is the person who has mothered the infant. The Dowager Empress is triumphant because, thanks to Catherine, the royal line has been continued. Nevertheless, just this far into the sequence, the film-maker has already established what seems to be an attitude of calculated playfulness concerning familiar standards of temporal and causal exposition. What is more, the last part of the segment is, if anything, more disorienting. First, we have the oddly moving and oddly uncommunicative scene in which Catherine lies in bed thinking her private thoughts. This is a rather characteristic moment in a von Sternberg film. The fact that Catherine's thoughts and feelings are veiled from view is visually signified by the veil-like bed hangings that blur and soften her unreadable expression. Clearly the reflections she is entertaining here are of some importance, since the camera lingers on her for an extended time, scrutinizing her impassive gaze. It is as if she were reaching some fundamental decision or conclusion, but we don't know what it might be. We do know from the action a moment before that her lover's locket has now been replaced by a jeweled political medallion, awarded to her for her splendid service to the state.

Presumably she is partly contemplating the ironic lessons implicated in that exchange (see figure 20).

Soon afterwards, we see Catherine who emerges again upon the public stage; but the Catherine who emerges in this scene is by now dramatically transformed. Gone is the wide-eyed virgin princess of the first half of the movie, and in her place we discover an altogether different being—a startling metamorphosis of Dietrich's character. To put it bluntly, we discover the powerful, well-established star persona of Marlene Dietrich, the persona we know and love so well from her earlier movies made with von Sternberg. Suddenly, up on the screen, we have Catherine the Great rendered in the familiar Dietrich style. One has had the feeling all along that the 'real' Dietrich has been withheld from us, hidden from us behind the implausible Princess Sophia façade. But, here at last, the real Dietrich, with very minimal motivation indeed, has been released into the story world. Sophia/Catherine has become the knowing, audacious, sexually exploitative figure who ambiguously seems to promise uncharted possibilities and who is coldly and exquisitely in complete control. One of the movie's odd, old-fashioned inter-titles explains that Catherine is presently consolidating her position in court and that she has "discarded all of her youthful ideals." This strikes me as another case of loopy understatement. Actually, it is more as if she had discarded the whole of her previous identity in the film. It is as if she has stepped, in the space of an inter-title, into an entirely new and yet oddly familiar role.

The transfigured Catherine is introduced to us conversing with a gray-bearded old man, and in this conversation she practices her new sexual and political sophistication

Figure 20 A veiled Catherine contemplates her medal

upon him. In a particularly sardonic stroke, the old fellow is the head of the Holy Russian Church, although he really doesn't seem, in any way, to be out of his league in negotiating cynically with her. Like a second-rate mobster, he assures her that he has considerable control of 'the political machine' at court, and, as he confides that assurance to her, he ostentatiously fingers the emblem of his grasp on power—the crucifix of the church. And Catherine, when she responds, likewise plays with the token of her newly realized power—the frothy, flirty handkerchief that she holds.

The obvious questions all this raises are: How is it that the Catherine character is so strikingly and abruptly transformed in this manner, suddenly stepping forth in this novel instantiation of the Dietrich persona? Why does this enormous change take place without any serious attempt at psychological elucidation or development? The transition here represented is, of course, the central minimally motivated narrative transformation in *The Scarlet Empress*. And, again, I want to raise the question "What interpretative rationale, if any, can be offered for this delirious stretch of film?"

In point of fact, the story of *The Scarlet Empress* is structured around a whole series of transformations, each having stylistic similarities to the key example I have just described. For instance, all of these scenes of transformation are punctuated by more or less elaborate montage sequences, sequences in which shots of the great tolling Russian bells recur and mark the passage of time. Thus, we have: (1) the transformation of Catherine as a young girl into Catherine as a sexually mature young woman; (2) the transformation of the young Catherine, at her wedding, into the wife of the czar-to-be; (3) the central transformation of Catherine's passage from sexual and political naïvety into worldly sophistication; (4) the death of her mother-in-law, which raises Catherine to a position of genuine political power and rivalry for political ascendancy with her husband; and, at the end of the movie, (5) Catherine's final and complete triumph— her apotheosis as the all-dominating Catherine the Great.

At each of these stages or stations in her development, there is little in the way of serious dramatic conflict. What conflict does exist is chiefly played out in terms of broad melodrama or farce. This aspect of the movie fits well with a shrewd remark that Mulvey makes about von Sternberg's storytelling. She says, "Despite Sternberg's insistence that his stories are irrelevant, it is significant that they are concerned with situation, not suspense, and cyclical rather than linear time, while plot complications revolve around misunderstanding rather than conflict."[15] However, each stage (or cycle) is a stage in the rise to power of Catherine the Great, and each stage marks a type of worldly knowledge and experience she has to acquire in order for her dominance at the drama's end to be possible at all. One wishes that Mulvey had applied her vague but insightful observation about the 'cyclic' structure of the von Sternberg stories to individual films like *The Scarlet Empress*. One wishes that the observation had encouraged her to further inquiry about the possible import of such

[15] Mulvey (1989), 22.

odd, narrative constructions and had checked her impulse to dismiss such inquiries about von Sternberg's use of narrative as beside the point.

From the very beginning, *The Scarlet Empress* makes it clear that it means to invoke for its audience the Legend of Catherine the Great and the associated myth of her political and sexual omnipotence. In the dialogue and in the absurd intertitles, the idea is repeatedly expressed that she is a character who has a fated, legendary destiny to fulfill. She is, the very first intertitle tells us, "the Messalina of the North." In the opening scene, following this title, the young Sophia falls asleep listening to fantastic tales and legends of past Russian rulers, tales whose violent content the movie encapsulates in a burst of Vorkapich-style montage. Catherine, we are later informed, is "chosen by destiny," but she, the intertitles assert further, "is unaware of the fate that awaits her." When she leaves for Russia, she is instructed by her father "to be worthy of her glorious destiny," and so on, from various sources, in the same vein. The narrative, defined in stages, charts out the fulfillment of that preordained destiny.

In this connection, I believe, we need to distinguish between the flesh-and-blood person from history, Catherine the Great, and the fictional character of the same name, created by myth and popular lore. Naturally, the fictional Catherine of legend is, in some sense, "based upon" or "derived from" the historical figure, but they are separate entities nonetheless. (They are related to one another in very much the same way that St. Nicholas, the storied Christmas character, is linked to the historical Saint Nicholas.) I suggest that we are meant to see and comprehend Marlene Dietrich, in this movie, as playing the *already* fictionalized Catherine and not as attempting to reenact the "real" Catherine at all.

In other words, *The Scarlet Empress* drops the standard pretense of biographical fiction film that the film-making will take us back in time and show us a selection of the historical events in question. That dramatic ambition is altogether forsworn in the present case. Actually, in the movie biographies of the classic period this imaginative pretense was almost always pretty shallow.[16] When George Arliss played Disraeli in *Disraeli* (Alfred E. Green, 1934), or Dolores del Rio played Madame DuBarry in *Madame DuBarry* (William Dieterle, 1934), they were cast for their roles principally because it was supposed that they carried with them, from other films, the kind of screen persona that would plausibly sustain the intended, usually stereotyped conception of the historical individual in question. Of course, this is just a special instance of the still more ubiquitous practice of conjuring up a major dramatic character on the basis of the star's already acquired motion-picture image. As usual, von Sternberg pushes this common movie-making practice to its limits. While Catherine is seen reflected in the 'Dietrich' figure, Dietrich is revealed to be a 'Catherine' counterpart, and each of the two 'roles' is played off against the other during the remainder of the film. This is an especially nice example of the way in which familiar, problematic

---

[16] For a helpful discussion of this and related issues concerning Hollywood film biographies, see Custen (1992).

dramatic devices were used by von Sternberg but were exaggerated, made especially salient, and exploited as a content-bearing stylistic motif.

Moreover, in this movie, it is very much the von Sternberg/Dietrich *version* of the legend of Catherine the Great that we are offered. And this version is idiosyncratic and highly stylized, constructing the figure of myth in its own terms of delirious parody and satirical fantasy. The character of Catherine is marked specifically as a creation of the film-making, erected from the bare framework of the fable of Catherine the Great, and is elaborated, in the movie's second half, in terms of the daunting screen persona of Miss Marlene Dietrich. If this interpretative proposal is right, then we already have some reason why we might expect *The Scarlet Empress* to deviate from our ordinary conceptions of the continuity of the self and of plausible dramatic evolution. The movie aspires to be, it seems to me, a kind of exemplary tale concerning the will to sexual and political power and, as such, its narration is fully prepared to abstract from ordinary ideas of psychological reality.

In fact, a moment early in the movie raises a brief uncertainty about the ontological status of its narrative, albeit playfully and in passing. That is, it is unclear at an early juncture whether the film is supposed to be recounting a piece of history, a legend, or Catherine's private fantasy. In the very first scene, Princess Sophia is ill, and, as the scene closes and Sophia falls asleep, her father is reading her tales of past Russian rulers. Sophia's image is then dissolved into the beginnings of an incredible montage of pillage, torture, and oppression, and these horrendous incidents are depicted as illustrations in a book whose pages appear to be turning on the screen. The last of the 'illustrations' shows a half-naked man being swung as the clapper in a huge, tolling bell, and this shot dissolves into a visually rhyming image of a teenaged Sophia being pushed by her companions in a garden swing. This image of Sophia (Dietrich's first appearance in the movie) surely represents a return from the montage to the main story, but, in visual terms, it is continuous with whatever it was the preceding montage had presented—a young girl's dream? anecdotes of violent Russian history? or cautionary fairy tales of cruelty? That is, nothing formally marks a definite point where the action re-emerges from the hallucinatory segment of the montage, and the formal indeterminacy this suggests is wholly appropriate to the preoccupations and strategies of the larger film. It is equally unclear what kind of 'reality' the movie as a whole presents.

The Scarlet Empress takes almost no interest in the 'realistic' depiction of any of its characters. Louise Dresser plays the Dowager Empress like an egregiously belligerent fishwife from 1930s Brooklyn. And, as Andrew Sarris once pointed out, Sam Jaffee's portrayal of Peter renders him as a kind of malignant Harpo Marx. As I observed in *Narration in Light*, all of these characters are presented, so to speak, as automatons made of flesh.[17] They all are driven, in the most crudely determined ways, by lust or greed or the will to power. The movie draws a broad contrast between the human characters,

---

[17] Wilson (1986), 96–97.

who seem devoid of significant emotional and spiritual life, and the huge statues by which they are constantly surrounded. The statues appear in poses of religious ecstasy and world-weary despair. They assume the postures of agony, shame, and grief. And these are states of mind and soul which the human characters seem largely incapable of experiencing.

If this film, whose scenes are obsessively filled with statues, dolls, and carved figurines, has an emblematic equivalent for the characters it portrays, these would probably be the grotesque mechanical figures that intermittently appear. One of them strips off its garments at midnight, a second pounds another with a club, and the members of a third group creep around in sinister circles, each tracking down the one ahead of it.[18] The metaphorical linkage of human behavior with the idea of the mechanical is extended in various other directions. For example, as I mentioned earlier, the old priest speaks anachronistically of "the political machine" in court that he controls. And, at the conclusion of the famous marriage scene, an inter-title reports that "the machinery of the wedding ceremony" grinds on to its conclusion.

It is not simply that the characters surround themselves with artifactual representations of human beings—the statues, dolls, paintings of human forms and faces, and mechanical figures; there is at least an equal emphasis on the theatricality of self-presentation and the continuous 'audience' scrutiny to which these dubious histrionic outbursts are subjected. For instance, when Count Alexey comes to fetch her from Germany, Sophia is subjected to a cold, critical inspection by the members of her own family. And, arriving in St. Petersburg, she is poked and peered at from all quarters of the court (see figure 21). A kind of culmination of this motif occurs at the spectacular marriage of Peter and Catherine. Here Catherine is offered up as the subject of a vast ceremonial spectacle and as the object of Alexey's private and penetrating stare. Moreover, at the same time, she is marrying a goggling idiot who stares blindly around and through her during the ceremony.

These considerations introduce another kind of concern about the adequacy of Mulvey's account of von Sternberg's work. It is curious that she says nothing about von Sternberg's own preoccupation—expressed again and again in his movies—with questions about the implications and potency of the sexualized 'gaze.' Thus, in *The Scarlet Empress*, the chief male protagonist, Count Alexey, is the bearer of the powerful 'male gaze,' although, through its very intensity and narcissism, it is presented as absurd. When Alexey first arrives in Germany to meet Sophia, he surveys her appraisingly with a fatuously forceful look that parodies the gaze of the supposedly dominating male, and, in the early parts of the movie, he repeats this kind of ridiculous self-absorbed

---

[18] There are several places in the movie in which the behavior of individual characters takes on a strange, mechanical character. For example, this occurs when Sophia meets Alexey in the stables, grabs hold of an adjacent, suspended rope, and, as if she were hypnotized, sways slowly back and forth while exchanging badinage with Alexey. However, the most striking case occurs during the marriage ceremony. As Peter stares glassy-eyed at the incredible wedding scene surrounding him, his head jerks mechanically around from one position to another without, it seems, even registering the presence of his bride beside him.

Figure 21 Sophia is inspected as she first appears in court

scrutiny of her several times. What is more, by the end of the movie, whatever power his look may have had for her is broken. As she progressively comes to rule the line of narrative action, she dismisses him and humiliates him, replacing him with a legion of other lovers, other controlling looks. By the time that she ascends to the throne, he is merely a minor aide to her final seizure of total power. And he figures as just one member of the audience that contemplates her culminating, triumphant transformation. In fact, after her crucial transformation to sexual maturity, it is Catherine herself who comes to be the one who surveys the male world with her own appraising and dominating gaze. For example, in the wonderful scene in which she inspects her troops, dressed herself in military garb, she looks over the more attractive specimens among them, accepting offerings from and awarding honors to those who seem as if they might perform most promisingly 'in action.' One soldier presents her with a bag of spectacular diamonds, and she gives him a spectacular stare of approving assessment in return. "Rich too!" she comments smilingly. So, it is not exactly as if 'the controlling gaze' is simply absent from the 'screen scene.' Rather, it is very much embodied in her parting look.

The potential implications of casting or averting one's gaze in one or another way are developed in the most elaborate fashion. When Alexey, Sophia, and her mother stop, en route to Russia, at an inn along the way, there is a bizarre scene between the lovers, where he warns her not to look him in the eyes, the power of the attraction in her mere glance being more than he can withstand. And, when she does look at him again, he demonstrates his complaint by being, it appears, so overmastered by passion that he grabs her and kisses her intensely on the lips. (All of this is accompanied by some fetching by-play with a whip.) Later, having arrived and settled in Russia, Alexey and Sophia have a rendezvous in the royal stables. She is holding on to a rope that hangs above her head and swaying her body in an odd, almost mechanical manner. She stares at Alexey as he approaches, looking as if she is hypnotized herself or has the aim of hypnotizing him. In this scene also, the impossibility of resisting the power of her gaze is humorously bruited once again, although in both of these scenes, the power in her look is to fire the passion of the man but not to dominate or control the interaction with him. But this will change. Even in the scene with the head of the church, just after her central transformation to maturity, we first begin to see her gaze that takes in the scene with calculating appraisal, one that expresses her intention to act on her own and for herself.

The issues of seeing and being seen reach a zenith of complexity in the famous wedding ceremony, and I won't attempt to analyze the many nuances that are involved in this elaborate setting. The spectacle of the marriage is virtually triangulated by three powerful lines of gaze. Catherine, moved by mixed but powerful emotions, stares straight ahead, the impact of her labored breathing almost causing the candle she is holding to be extinguished. Count Alexey glowers balefully at the proceedings from a position in the crowd that is never clearly specified, but, by means of the editing, one is given the impression that metaphorically he is looking into her eyes—his gaze being one chief cause of Catherine's emotional response. In one way, he still can control her feelings to a significant degree, but in the sphere of action he is helpless. He is helpless to stop the course of the monstrous ceremony. And, presiding over the whole affair, dominating the spectacle as a whole, is Elizabeth, watching triumphantly as the union she alone desires is brought to culmination. Ironically, the idiot groom, Peter, stares around the church, grinning vacuously, but his vision, overwhelmed by spectacle, has no power to effect anything, and it takes in nothing but an overwhelming chaos of sight and sound. Of course, Peter is a male, but, here and elsewhere in the movie, his voyeuristic gaze is impotent.

In Mulvey's short analysis, the Dietrich/von Sternberg films are simply treated as symptomatic manifestations of a recurring proclivity for a purportedly basic perceptual regime of scopophilia. But really, there is every reason to suppose that von Sternberg was very much alive to many of the issues that she seeks, in her much later article, to raise. No doubt his conception of the issues and their broader import was very different from hers, and, no doubt, various aspects of his views on such matters were, to put it mildly, problematic and perverse. Nevertheless, these themes, along with many variations, are present in *The Scarlet Empress*, and von Sternberg's treatment of them achieves a certain level of complication and sophistication.

Similarly, much attention is devoted to the various roles that the main characters themselves undertake or, alternatively, to the roles that others expect or require them to perform. The central conflict between the Dowager Empress and Catherine lies in this range. On the one hand, Empress Elizabeth repeatedly demands that Catherine learn her proper role as a royal Russian wife. That role demands the observance of established forms of duty, submission, and female enticement. Above all, it demands an outcome—the breeding of male heirs. On the other hand, Catherine's successful acquisition of supreme power depends, as she herself remarks, upon mastering a very different role. Catherine must learn the highest arts of sexual politics, at least as von Sternberg conceives of these. She learns the maneuvers of ambiguous sexual promise and the payoffs of strategic manipulation. She acquires freedom from romantic illusion, and she learns to wear the countenance of self-control and to wield the power of the dominating gaze. At the end of our highlighted segment, she tells the priest: "You need have no fears for me. Now that I know how Russia expects me to behave—I like it here." Somewhat later on, she adds, "And I am taking lessons [in the expected behavior, she means] as quickly as I can."

One lesson that Catherine apparently has to learn is given by her formidable mother-in-law. Elizabeth humiliates Catherine by having her prepare the way for the entrance of Count Alexey into her (the Empress's) boudoir. Now, this piece of cruel instruction is quite effective. The humiliation leads to Catherine's seduction; and her seduction leads, as we have seen, to the crucial transformation of the Dietrich character. What is more, the transfigured Catherine actually replays this same scenario later, recasting Alexey in the role that she originally had played. In fact, it is my proposal that her subsequent transformation is itself to be conceived as her self-conscious adoption of a radically new role. Seen in this fashion, its minimally motivated nature makes an obvious sort of sense. Normally, we do not expect that a person's character, outlook, and sensibility can alter so swiftly and extensively. But if we assume that the fictional characters in The Scarlet Empress are largely empty of any significant core from the outset, then it is not implausible that the canniest among them should drop one role and take up another better suited to her needs and circumstances. This is what I make of the musings of Catherine, veiled by the delicate curtains around her bed. I see her as making just this sort of calculation about the content of her future performances.

At one juncture, the Dowager Empress says to Catherine, "We women are too much creatures of the heart," and Catherine has to comprehend the hypocritical posturing expressed in such a speech. And this is just one facet of the expertise in histrionic self-presentation she acquires. In the course of the whole movie, Catherine's progressive acquisition of her fated role as "Catherine the Great" demands the blurring or, perhaps, even the obliteration of many standard roles, and gender roles are definitely among those left behind in the rubble. Czar Peter progressively rages and dithers more and more hysterically as Catherine grows correspondingly more assured and self-controlled. This double transformation culminates at the instant when Peter, in his billowing white robe and flowing white hair, is struck down helplessly before the crucifix in his bedroom (see figure 22). And, at this moment, Catherine, mounted on her white stallion and wearing her white soldier's gear, takes her place upon the throne. Even Count Alexey characterizes these changes in theatrical terms. "Exit Peter. Enter Catherine," he announces, and the revolution (of several kinds) is now complete. In

Figure 22 Peter is strangled in front of a cross

the world of *The Scarlet Empress*, Catherine enjoys an almost alchemical mutability, a power available to "those extraordinary people" (this is Alexey's phrase) who have the intelligence to discern their theatrical options and go on, as Alexey says, "to create their own laws and logic." He means, of course, the laws of conduct and the logic of high style.

IV. Conclusion

I have maintained at some length that both *The Devil Is a Woman* and *The Scarlet Empress* exhibit a sophisticated mode of self-conscious narration and self-reflexive content, but I suspect that there will be lingering doubts about whether it is plausible to presuppose that von Sternberg really possessed the requisite level of philosophical erudition and cared about such experiments in form. However, there certainly is evidence that von Sternberg was attracted to these odd configurations of narrative and narration and aspired to investigate them in film. For example, we know from his autobiography, *Fun in a Chinese Laundry*, that he had plans to make a movie of Luigi Pirandello's *Six Characters in Search of an Author*, and that he failed to do so only because he was unable to obtain the rights to the play.[19] Now *Empress* and *Devil* do not exhibit the same overt, self-conscious concern with fictionality and related topics that one finds

---

[19] von Sternberg (1965), 48.

in *Six Characters* and in certain other products of early modernism. Nevertheless, as I have tried to establish, there is a broad, important affiliation between the relevant modernist works and von Sternberg's final films starring Dietrich. Von Sternberg, we also know, took great pride in being a friend of Max Reinhardt, and there is every reason to suppose that he was acquainted with a range of the theatrical experiments in the early part of the twentieth century that broke with conventional forms of dramatic narrative. And many of these productions also experimented with various forms of non-naturalistic acting, abstract and/or symbolic staging, and the expressive possibilities of sets and lighting. It is unfortunate that in his autobiography and in interviews von Sternberg was so grudging about admitting that he learned much of anything from anyone, or that he was significantly influenced by specific antecedents and contemporaries. Nevertheless, we can be sure that he was acquainted with some range of avant-garde work in theater and cinema, and the thematic preoccupations I have attributed to his last two Dietrich films are not at all beyond his ken.

Of course, von Sternberg's own artistic experiments were conducted in the seedier confines of Hollywood romance and melodrama; he was not, after all, directing experimental productions for the sophisticated theater in Paris, Rome, or Berlin; he was making motion pictures for Paramount Studios, and he was employing one of that company's hottest, most valuable properties. These movies were expected to play profitably in Bangor, Maine, and Boise, Idaho, and it is amazing to me that von Sternberg got away with making movies as excessive and outrageous as he did. Actually, by the time he and Dietrich were making their last two films together, Paramount had pretty much given up on his ability to continue to turn out massive popular successes like *Morocco* (1930) and *Shanghai Express* (1932). The studio was eager to transfer Dietrich into more reliable hands, and von Sternberg was very much aware of the situation. Letting their contractual commitments to him play out, the bosses at Paramount allowed him relative freedom in making *Empress* and *Devil*. No doubt this was more a matter of resignation on their part than deference to his artistic aspirations. Whatever the reasons, von Sternberg delivered the most complex and carefully crafted movies of his career.

These films are the stunning result of two conflicting forces: von Sternberg's elaborate, sometimes pretentious artistic impulses, for one, and the commercial pressures under which he worked, for the other. If my interpretations of the movies are correct, then what is most striking about them is the complexity and ambition of their artistic objectives, especially when those objectives are matched against the superficial poverty of the literary resources with which the director had to work. I have emphasized the fact that the three films I have considered are very much movies that belong to certain genres, genres which fairly often veered toward the tawdry and the dumb. In the first place, many movies that fall within these genres contain implausible and murky plot connections, and the same movies commonly involve characters whose changes of heart and mind are, to put it mildly, imperfectly explained. For this reason, the segments of minimally motivated narrative transformation in the von Sternberg films do not stand out egregiously in the context of their genres; and, in point of fact, these segments are reasonably understood to be von Sternberg's own reworking, as a kind of strategic ellipsis, of the incompleteness or vagueness featured in so many genre movie story lines. Second, I have elaborated the ways in which Dietrich's 'star' persona was utilized to complicate the identity and ontological status of that celebrated female figure on the screen. And this, I have argued, represents an intricate use of the ubiquitous Hollywood practice of casting parts in terms of the actors' pre-established identities as well-known stars. Third, it is an equally familiar fact that sets and staging in certain types of Hollywood studio films are often designed less to achieve, say, a high level of dramatic verisimilitude than to create an engaging context of visual spectacle. Von Sternberg's strong proclivity for spectacle and painterly visual design is probably the most celebrated feature of his work, but I have not focused a great deal on this much-noticed aspect of his late work. Rather, I have argued that his curious narratives have an extremely articulated structure and convey a much richer thematic content than his commentators have supposed.

It is a fascinating aspect of the Dietrich/von Sternberg films that, bizarre and stylized as they unquestionably are, they are not, on the surface at least, more bizarre and stylized than many other films from the same genre and period. This is exactly the reason why the case of von Sternberg is so fascinating, on the one hand, and so hard to argue persuasively, on the other. It would be instructive in this regard to compare von Sternberg's work with that of his contemporary at Paramount, Cecil B. de Mille. Rated simply on a scale of narrative flamboyance, *The Scarlet Empress* and *Cleopatra* (1932) and *The Sign of the Cross* (1934) might tie. Indeed, the fantastic fictionality of the de Mille movies would make it a tricky matter to explain why the fictional worlds of *Cleopatra* or *The Sign of the Cross* count as ontologically self-subsistent, in the sense I have defined, while the world of *Empress* does not. Unfortunately, I don't think there is any short way of arguing that there is more method to von Sternberg's madness than there is to de Mille's. What we know of de Mille's personality, character, and interests does not hint at avant-garde aspirations, and I think it is preposterous to imagine that close interpretative scrutiny of his films would uncover anything like the density and richness of late von Sternberg. In particular, one does not find, for example, a methodical effort to stylize the acting of the whole ensemble in relation to one another. One does not discover a regular playing off of the visuals against the dialogue, and conversely. And, one does not encounter fragments of mischievous unreliability in the visual narration. In other words, one would not find evidence of any systematic aim of highlighting the fictionality of the characters and capricious nature of the narrative action. Still, these are only my impressions of the matter, and nothing can replace the hard labor of interpretative examination and comparison.

No matter what such a comparison might reveal, I want to stress one last time the extent to which von Sternberg adopted and adapted the typical apparatus of his chosen genres, shaping, reworking, and exaggerating these materials in the service of his own highly wrought, personal projects. Where others have thought, with some justice, that these well-worn devices of the Hollywood storytelling apparatus normally limited or compromised the movies that incorporate them, von Sternberg employed the very same resources, after his own fashion of course, to construct the self-conscious narrational frameworks I have tried to elucidate in this chapter. I have tried to explain why I believe that most critics, critics as sophisticated as Wollen, Studlar, and Mulvey have paid far too little attention to the details of his narrative and narrational strategies, and, as a consequence, they have misidentified some of the main sources of the special originality in his work. When the subtlety and audaciousness of von Sternberg's cinematic projects are set beside his quite ingenious use of otherwise dubious materials, it becomes clear that these films he made with Dietrich constitute the products of an amazing artistic balancing act. They are, to my mind, among the more spectacular instances of sheer formal inventiveness in the history of the Hollywood cinema.

9

Love and Bullshit in Santa Rosa: *Pastiche* in *The Man Who Wasn't There*

In the Coen brothers' movie, *The Man Who Wasn't There* (hereafter *MWWT*, 2001) there are flying saucers cruising the night skies over Santa Rosa. Or are there? Is it rather that there are flying saucers cruising around in the mind of the protagonist and voice-over narrator, Ed Crane (Billy Bob Thornton)? Well, wherever we think the saucers figure in the world of the film, there is surely a question about what they are doing there in the first place. What function do these science fiction images and narrative fragments serve in the movie anyway? In a review of *MWWT* in the *Village Voice*, the reviewer complains about its inclusion of "a tediously sub-Lynchian UFO subplot."[1] But, first, the various appearances of and references to the saucers are so brief and scattered that they don't really amount to a determinate subplot at all. This makes them especially puzzling. Second, the notion that they are there to provide some 'Lynchian' frisson is utterly unclear. Still, the basic worry behind the complaint by this reviewer and others is intelligible enough. The space invasion motif in *MWWT* is liable to seem pointless, silly, and even internally incoherent.

The story of *MWWT* is predominantly a *noir* style tale of a downtrodden, deluded, and doomed barber who commits a murder for which his wife is wrongly blamed and who is himself subsequently convicted of another murder of which he is innocent. The Coens were influenced, in making the movie, by the novels of James M. Cain, and there are broad similarities to the twists and ironies of *Double Indemnity* and *The Postman Always Rings Twice*. Like the film versions of these novels[2] (and many other *noirs* of the period), the protagonist of *MWWT* provides a retrospective voice-over commentary on the dramatic action, a commentary in which he attempts to make some sense of the critical ill-fated incidents of his life. Of course, this is a narrative that spoofs the labyrinthine plots of the *noirs* it emulates, and the barber's voice-over parodies the gloomy, deterministic philosophizing that is characteristic of the verbal narration in similar films. Still, the objective of spoof and parody don't do much to

---

[1] Hoberman (2001).
[2] *Double Indemnity* (Billy Wilder, 1944), *The Postman Always Rings Twice* (Tay Garnett, 1946).

explain why aliens from outer space should enter into the enterprise. In one interview, the Coens say, "With this one, we were thinking *noir* to a certain extent, but we were thinking about science fiction movies from the early 1950's. You know, the flying saucers and the pod people."[3] No doubt they *were* thinking of both genres, but the film-makers don't explain why these two lines of 'thought' have been joined together in their film.[4]

Aficionados of the Coen brothers are likely to remind one that many of their other films involve a *pastiche* of genres and reject the supposition that some kind of coherent explanation of the genre grafting is even called for here. *Pastiche* is the mixing of incongruous genres, normally done with the aim of subverting traditional outlooks and values usually associated with the relevant genres. Now, *pastiche* we certainly have in *MWWT*, but it strikes me as too facile to propose that its amalgamation of genres is simply the upshot of some sort of ironic postmodern playfulness. If a saucy mix of elements from genres popular in the period were the basic inspiration in this case, then why, for example, wouldn't the intermittent appearance of a Randolph Scott-like cowboy who tames the town of Santa Rosa effectively enrich and amplify the fun? Why would such an augmentation completely violate the spirit and texture of the film? In what follows I will argue that the motif of 'invasion from outer space' plays an important role in structuring the key thematic materials of the movie. The aliens in their saucers, whether they are real or products of fantasy, serve as a counterpointing frame of reference for the alienated sensibility that afflicts Ed Crane and the alienating behavior of the other 'humans' with whom he deals. Naturally, this claim calls for amplification and defense. In other words, I argue that the film actually has a kind of recessive thematic unity that one would not have expected. What is more, it offers an odd affirmation of love in marriage. At least, the relationship between them offers Ed Crane and his wife a respite and shelter from the empty and manipulative social order of the Santa Rosa in which they reside.

A prototypical storyline in a 1950s space invasion movie, e.g., *Invaders from Mars*, *It Came from Outer Space*, has the following rough structure. The aliens arrive in a small community, and a human protagonist comes to know that an invasion of Earth has occurred. The protagonist becomes aware that the aliens are gradually gaining control of the community by occupying or otherwise gaining control of the bodies of the

---

[3] Smriti Mundhra, "Interview with Joel Coen," *FilmForce*, November 2, 2001, http://filmforce.ign.com. Reprinted in Allen (2006), 189.

[4] In the interview cited in fn. 3, Joel Coen explains the purpose of adding science fiction elements as follows: "We were interested in the whole idea of post-war anxiety, you know, atom bombing anxiety and the existential dread you see in '50's movies, which curiously seems appropriate now." See p. 189 in the reprinted version. But, Coen's purported explanation is not very helpful. Frankie notes a story about the first Russian test explosion of the A-bomb in the newspaper, and Anne Nerdlinger, Big Dave's wife, is unquestionably paranoid about attacks from flying saucers. Nevertheless, anxiety about these matters and other contemporary objects of dread do not play a major role in motivating the actions of the central characters. Coen may be describing an aspect of the tone of the film, but he doesn't account for the specific role of the 'science fiction elements' in the last third of the story.

community's human members. The realization that the protagonist and his allies must face is that the familiar human figures that have been their friends, neighbors, and lovers may be currently housing the malevolent minds of unearthly creatures bent on conquest. What is more, the protagonist is in danger that the same fate of alien transformation imperils him as well. The film viewer's knowledge of the dangerous situation is closely tied to the unfolding experiences of the protagonist, and the viewer is expected to identify sympathetically with this character and his plight. The humanity of the protagonist and other members of the community is vulnerable to attack, and their shared humanity is the supremely valued attribute under threat from the invasion. Correlatively, the anguish of the protagonist in the face of this threat is the emotion that does most to bind the audience to him in his struggle against the creatures from outer space.

Ed Crane is the protagonist of *MWWT*, and, throughout the film, the narrative action is depicted and commented upon from his idiosyncratic perspective. Moreover, he is the character who makes the 'discovery' that aliens have arrived in the vicinity of Santa Rosa. Beyond this, however, Ed is scarcely the sturdy hero familiar from the space invasion melodramas. First, the local incursion of extraterrestrial visitors is not a development that Ed views with either alarm or fear. On the contrary, at the end of the movie, his belief in their presence and his expectation that they will carry him away appear to be a source of hope and comfort to him. We will discuss this point later on. Second, Ed is presented from the outset as a distinctly alien sensibility within the human community. It is a commonplace of *film noirs* from the 1940s and 50s that their protagonists are seriously 'alienated' either from their own emotional lives, from the social contexts in which they live, or from both. But *MWWT* introduces the striking conceit that the protagonist could be an alien himself or, in any event, has a psychological profile more fitting for an inscrutable extraterrestrial. In fact, it is unlikely that we are meant to imagine that Ed has literally come from outer space, but he is unquestionably 'from outer space' in the figurative construction of that phrase. Wherever he is from, he is very weird.

Some aspects of his alienation constitute pretty familiar fare in traditional *noir* narratives. Ed is a man who is estranged from his life in 1940s Santa Rosa. He is stifled by his job as a second string barber, emotionally and sexually paralyzed in his marriage to his wife, Doris (Frances McDormand), and completely distanced from the self-absorbed and manipulative acquaintances that constitute his severely constricted social life. Although Ed's estrangement and isolation are extreme even by the usual standards of *noir* plotting, these facts about his circumstances still fail to capture the thoroughgoing oddness—the patent creepiness—of the Ed Crane character. They don't explain one's sense of him as someone who functions like a foreign exchange student who is visiting northern California from Mars.

The creepiness resides chiefly in his actions and demeanor. As played by Billy Bob Thornton, Ed bears some resemblance to a gaunt, muted, and haunted version of

Humphrey Bogart.[5] The character moves through his life as if he were under some sort of emotional anesthesia. When another person expresses a genuine, recognizable emotion—anger, distress, or fear, for instance—Ed seems to have only a glimmer of comprehension of the feeling that has been elicited. Similarly, the mechanisms that should register whatever emotions he might experience seem to have been massively short-circuited. He views the world with a blank impassive stare, often acknowledging the most outrageous occurrences in the story with a characteristic enigmatic nod of his head. Most notably, the man is preternaturally terse. "Me, I don't talk much," he says at the beginning of the film, "I just cut hair." Instead of speaking, he mostly smokes: it is as if the flow of smoke that he constantly exhales replaces the words he might but doesn't utter. In fact, his exhaled smoke seems like a weird caricature of all of the obfuscating hot air that his more voluble compatriots produce. Ed doesn't like the talk of other people much either. He is mystified and often distressed by all the elaborate verbal baloney to which he is constantly subjected. This is an important subject of the movie, and we'll explore it at some length.

So, the protagonist of *MWWT* has a capacity for emotional response that is functionally equivalent to that of a being from another galaxy, and, by rendering him in this way, the film reverses a fundamental strategy of the kind of space invasion movies sketched above. If Ed Crane were replaced by a pod duplicate, it is not immediately obvious just what difference in him the replacement would effect. It is no wonder that, at the end of the movie, he seems to welcome the presence of visitors from outer space. Now, it's not clear whether alien intruders have really arrived in the Sonoma valley, but Ed undoubtedly imagines that they have. The idea is planted in his mind when Big Dave's wife, Ann Nirdlinger (Katherine Borowitz), tells him that she and her husband had been captured and released by creatures in a flying saucer during a camping trip outside of Eugene, Oregon. She believes that Big Dave has been fundamentally transformed by the spacemen during the encounter. Her manner and testimony is so hysterical and bizarre that Ed himself is puzzled by it, but the idea of an invasion by extraterrestrials has been broached emphatically. Later, Ed glances at an article in *Life* magazine concerning the mysterious events at Roswell, New Mexico, although he evinces no reaction to the story. By the end of the movie, there is a scene that shows a flying saucer hovering over the prison in which Ed is incarcerated, but it may well be that this scene merely reflects the workings of Ed's imagination shortly before he is due to die. Nevertheless, whether the aliens are real or not, we will see that Ed feels some affinity for them—in fact, much more affinity than he feels for his fellow citizens in Santa Rosa. This, of course, is a reversal of the protagonist's normal allegiances in the face of an incursion from outer space.

---

[5] In an interview, Billy Bob Thornton says, "For this movie, I didn't try to look like Bogart. I was thinking more about Frank Sinatra." Gerald Perry interview with Joel and Ethan Coen, *Boston Phoenix*, November 2001, reprinted in the collection by Allen (2006), 161. Especially if Thornton is thinking of the Sinatra of the 1940s, one sees his point. However, it is a pretty worn and haunted version of the young Sinatra.

At the same time, it is easy to feel some sympathy for Ed's estrangement from the other characters. As Hoberman puts the point, Ed is surrounded by "a gaggle of garrulous gargoyles" in this movie, and his retreat into a policy of conversational minimalism can strike one as a reasonable response to their nonstop self-aggrandizing verbiage. It is worth reviewing the more prominent of these garrulous gargoyles, briefly sketching the dreadfulness of each man and his distinctive style of loopy chatter.

FRANKIE RAFFO (Michael Badalalucco), Ed's brother-in-law and fellow barber, is the most benign of the gargoyles, but he is also the paradigmatic producer of pure unmitigated balderdash. In the opening scene, Ed introduces him with the following remarks. "And man, could he talk . . . Now maybe if you are eleven or twelve years old, Frank's got an interesting point of view. But sometimes it got on my nerves." Here is a sample of Frankie's nerve-wracking barber chair discourse.

FRANK: . . . so you tie your own flies, Ed. I mean, if you're really serious. You tie your own flies, you do a—I know it's matickless, I know, people say, hey, you can buy flies at the store— but you can buy *fish* at the store, Ed, you see what I'm saying? ED: Uh-huh. FRANK: The point is that there's a certain art to the process. The point is not merely to provide, and let me point out, these fish are not as dumb as you might think. ED: Uh-huh.

Frankie, unlike some of the other gargoyles, is not exactly a humbug or a liar, but his discourse is wholly unconstrained by even the laxest maxims of conversational relevance and audience attention.

BIG DAVE BREWSTER (James Gandofini), on the other hand, lies a lot. He is a vulgar, loudmouthed liar who tells incredible tales of fighting the 'Japs' in World War Two. These wartime stories are produced with the aim of establishing for Doris and others that he is a 'real man.' He is a paradigm of small-town male braggadocio and swagger—a thoroughly duplicitous windbag. Fairly late in the movie, it emerges that Big Dave was actually stationed in San Diego throughout the war and didn't see combat at all. He is married to Ann Nirdlinger, whose family owns the department store he manages. He is also having an affair with Doris, and this fact leads, through a couple of notable narrative complications, to his being stabbed to death by Ed. It is altogether fitting, by the way, that Ed stabs this hot air specialist in the throat.

CREIGHTON TOLLIVER (Jon Polito): is a traveling 'entrepreneur' who convinces Ed to invest in his prospective dry-cleaning business. Creighton fancies himself to be a suave, slick talker, and, plausibly enough, he wants Ed to be his 'silent' partner in the scheme. Creighton is a classic American huckster, and his pitch is as elaborate and phony as his toupee, "handcrafted by Jacques of San Francisco." In pitching his investment opportunity to Ed, he says:

CREIGHTON: It's called dry cleaning. You heard me right, brother, '*dry-cleaning*'—wash without water, no suds, no tumble, no stress on the clothes. It's all done with chemicals, friend, and your garments end up crisp and fresh. And here's the capper: no shrinkage. ED: Huh. CREIGHTON: That's right! Dry-cleaning—remember the name. It's going to revolutionize the laundry industry, and those that get in early are gonna bear the fruit away. All I need is

$10,000 to open my first store, then I use its cash flow to finance another, and so on—leapfrog, bootstrap myself a whole chain. Well, me and a partner.

We never really find out whether Creighton means to be scamming Ed, since Big Dave, wrongly thinking that Creighton is blackmailing him, strangles him first. So, another big talker in the movie meets his end from a fatal attack directed at his throat.[6]

FREDDY RIEDENSCHNEIDER (Tony Shalhoub) is a resourceful lawyer with grand philosophical pretensions. As such, he is the pre-eminent artiste of bullshit in the film. He is the unbeatable big city attorney who Ed hires to defend Doris after she has been charged with murdering Big Dave. Later Ed is tried for Creighton's murder, and, at least until Ed's money gives out, Freddy mounts a dazzling if utterly incredible defense of him.[7] Freddy refers to the trial as "the Big Show," and he is the biggest legal showboat in all of northern California. His specialty is a kind of outlandish, philosophical boilerplate, and his philosophical predilections tend toward arguing that the defense lawyer's standard of Reasonable Doubt undergirds the universe. Discussing his envisaged defense with Doris and Ed in prison (see figure 23), he explains his basic thought:

Figure 23 Freddy Riedenschneider orates in a cone of light

---

[6] Doris, who kills herself, dies from hanging. So her death is caused by still another injury to the throat. I'm not sure what to make of this. She is not among the paradigmatic bullshit artists in the movie. However, I believe it is important that she has chosen to *silence* herself, but her specific motives for doing so are difficult to construe.

[7] Freddy is in the lineage of shyster lawyers in *film noir*. Three well-known antecedents are Arthur Keats (Hume Cronyn) in *The Postman Always Rings Twice* (Tay Garnett, 1946), Fred Barrett (Leon Ames) in *Angel Face* (Otto Preminger, 1952), and George Grisby (Glenn Anders) in *The Lady from Shanghai* (Orson Welles, 1947). It seems likely that the grotesque courtroom scene in the last of these movies had some influence on the courtroom scenes in *MWWT*.

FREDDY: ... They got this guy in Germany, Fritz something-or-other. Or is it? Maybe it's Werner. Anyway, he's got this theory, you wanna test something, you know scientifically—how the planets go round the sun, what sunspots are made of, why the water comes out of the tap—well, you gotta look at it. But sometimes, you look at it, your looking *changes* it. You can't know the reality of what happened, or what *would've* happened if you hadden a stuck in your own goddam schnozz. So there *is* no 'what happened.' Not in any sense that we can grasp with our puny minds. Because our minds ... our minds get in the way. Looking at something changes it. They call it the 'Uncertainty Principle.' Sure, it sounds screwy, but even Einstein says the guy's onto something ... Science. Perception. Reality. Doubt.

This is Freddy's normal grandiloquent mode, and, as he tries out this line of argument in Doris's prison, he stands in a glaring cone of light—a theatrical spotlight, as it were, improbably formed by the way that the sun is entering the barred room. When Freddy visits Santa Rosa, he stays in the Turandot Suite of the Hotel Metropole ("Yeah, it's goofy, the suites are named after operas"). In one brief scene, the camera tracks through his suite and reveals the stills that cover the rooms of the wall. They are stills of costumed opera singers, straining at their own virtuoso performances.

Thus, *MWWT* offers us these four iconic figures from the Pantheon of American Bullshit—the Chattering Barber, the Blowhard, the Huckster, and the Shyster—each with his distinctive style of verbiage and rhetorical ambition.[8] These are the leading bullshit artists in the movie, but they are not the only able practitioners by any means. When Frankie stops working because of his depression over the fate of his sister, Doris, Ed is forced to hire someone else to take his place. Although Ed hires the candidate who "... did the least gabbing when he came in for the interview," the new barber, when he starts work, talks incessantly from the minute the shop is opened in the morning until it is closed again at night. Naturally, this development drives Ed nuts. Or again, Ed goes to see a psychic hoping to establish some kind of contact with his dead wife, Doris. This venture is mildly startling. Since communication with Doris or with anyone else has never been Ed's normal practice, it is surprising that, after her death, he should search out such a desperate way of getting back in touch with her.[9] In any case, the attempt is a miserable failure. The old crone just offers him some disappointing spiritual mumbo jumbo while failing even to keep his wife's name straight. As Ed leaves the ersatz medium's room, he says, "She was a phony. Just another gabber." For him, the ubiquitous gabbing is inescapable, and in the face of the endless linguistic hogwash with which Ed is assaulted by these characters and others, it is hardly surprising that he retreats into an impassive and apparently defeated silence.

---

[8] Outrageous bullshitters are a staple of Coen brothers' movies. It appears to be their view that Los Angeles produces a huge crop of them. See *Barton Fink* (1991), *The Big Lebowski* (1998), and *Intolerable Cruelty* (2003). Nevertheless, their other films make it amply plain that fortunately they don't suppose that bullshit artists are endemic only to the state of California.

[9] His hope of being reunited with Doris is expressed again in the closing words of his voice-over narration. This hope is important, and I will return to Ed's closing words and some questions they raise in the last part of the chapter.

At the beginning of his famous essay, "On Bullshit," Harry Frankfurt says the following: "One of the most salient features of our culture is that there is so much bullshit. Everyone knows this. Each of us contributes his share."[10] For Frankfurt, bullshit is any mode of groundless speechifying in which the speaker proceeds in more or less complete indifference to the truth of what he says. Certainly this describes the typical mode of discourse practiced in *MWWT* by the citizens of an emotionally blighted Santa Rosa. Bullshit is overwhelmingly prevalent there, and Ed Crane is a human lightning rod for the stuff. This is apparently a chief reason why he is as deeply alienated as he is. But, if bullshit is utterly off-putting to Ed, it comes quite naturally to most of the other characters. The naturalness of bullshit to them seems to constitute a fundamental trait of their otherwise undoubted humanity.[11] But, this fact marks still another reversal of a chief assumption of standard space invasion movies. The humanity of the human characters in this film is not depicted as something especially valuable— something that deserves to be protected from an attack from outside forces. These humans are too corrupted and damaged by their thoroughgoing proclivity for bombast and blarney to be of special merit or appeal. In fact, the humans in the movie are, in various ways, quite foreign to the ideal we have of what our humanity ought to amount to. The protagonist here is alienated from his fellow human beings and comes to feel some fundamental connection with the ambient aliens (whether they are ambient in Santa Rosa or only in his head). It is these humans that arouse Ed's puzzlement and even dismay. They move him to search for some escape route from the unpleasant morass of quotidian human affairs. However, I want to emphasize that it is not the aspects of unquestionable moral squalor that most offend Ed Crane. After all, he is readily prepared to resort to blackmail himself, and he seems to take murder, infidelity, and blatant lying pretty much in his stride. What does paralyze him is all the bullshit—the battery of unfounded verbal banality he constantly endures.

In a well-known and influential book on *film noir*, *Voices in the Dark*, J. P. Telotte has argued that it is a central concern of many *noir* films that the characters are forced to face and survive the vast potential for duplicity in speech and language. For example, he states, "... the characters in these films seem singularly distanced from each other and unable to achieve any kind of intimate or meaningful communication. As a result, this world seems largely populated by isolates, and the ability to reverse the situation or to communicate any vital truths at all appears increasingly unlikely." Or again, a little

---

[10] These are the well-known opening lines of Frankfurt's essay (2005). In the following, I have relied a good deal on Frankfurt's elaboration of the concept of 'bullshit' without attempting to spell out the details of his account.

[11] Chris Grau has made the striking suggestion to me that Heidegger's discussion of *Gerede* (usually translated as 'idle talk' or 'idle chatter') in *Being and Time* (Heidegger (1962), 211–214) is of particular relevance in this connection. The concept of 'idle chatter,' for Heidegger, seems to include bullshit (roughly as Frankfurt understands the notion), although it may be significantly wider in its application. Moreover, the ubiquitous character of idle talk is held to be similar in its deleterious effects on the human psyche. At least, it's bad for our relationship to *Dasein*. This topic deserves much more extensive investigation.

later, "Through a thematic focus on our discourse, these films show how fundamentally our communications, even the movies themselves, carry a certain estranging force, one that renders all discourse precarious and every effort at human communication a risky wager against misunderstanding and alienation."[12] Although these passages from Telotte may somewhat inflate the matter, he has, in my opinion, identified a basic pattern that recurs across a significant range of *noir* movies. I prefer a Frankfurt style of formulation of his point. As I would put it, the struggling, isolated characters in these movies are forced to solve their mysteries and negotiate the hazards that they face by coping with the massive amounts of bullshit that cloud their comprehension of their threatening circumstances. What the Coens have done in *MWWT* is to give a penetrating focus and salience to this pattern, taking 'the prevalence of bullshit' as their major subject and source of parody.[13]

The question of the nature and extent of Ed's alienation is voiced directly within the film. The other characters recognize that he is a creature who is directed by psychic forces that they find incomprehensible. In fact, he is angrily asked the perfectly reasonable question, "What kind of man are you?" on two occasions when his unprecedented strangeness has roused someone into rage. First, when Big Dave discovers that it is Ed that has been blackmailing him over his affair with Doris, he repeats this query four times before he attacks Ed and, during their struggle, he is stabbed to death. Second, even Frankie, who has heretofore been faithful and supportive to Ed, asks him the very same thing twice when, late in Ed's trial for murdering Creighton, he wrathfully explodes and knocks Ed onto the courtroom floor. Actually, Frankie seems to be aroused to his angry question in part by Freddy's extravagant attempts to portray to Ed to the jury as both a typical guy and a kind of cosmic conundrum at the same time. Here, in Ed's voice-over account of it, is part of what Freddy has declared:

ED (voice-over): He talked about how I had lost my place in the universe . . . I was just like them, an ordinary man, guilty of living in a world that had no place for me, guilty of wanting to be a dry-cleaner, sure, but not of murder . . . He said I *was* Modern Man, and if they voted to convict me, they'd be practically cinching the noose around their own necks.

Given everything that has happened up to this point, it is no wonder that poor Frankie, provoked by Freddy's philosophical pyrotechnics, should want to know 'what kind of a man' Ed might be anyway. Indeed, at the very beginning of the film, the issue of the 'kind of man' that one might be or become has already been fleetingly signaled in the visuals. On the wall behind Frankie in the barbershop, there is a Charles Atlas-like bodybuilding ad that says, "Lend me 15 minutes a day . . . and I'll prove I can make you a NEW MAN."

---

[12] Telotte (1989). The first quote is on pp. 27–28 and the second on p. 30.
[13] Telotte's book is quite well known, and it came out in 1989. So, it is possible they knew the work and the key thesis I have sketched.

The strangeness of Ed's relationship to humanity, however, is hardly confined to his hypersensitive negative reactions to bullshit and false forms of conventional sociability. In fact, Ed seems to have a rather perplexed distaste for the basic biological facts of birth, growth, sex, and death. Some of this is expressed most directly in Ed's inscrutable excurses on the subject of human hair. The first of these is presented in Ed's uncharacteristically lengthy outburst to Frankie while he (Ed) is giving a haircut to a boy who is glumly reading a *Dead-eye Western* comic book. Frankie is sitting in a customer's chair leafing through a magazine. Ed and Frankie have the following exchange:

ED: Frank. FRANK: Huh? ED: This hair. FRANK: Yeah. ED: . . . You ever wonder about it? FRANK: Whuddya mean? ED: I don't know . . . How it keeps on coming. It just keeps growing. FRANK: Yeah—lucky for us, huh, pal? ED: No, I mean it's growing, it's part of us. And we cut it off. And throw it away. FRANK: Come on, Eddie, you're gonna scare the kid. ED: (to the boy in the chair) OK, bud, you're through. (And then continuing to Frank) . . . I'm going to take this hair and throw it out in the dirt. FRANK: What the—? ED: I'm gonna mingle it with common house dirt. FRANK: What the hell are you talking about? ED: I don't know. Skip it.

Much later in the movie, just after his almost fatal car accident with Birdy, Ed returns to philosophical reflections on the topic of hair. He reports in voice-over that, while he was unconscious from the crash, he remembered that an undertaker had once told him that a person's hair keeps growing for a while after the person's death and then it inexplicably just stops. Still unconscious, Ed is led to wonder, "Is it [the hair, he means] like a plant in the soil? What goes out of the soil? The soul? And when does the hair realize that it's gone?" In fact, hair seems almost to symbolize the condition of brute biological life on earth as Ed is inclined to understand it. That is, hair is something that keeps on growing endlessly and purposelessly, requiring the existence of barbers to cut it back, to shape it, and to dispose of the shaggy waste. Hair is living stuff that does not have a life of its own.[14] Moreover, human vanity being what it is, it is the barber's job to coif a person's hair into one of various fashionable configurations. In defiance of the silent, inexorable, unruly growth of hair, barbers give haircuts (e.g., the Flat Top, the Executive Contour, and the Duck Butt) that express, within a narrow and stereotyped semiotics, the vacuous self-images of their clients. In *MWWT*, the women tend to go in for ridiculously constructed hats that top them off in a similar way.[15]

In a particularly eccentric scene, Doris is taking a bath and Ed stands leaning on the bathroom door, smoking. There is no overt interaction in speech or gesture between the two until Doris asks Ed to shave her legs. Without uttering a word, Ed fetches the razor, soaps up her lower legs, and carefully and expertly does as she has asked. We see the shaved hairs fall like splinters into the bathwater. Despite the general chilliness of

[14] Dick Moran has pointed out the resemblance to Roquentin's reflections on the growth of the roots of the chestnut tree in Sartre's *Nausée*.

[15] See especially the women in the jury at Ed's trial. Anne Nirdlinger's veiled chapeau, during her nighttime visit to Ed, is particularly bizarre.

their interaction, there is also the hint that it has some shared significance between them. After the shaving is finished, Doris shares Ed's cigarette with him and says with a placid smile, "Love ya, honey." Later in the film, we learn that they have not performed together what Ed refers to as "the sex act" for many years. However, one gets the impression that this little episode of leg shaving has for them a kind of distanced but comfortable intimacy that takes the place of more conventional love-making. If this is right, it says something about the attachment between Ed and Doris, a topic to which I will return in due course.

So Ed and Doris don't have sex, and they don't have children either. In a later scene, Ed and Doris go to a picnic in honor of Doris's cousin Gina who has just been married. Ed and Doris are characteristically disgruntled about the social occasion. Ed says, "Doris didn't much feel like going, and I didn't either, but, like she said, we had a Commitment [capitalization in the script]." Doris, whose family is Italian, says, "I hate wops!" and she adds, "You didn't have to grow up with them. Family! Boy!" This dim view of family life and its Commitments is borne out by what we see of the inauspicious gathering. In the movie, Frankie is the explicit advocate of the importance of family ties, and he is specially featured in the scene. His behavior is cheerful, frenetic and repugnant. He delights the raucous, squealing children who dominate the gathering by riding bronco-style upon an enormous hog. After the pig ride, the young boys of the family take part in a revolting pie-eating contest, and Frankie is persuaded to join in. At the signal to start, the contestants all plunge their faces into the pies and devour them ravenously. Frankie wins the contest face down, so to speak, and, inebriated before the contest began, he caps his victory by falling asleep in the car, drunkenly clutching his pie contest trophy to his chest.

One of Doris's older female relatives cannot even remember what Ed's name is, and she obnoxiously demands of Doris, "So, how come you got no kids?" This exchange is chilly and unpleasant, but Doris herself is hardly more pleasant to the new bride. "Congratulations, Gina," she says sourly, "It's so goddam wonderful ... Life is so goddam wonderful, you almost won't believe it ... It's just a goddam bowl of cherries, I'm sure ... Congratulations on your goddam cherries." The pretext of family affection and conviviality is shallow. Rather, the occasion is hostile and even sordid, consisting mostly of a mutually tolerated social belligerence among the kinfolks. Although it is Doris who mostly voices the negative sentiments on the subject of one's commitment to relatives, she and Ed are surely one on this point. So, sex, marriage, and family are pretty repellant to them both, and religion apparently fares no better. Ed has told us earlier, "Doris wasn't big on divine worship ... and I doubt if she believed in life everlasting: she'd most likely tell you that our reward is on this earth, and bingo is probably the extent of it ... " Ed, by contrast, doesn't even like the bingo.

The opaque relationship between Ed and Birdy Abundas (Scarlett Johansson), the teenage daughter of an alcoholic local lawyer, might seem to require some qualification here concerning Ed's sentiments toward love and sex. After all, Birdy is an extremely attractive young woman in whom Ed takes an intense proprietary interest. However, the brief subplot is hard to construe. I am inclined to take Ed's actions toward her as chiefly having the non-sexual motivation he assigns them. First, as circumstances close down on him, he is moved by the thought of her youth and his sense of what life might potentially bring her in the future. Second, what most immediately attracts him to her is her 'beautiful' playing of classical piano. Third, he also seems to be taken by her apparent All-American innocence and her candid trust in him. On both of these last two scores, Ed is under an illusion, and he is seriously out of touch with both the music and the musician. It really is a symptom of Ed's broad estrangement from genuine manifestations of human emotion that he can listen to Birdy's playing and suppose that she has any noteworthy musical talent. As Monsieur Carcanogues, the foremost San Francisco piano teacher, has to explain to him, Birdy, with sufficient practice, can learn to hit the right notes, but her playing is utterly devoid of emotion or the expression of anything significant 'inside' her. Indeed, there is probably not much 'inside' for her to express. (The film's viewer, it seems to me, is meant to recognize immediately the vacant character of Birdy's playing and to grasp the minor pathos of Ed's illusion on this score.) Carcanogues says, "She ztinks... Someday, I think, maybe, she make a very good typist." Naturally, this mode of lacking musical talent, inexpressiveness, is precisely the sort of failing that Ed cannot discern.

One can certainly understand how the idea of classical music—especially music composed by a deaf composer—would have a kind of profound attraction to him. The idea promises some kind of aesthetic alternative—some kind of spiritual release—from all the hokum and claptrap that afflicts him. Ed tells us that he found something when he listened to Birdy play: "Some kind of escape. Some kind of peace." But, whatever solace he may find in listening to her playing, Birdy really has no music in her. In fact, we learn after the visit to Carcanogues that she is not seriously interested in music anyway. Moreover, in idealizing Birdy, Ed misses the fact that she is, at a minimum, a pretty normal teenage girl with an interest in boys and smoking and a dim ambition of taking care of small animals some day. Indeed, the incident that causes the car accident after the failed piano audition—her attempt to give him a blowjob on the return drive home—strongly suggests that Birdy's interest in sex enthusiastically exceeds the norm. For all of Ed's glum passiveness and minimal emotional life, he does have an aspiration for self-improvement. He plainly hopes that Creighton's dry-cleaning scheme will strengthen his economic status, and he anticipates, it seems to me, that Birdy and her music will elevate his spiritual life. The visit to the music teacher and the car accident afterwards bring his expectations concerning her to an abrupt end.

It would be a stretch, I suppose, to think of Birdy as a *femme fatale* in *MWWT*, but I'm inclined to stretch a bit here. It is amusing to consider the fact that she is the woman whose façade of deceptive attractiveness seduces the protagonist into illusion and eventual calamity. Of course, the seductive attractions in *film noir* do not usually consist in a brand of well-mannered, female insouciance combined with a less than modest talent for the piano. And normally, the illusory desire of the male is not focused on shepherding the woman's envisaged national career at the keyboard. Certainly, the man's culminating disillusionment does not consist in learning that the woman is much less interested in instrumental music than in oral sex. The specific pattern of attraction, seduction, and devastating revelation here is decidedly non-standard, but the pattern *is* present, culminating, as it usually does, in physical catastrophe for the doomed lovers. In fact, the relationship between Ed and Birdy is ended by an almost fatal car accident—an accident that echoes similar passion-shattering crashes in *Angel Face* (Otto Preminger, 1953), *Out of the Past* (Jacques Tourneur, 1947), *The File on Thelma Jorden* (Robert Siodimak, 1950), and *The Postman Always Rings Twice* (1946).[16] Indeed, in *MWWT*, as in *Postman*, the crash is caused by an ill-considered last kiss between the protagonist and his flame. Hence, the dramatic pattern of this quirky relationship between Ed and Birdy may lack the expected heat, but, for the Coen brothers, it still may represent the darkness of romantic infatuation as it occurs in the Humpty Dumpty setting of this movie.

Almost killed in the crash, Ed has a bizarre near-death experience. As he explains in voice-over, "Time slows down right before an accident, and I had time to think about things." While he is unconscious after the crash, he has a dream in which Doris, in effect, comes back from death and revisits him in their home.[17] The dream, it seems to me, has a kind of emblematic significance, and it conveys something crucial about the emotional structure of their relationship.[18] It represents, I believe, some of the 'thinking about things' that the accident induces in Ed. Very briefly, the dream unfolds as follows. Ed is sitting on the front porch of their house on Napa Street, when he notices a man inspecting his driveway and seeming to take some notes. It emerges that the stranger is a door-to-door salesman who is selling Macadam tar for resurfacing driveways. He begins to make a sales pitch for the tar treatment, and, although Ed mildly demurs, Ed seems unable to extricate himself from the increasingly aggressive pitch. It is at this juncture that Doris drives up, gets out of her car, and asks the salesman what he is selling. Just as he begins to respond to her, she snatches his brochure, tears it up, and snarls, "Get lost!" The salesman flees from this attack, and Doris turns and stalks grumpily into the house. Ed follows her inside, and he sits on the sofa in the living room, listening to the clinking of ice cubes as Doris, in the kitchen, fixes her first drink of the night. She joins him in the living room with her drink, and they sit together on

[16] Also in *Postman*, the image of Cora's lipstick case rolling out of the ruined car is oddly replicated by the hubcap that rolls off the car and spins away in *MWWT*.

[17] Although I think this is most plausibly taken as Ed's dream or fantasy, it could be a memory of some incident in their past. It would not significantly affect my interpretation here if that were so.

[18] This scene is a good example of what I dub 'a rhetorical figure of narrational instruction' in *Narration in Light*, Wilson (1986), 49. That is, it is a scene or segment that exemplifies and foregrounds a structure of narrative or narration that is reiterated and elaborated within the wider context of the movie. It thereby offers the audience some 'instruction' as to how the film may hang together in surprising ways.

the sofa staring impassively ahead.[19] As the screenplay tersely puts it, "She sips. He puffs." After a moment, he ventures a hesitant, "Doris...?", but she cuts him off with, "Nah, don't say anything. I'm all right." They continue sitting together, smoking and drinking in the fading afternoon light (see figure 24).

The scene, in its context, is very peculiar, and it can seem gratuitous. But, for one thing, it is the point at which the movie's narration begins to depict directly subjective or subjectively inflected episodes from Ed's retrospective narrative. As noted above, the cinematic narration of *MWWT* follows Ed's epistemic point of view throughout. The viewer consistently accompanies Ed, and the visual information that the viewer acquires thereby corresponds to visual information available to Ed. Before the accident, this visual information is transparent information about the 'objective' world of the film. After the accident, the narrational strategy changes, and the epistemic status of several of the culminating scenes is significantly ambiguous: either they depict Ed's fantasies or, at least, they are subjectively inflected in a major way. We will discuss some of this subjective inflection shortly. In any case, it is no accident that, in these episodes, the imagery of and references to alien invasion move into prominence.

So, the onset of this modulation into more subjective cinematic narration is introduced by Ed's dream of Doris's return. Moreover, as mentioned above, the pattern of the action in this dream of his strikes me as a paradigmatic instance of the personal connection between the Cranes. Even in the privacy of his 'bungalow,' Ed is accosted

Figure 24 Ed and Doris at peace at home

---

[19] In fact, Doris sits on the sofa first, and Ed joins her there. However, as several people emphasized to me, he seats himself on the far end of sofa away from Doris. Thus, despite the fact that this is a scene that marks their solidarity together, it also marks their physical and emotional distance.

by still another bullshit artist: the Macadam tar salesman in this instance. Ed is dismayed by this new eruption of bullshit but doesn't know how to deal with it. However, Doris, always the more active and socially effective of the two, dispatches the salesman immediately. In effect, she protects her husband from the unwanted assault, and, as I read the scene, when they settle down afterwards on the sofa, they stolidly acknowledge the significance of what has just occurred and the implicit bond that exists between them. Measured in terms of all the usual parameters, Ed and Doris's marriage seems bleak. And, in fact, it *is* pretty bleak, but, as the scene reminds us, their relationship serves certain basic needs and purposes for each of them. For one thing, they offer one another a certain level of tacit understanding and practical complicity.

This scene should be linked with the scene, discussed earlier, in which Ed shaves Doris's legs in the bathtub. No doubt, this is a pathetic instance of physical intimacy between a man and his wife, but, the scene, especially when it is re-viewed in terms of what we eventually learn about the two of them, suggests that there is a bizarre, reserved but harmonious accord that each feels for the other. After the ghastly family picnic, Doris has passed out drunk, and Ed carries her from their car and puts her into bed. As he stands there watching her sleep, he begins to reflect upon the way that they met and got married. These reflections are interrupted by a phone call from Big Dave who summons Ed to meet him at Nirdlinger's, and it is during the meeting that Ed stabs Big Dave. After the murder, Ed goes back home to Doris and resumes his contemplation of her sleeping form. In the first of these voice-overs, Ed says, "I'd met Doris blind on a double-date with a loudmouthed buddy of mine . . . At the end of the night she said she liked it I didn't talk too much." In the second part of these voice-over reflections, he continues:

ED: . . . it was only a couple of weeks after we met that Doris suggested getting married. I said, Don't you wanna get to know me more? She said, "Why, does it get any better?" She looked at me like I was a dope, which I've never really minded from her. And she had a point, I guess. We knew each other as well then as now . . . Anyway, well enough.

Thus, certain basic terms of the relationship have been established from the outset. There is no expectation on either side that a lot of words are to be exchanged between them, and, beyond that, there is no idea of reaching some depth of psychological or spiritual comprehension. In fact, there may not be a lot to grasp on either side, but the knowledge that they have of each other is, he informs us, sufficient for getting on in the marriage. The knowledge that they have serves them "well enough."[20]

[20] It is worth comparing Ed and Doris's marriage with the much warmer but still muted marriage of the Gundersons in *Fargo*. See, for instance, the discussion of the relationship between the Gundersons on the concluding pages, 290–291, of George Toles's marvelous essay, "Obvious Mysteries in *Fargo*," Toles (2001). Toles is more broadly concerned with the way in which the Coen brothers work their way to a positive affirmation of human value within the intricate structures of irony that they deploy in *Fargo*. The structures are quite different in *MWWT* and the values affirmed are different as well, but much that Toles says in his analysis is highly instructive in relation to the later movie.

Ed's outlook on the world has a certain curious trajectory in the course of the movie. After Big Dave's murder, Ed begins to express his sense of having some special grasp of some larger pattern in his life. Looking out of his car at a band of anonymous pedestrians in the street, he says, "All [he is referring to the people he sees] going about their business. It seemed like I knew a secret...something none of them knew......Like I had made it to the outside, somehow, and they were all still struggling, way down below." Notice that Ed's privileged outlook is here described in terms of constituting a view for him from 'up above.' This notion of his that he is acquiring the capacity to see things from a distanced and higher position comes to be more and more articulated. As it does so, Ed also comes to associate this new superior perspective with the point of view that the invaders from outer space would naturally enjoy. During the same period, Ed progressively acquires the sense that he is disappearing from the world. Somewhat later he announces, "I was a ghost walking down the street...I was a ghost: I didn't see anyone; no one saw me...I was the barber." These patterns reach a partial culmination in his near-death experience. After the car accident, we see a hubcap spinning in slow motion down the road and over an embankment. From the spinning hubcap, we cut to a very high shot looking down into the car and showing Ed who is lying unconscious at the wheel. The camera booms down closer and closer to Ed's face until the face itself blurs out and the blurry shape that supersedes it starts spinning away, a bright revolving disc moving off into the darkness. It looks for everything like a flying saucer disappearing into distant space. It is a fade-in from this image that takes us into Ed's dream about Doris's coming home.

I have already explained why I think that this scene encapsulates for Ed and for us the essence of the Cranes' togetherness. The shot of the receding alien spacecraft enigmatically connects Ed's experience with the presence, real or imagined, of the visiting creatures from outer space. Moreover, at the end of the scene, the saucer-like white form reappears in Ed's field of vision as he recovers consciousness, but it resolves itself into the light-reflecting disk on the visor of the doctor who is peering down into his eyes. In several of the concluding scenes, it becomes unclear whether what we are seeing are supposed to be mysterious but real events or the products of the fantasies of Ed's last days on earth.

For example, Ed is in prison waiting for his execution when he has what seems to be another dream. In the dream (or whatever it is), Ed hears the mysterious treble hum of the spacecraft, and the doors of his cell and the outer doors of the prison inexplicably open up. Ed wanders out into the prison yard, and he is almost blinded by an intense searchlight glaring down into his eyes, and we see, as he does, what is unquestionably a flying saucer hovering above the walls. The spaceship has the rather tacky look that is familiar from low budget 1950s sci-fi movies. The saucer is motionless except for a slight wobbling movement and the rotation of its upper deck (see figure 25). As we see Ed walking out of the prison, we hear him say in voice-over, "But now all the disconnected things seem to hook up." Staring blankly at the saucer above him, Ed

Figure 25 Ed 'sees' a spacecraft hovering above the prison

simply gives his characteristic and inscrutable nod—nodding as if he were acquiescing in something that the spaceship has somehow communicated to him. In any case, this is the beginning of Ed's ultimate epiphany—the heightened perspective on his life that he thinks he has finally achieved. An instant later, he goes on (continuing in voice-over) to explain:

ED: . . . Well, it's like pulling away from a maze. While you're in the maze you go through willy-nilly, turning where you think you have to turn, banging into the dead ends, one thing after another . . . But get some distance on it, and all those twists and turns, why, they're the shape of your life. It's hard to explain . . . But seeing it whole gives you some peace.

Completing this little speech, he turns and goes back to his cell.

Plainly no break from prison is envisaged here, but only the dawning of a new sense of spiritual release. We should be careful not to equate Ed's final perspective with some sort of religious epiphany. Earlier in the movie, it's been established that he and Doris regard all that as crap, and here he seems to imagine his release as a matter of being taken away by the space invaders. Of course, Ed has been an enigma throughout the film, and he remains an enigma at the end. Indeed, his rather touching final perspective is profoundly enigmatic as well. What is the significant configuration of these events that he takes himself to discern? Perhaps, Freddy Riedenschneider's final remarks to the jury at Ed's trial give us our best hermeneutic advice on this point. Freddie affirms to the jury that Ed's case exhibits " . . . the chaos of a work of modern art," and Ed reports that the lawyer " . . . told them to look not at the facts but at the meaning of the facts, and then he said that the facts *had* no meaning." But whether Freddy is actually right about this or not, Ed, in the end, comes to suppose otherwise.

Here, in any event, is what Ed relates to us about his perspective, as he enters the execution chamber and seats himself in the electric chair.

ED (in voice over): . . . I don't know where I'm being taken . . . I don't know what waits for me, beyond the earth and sky. But I'm not afraid to go . . . Maybe the things I don't understand will be clearer there, like when a fog blows away . . . Maybe Doris will be there . . . And maybe there I can tell her . . . all those things . . . they don't have words for here.

Now, much of this concluding speech sounds a lot like conventional movie stuff—the summary philosophical reflections of the condemned *film noir* protagonist before his death. In fact, these words may well be the last that Ed has penned on commission for the tabloid men's magazines that have paid him for a rendering of his final thoughts and feelings. In his cell, we see scattered samples of the tacky confessional genre to which he has committed to contribute. They include: in *Stalwart* magazine, the story, "After 10 years of married life . . . I discover I am escaped lunatic," and in another tabloid, *The Unheard-of,* the tale, "I was abducted by aliens." So, maybe we are supposed to think that his final voice-over speech is only a culminating burst of sub-literary baloney. Maybe, we are to conclude that the whole surprisingly loquacious voice-over narration has been nothing more than some type of fictionalizing bullshit itself.

I don't believe, however, that this is the irony intended. More likely is the irony that Ed's weird narration, which fictionally we know to give the truth of the affair, will appear in the tabloids and then effectively get lost in the garbage heaps of lurid, trashy journalism. His honest words will be engulfed within the predominating tide of bullshit. Given the patterns in the movie that I have traced out at some length, these words, whatever the conventional character of their content and rhetoric, do complete some of the motifs I have emphasized in the course of this discussion. First, there is the hope that, when he is taken away, he will escape the debasing effects on thought and speech of the all-encompassing posturing and pretense. He hopes that he will finally be able to find words that allow him to say important things he cannot express on earth. Second, there is the hope that Doris will be with him in the new place, and that he will be able to tell *her,* specifically, what he has not been able to say before. Presumably, some of this would concern his thoughts and feelings for her. It would concern the significance of the muted connection with which they have lived together and about which, by mutual agreement, they have hitherto been silent. The fact that Ed's last musings include this wish to be with Doris underscores, I believe, the point that their marriage, however distant and cheerless it has seemed, has involved some kind of alienated unity between them.

There is a scene occurring much earlier in the movie, in which the bullshitter's endemic indifference to truth is contrasted with the repressed resonance for the Cranes of a personal truth that they are forced to share. When Riedenschneider first visits Doris and Ed in prison to begin to work out the basis for her defense, we are given a somewhat opaque glance at a dimension of the personal feelings that the Cranes may have for one another—feelings they almost totally suppress. In the exchange, Ed tries to speak the truth. He confesses that he committed the murder, explains his motives, and describes how the crime took place. On the one hand, the lawyer has absolutely no interest in Ed's account. He dismisses it contemptuously on the grounds that it constitutes a story that cannot possibly play successfully before a jury. Freddy says, " . . . Yeah. OK. Forget the jealous husband thing, that's silly; we're going with the blackmail. I'll be in touch." With that remark, he exits the cell. On the one hand, for him the truth of the story is a matter of complete indifference if it cannot fit within a rhetorically effective piece of courtroom bullshit. On the other hand, in the course of giving his account, Ed reveals to Doris for the first time that he has known about her affair with Big Dave. As this information is disclosed, the camera cuts back and forth between shots of Ed and Doris, each looking at the other intently but with utterly impassive countenances, until, in the last of the shots, Doris makes a quick and barely detectable grimace. With any other couple, one would suppose that no notable emotion had been registered between them. With Ed and Doris, however, the truthful exchange amounts to an almost operatic expression of surprise and shame, although it is only with hindsight that we can discern the feelings that seem to be in play.

In any case, the epistemic status of the culminating scene in the execution chamber is particularly perplexing. It depicts the last moments before Ed's electrocution, but it mixes some elements, realistic in its *film noir* terms, with a setting that is thoroughly and eccentrically infused with the science fiction motif.[21] On the one hand, the chamber contains what looks like a 1940s electric chair, and the executioners are wearing contemporary garb. But, on the other hand, the chamber itself is quite fantastic. It is an elegant circular space of spare, futuristic design. The room is uniformly and intensively lit, and the walls are made out of some glossy, slick, white material. As a result, the preparations for the execution take place in an almost blinding whiteness. Cut into one of the walls of the chamber, there is a thin, long rectangular window in front of an observation room for official spectators of the electrocution. Although the figures behind the observation window look like typical (male) citizens of Santa Rosa, they also have the frozen guise of aliens who are embodied in human forms. Each of them looks out through the window with a fixed and inexpressive stare, as if the execution about to take place is an event that they can only register with mesmerized, vacuous attention. These witnesses are also dressed in conventional business suits, and each man has had his hair coiffed rigidly into one of the snappy styles that Ed and Frankie's shop has featured, but their immobile postures and blank demeanors are unquestionably spooky. So, this execution chamber looks as if it were the central inner compartment of a flying saucer. It is as if Ed is being readied for a take-off as the denizens of the spacecraft observe his reactions.

---

[21] The row of lights on the ceiling of the hallway outside his cell looks like a series of little flying saucers. When, in the very end, he walks along that hallway to the room that holds the electric chair, they guide him down the pathway to his execution.

At the same time, the electric chair is a sinister double of a barber's chair, a point that is emphasized when Ed is given a final shave after he has been seated in the chair. That is, a patch of hair from his leg is shaved, invoking the earlier scene in which Ed, with gentler aims, had shaved Doris's legs in the bathtub. So, the room, in its gleaming, antiseptic whiteness also seems like a kind of dead-end barbershop for the doomed. The barber is himself being barbered and will shortly be barbecued, while the event is monitored by creatures that look as if they might be replicants of his former customers. Thus, Ed's past and his possible future are both implicitly present in this glistening room where he will die. The effect is very odd.

So, what are we seeing in this extraordinary scene? Is Ed in an execution chamber or a flying saucer? And who are the observers behind the window? Are they creatures from outer space or are they human beings who are so removed from any natural sentiment or concern with Ed that they sit there like mannequins in a Nirdlinger window display? (Are they reflections of the movie's audience, perhaps?) Maybe, the point is just that there is no notable difference between extraterrestrials who have assumed human bodies and 'genuine' humans who, in their complete emotional vacuity, are as alarming as any possible invader from another planet. And what is the epistemic status of the shots in this last scene? Is this really supposed to be a believable Californian execution chamber in 1947?[22] Even allowing for the extent of stylization in this movie, this is surely not the case. Or, are we seeing Ed's execution in a manner that reflects his own fantasy-driven perception of where he is and what is happening to him? Are these final shots subjectively inflected by *his* visual imagination as he experiences his imminent death as a liberating take-off in a flying saucer? Since the movie has progressively veered into more frequently deploying segments that depict, directly or indirectly, the contents of Ed's mind, it may be that this trajectory in the visual narration of *MWWT* reaches its intensely subjective culmination in the present scene. Or, finally, does the scene construct an elaborate visual metaphor put forward at the conclusion by the Coen brothers to foreground, meld, and summarize the elements of *film noir* plot and science fiction imagery that they have interwoven in their film? Is it *their* vision of Ed's execution that is here figuratively embodied and affirmed?

Actually, I doubt that we have grounds for choosing between these last two alternatives. In the final third of the movie, as the story becomes more and more fantastic, it is more and more difficult to be sure what sort of reality is being offered to us on the screen. It is probably impossible to resolve the issue when we arrive at these closing shots of the film, and it probably doesn't matter much what we decide. It does matter that the movie ends by making a transition into *some* new epistemic plane. The movie has operated within a *pastiche* of narrative genres, but more and more, the audio–visual narration operates in a *pastiche* of epistemic modes. If in the early part of the movie, we see (as it were) the objective 'reality' of Santa Rosa, in the last third, we

---

[22] In point of fact, the state of California has never used the electric chair in executions.

move more and more into a mix of dream, memory, hallucination, and filmic quotation. The scene of Ed's execution is the culmination of the accelerating trajectory in the fluctuating modes of the narration.

In his final voice-over declaration, Ed says he hopes to find Doris in the life beyond. Should we conclude from this and other evidence that Ed loves Doris after all? Actually, I think this is a lousy question. In *film noir*, the central sexual/romantic relationship is almost always too ambiguous and tortured to fit or fail to fit the concept of 'love' very well. In *MWWT*, on the other hand, Ed and Doris's relationship is too ambiguous and inert to classify in terms of 'love' either. Nevertheless, as I indicated above, we are led to understand that their marriage has rested on a certain crucial cohesion between them. Perhaps we can say that their relationship is meant to offer an instance of what a merely 'companionate marriage' could amount to under conditions of maximal alienation and repression on both sides. Husband and wife support and protect each other in the face of outside forces of manipulation, duplicity, and violence, and, above all, in the face of unremitting bullshit. Moreover, they understand quite well that this is so. Of course, their relationship is categorically not a Miltonic marriage whose ideal is a "meet and happy conversation" between the partners. This couple does not go in much for conversation of any sort. But really, that seems to be a key part of the point. The Cranes have coped with their odious lives in sunny Santa Rosa by establishing a tacit solidarity, and there hasn't been any great need to talk about it.

Bibliography

Adorno, T.W. (1991). *The Culture Industry: Selected Essays on Mass Culture*. London: Routledge.

—— and M. Horkheimer (1990). "The Culture Industry: Enlightenment as Mass Deception," in *Dialectic of Enlightenment*. New York: Continuum Press.

Allen, W. R. (ed.) (2006). *The Coen Brothers Interviews*. Jackson: University of Mississippi Press.

Altman, R. (2008). *A Theory of Narrative*. New York: Columbia University Press.

Auiller, D. (1998). *Vertigo: The Making of a Hitchcock Classic*. New York: St. Martin's Press.

Bal, M. (1985). *Narratology: Introduction to the Theory of Narrative*. Toronto: University of Toronto Press.

Barthes, R. (1974). *S/Z*. New York: Hill & Wang.

—— (1977). "An Introduction to the Structural Analysis of Narrative," in *Image-Music-Text*, trans. S. Heath. New York: Hill & Wang.

Baxter, P. (1994). *Just Watch! Sternberg, Paramount, and America in 1932*. London: British Film Institute.

Bazin, A. (2004). *What is Cinema? Vol. 1*, trans. Hugh Gray. Berkeley: University of California Press.

Booth, W. (1983). *The Rhetoric of Fiction*, rev. edn. Chicago: University of Chicago Press.

—— (1988). *The Company We Keep: An Ethics of Fiction*. Berkeley: University of California Press.

Bordwell, D. (1985). *Narration in the Fiction Film*. Madison, WI: University of Wisconsin Press.

—— (1991). *Making Meaning*. Cambridge, MA: Harvard University Press.

Branigan, E. (1984). *Point of View in the Cinema*. Berlin: Mouton Publishers.

—— (1992). *Narrative Comprehension and Film*. London: Routledge.

—— (2006). *Projecting a Camera: Language-Games in Film Theory*. Oxford: Routledge.

Brooks, P. (1984). *Reading for the Plot: Design and Intention in Narrative*. New York: Knopf.

Budd, M. (1995). *Values of Art: Pictures, Poetry and Music*. London: Penguin Books.

Carroll, N. (1998). *The Philosophy of Mass Art*. New York: Oxford University Press.

—— (2003). "Forget the Medium!" in *Engaging the Moving Image*. New Haven, CT: Yale University Press.

—— (2006). "Introduction to Part IV (Film Narrative/Narration)," in *Philosophy of Film and Motion Pictures: An Anthology*, ed. N. Carroll and J. Choi. Oxford: Blackwell.

—— (2009). "Narration," in *The Routledge Companion of Philosophy and Film*, ed. P. Livingstone and C. Plantinga. London: Routledge.

Chatman, S. (1978). *Story and Discourse: Structure in Fiction and Film*. Ithaca, NY: Cornell University Press.

—— (1990). *Coming to Terms: The Rhetoric of Narrative in Fiction and Film*. Ithaca, NY: Cornell University Press.

Culler, J. (1975). *Structuralist Poetics*. Ithaca, NY: Cornell University Press.

—— (1997). *Literary Theory: A Very Short Introduction*. Oxford: Oxford University Press.

Currie, G. (1990). *The Nature of Fiction*. Cambridge: Cambridge University Press.

—— (1995). *Image and Mind: Film, Philosophy, and Cognitive Science*. New York: Cambridge University Press.

Currie, G. (2010). *Narratives & Narrators: A Philosophy of Stories*. Oxford: Oxford University Press.

Custen, G. F. (1992). *Bio/Pics: How Hollywood Constructed Public History*. New Brunswick, NJ: Rutgers University Press.

Fleishman, A. (1991). *Narrated Film: Storytelling Situations in Cinema History*. Baltimore: Johns Hopkins University Press.

Forster, E. M. (1927). *Aspects of the Novel*. New York: Harcourt, Brace.

Frankfurt, H. (2005). *On Bullshit*. Princeton, NJ: Princeton University Press.

Gaudreault, A. and F. Jost (1990*). Le Recit cinématographique*. Paris: Nathan.

Gaut, B. (2004). "The Philosophy of the Movies: Cinematic Narration," in *The Blackwell Guide to Aesthetics*. Oxford: Blackwell.

—— (2010). *A Philosophy of the Cinematic Art*. Cambridge: Cambridge University Press.

Genette, G. (1980). *Narrative Discourse: An Essay in Method*, trans. J. E. Lewin. Ithaca, NY: Cornell University Press.

—— (1982). *Figures of Literary Discourse*, trans. A. Sheridan. New York: Columbia University Press.

—— (1988). *Narrative Discourse Revisited*, trans. J. E. Lewin. Ithaca, NY: Cornell University Press.

Gibbs, J. (2006). "Filmmakers' Choices," in *Close-up 01*. London: Wallflower Press.

Greenberg, C. (1986). "*Avant-Garde* and Kitsch," in *The Collected Essays and Criticism*, ed. J. O'Brien. Chicago: University of Chicago Press.

Greimas, A. J. (1981). *On Meaning: Selected Writings in Semiotic Theory*. Minneapolis: University of Minnesota Press.

Heidegger, M. (1962). *Being and Time*, trans. J. Macquarrie and E. Robinson. New York and Evanston: Harper & Row.

Hoberman, J. (2001). "Toy Stories" (reviews of *Amélie* and *The Man Who Wasn't There*), *The Village Voice*, Oct. 31–Nov. 6.

Hopkins, R. (2008). "What Do We See in Film?" *The Journal of Aesthetics and Art Criticism*, 66/2: 149–159.

Hyman, J. (1992). "Perspective," in *A Companion to Aesthetics*, ed. D. Cooper. Oxford: Basil Blackwell.

Iser, W. (1974). *The Implied Reader*. Baltimore: Johns Hopkins University Press.

—— (1993). *The Fictive and the Imaginary*. Baltimore: Johns Hopkins University Press.

James, H. (1986). *The Art of Criticism*, ed. W. Veeder and S. M. Griffin. Chicago: University of Chicago Press.

Jameson, F. (1981). *The Political Unconscious: Narrative as a Socially Symbolic Act*. Ithaca, NY: Cornell University Press.

Kania, A. (2005). "Against the Ubiquity of Fictional Narrators," *The Journal of Aesthetics and Art Criticism*, 63/1: 47–54.

—— (forthcoming). "Our Wildest Imaginings: Two Theories of Our Engagement with (Narrative) Fictions."

Kawin, B. (1978). *Mindscreen*. Princeton, NJ: Princeton University Press.

Kermode, F. (2000). *The Sense of an Ending*, 2nd edn. with new epilogue. Oxford: Oxford University Press.

Kozloff, S. (1988). *Invisible Storytellers*. Berkeley: University of California Press.

Lamarque, P. (1990). "Narrative and Invention," in *Narrative in Culture: The Uses of Storytelling in the Sciences, Philosophy, and Literature*, ed. C. Nash. London: Routledge.

—— (1996). *Fictional Points of View*. Ithaca, NY: Cornell University Press.

—— (2004). "On Not Expecting Too Much of Narrative," *Mind and Language*, 17: 393–408.

Lemon, L. and McLaughlin, T. (eds.) (1965). *Russian Formalist Criticism: Four Essays*. Lincoln, NE: University of Nebraska Press.

Levinson, J. (1996). "Film Music and Narrative Agency," in *Post-Theory: Reconstructing Film Studies*, ed. D. Bordwell and N. Carroll. Madison, WI: University of Wisconsin Press.

—— (1998). "Wollheim on Pictorial Representations," *The Journal of Aesthetics and Art Criticism*, 56/3: 217–226.

Lewis, D. (1983). "Truth in Fiction," in *Philosophical Papers, Vol. 1*. Oxford: Oxford University Press.

Livingstone, P. (2009). *Cinema, Philosophy, Bergman: On Film as Philosophy*. Oxford: Oxford University Press.

Lotman, J. (1977). *The Structure of the Artistic Text*. Ann Arbor, MI: University of Michigan Press.

Lubbock, P. (1921). *The Craft of Fiction*. New York: Charles Scribner.

Martin, W. (1986). *Recent Theories of Narrative*. Ithaca, NY: Cornell University Press.

McGinn, C. (2005). *The Power of the Movies: How Screen and Mind Interact*. New York: Pantheon Books.

McGowan, T. (2004). "Lost on Mulholland Drive: Navigating David Lynch's Panegyric to Hollywood," *Cinema Journal*, 43: 67–90.

Metz, Christian (1974). "Notes Toward a Phenomenology of the Narrative," in *Film Language: A Semiotics of the Cinema*, trans. Michael Taylor. New York: Oxford University Press.

Miller, D. A. (1981). *Narrative and its Discontents: Problems of Closure in the Traditional Novel*. Princeton, NJ: Princeton University Press.

Mitchell, W. J. T. (ed.) (1981). *On Narrative*. Chicago: University of Chicago Press.

Mitry, J. (1997). *The Aesthetics and Psychology of the Cinema*, trans. Christopher King. Bloomington, IN: Indiana University Press.

Mulvey, L. (1989). "Visual Pleasure and Narrative Cinema," in *Visual and Other Pleasures*. Bloomington, IN: Indiana University Press.

Nussbaum, M. (1990). *Love's Knowledge: Essays on Philosophy and Literature*. Oxford: Oxford University Press.

Pavel, T. (1986). *Fictional Worlds*. Cambridge, MA: Harvard University Press.

Perez, G. (1998). "The Narrative Sequence," in *The Material Ghost: Films and Their Medium*. Baltimore: Johns Hopkins University Press.

Perkins, V. (1972). *Film as Film: Understanding and Judging Movies*. Harmondsworth: Penguin Books.

Prince, G. (1982). *Narratology: The Form and Functioning of Narrative*. Amsterdam: Mouton.

—— (1987). *A Dictionary of Narratology*. Lincoln, NE: University of Nebraska Press.

Propp, V. (1968). *Morphology of the Russian Folktale*. Austin: University of Texas Press.

Pye, D. (2007). "Movies and Tone," in *Close-up 02*. London: Wallflower Press.

Richardson, B. (2000). "Narrative Poetics and Postmodern Transgression: Theorizing the Collapse of Time, Voice, and Frame," *Narrative*, 8: 23–42.

Ricoeur, P. (1984, 1985). *Time and Narrative, Vols. 1 and 2*, trans. K. McLaughlin and D. Pellauer. Chicago: University of Chicago Press.

Rimmon-Kenan, S. (1983). *Narrative Fiction: Contemporary Poetics*. London: Methuen.

Sacks, S. (1964). *Fiction and the Shape of Belief*. Chicago: University of Chicago Press.

Salmon, N. (2005). "Non-Existence," in *Metaphysics, Mathematics and Meaning*. Oxford: Oxford University Press.

Savile, A. (1989). "Narrative Theory: Ancient or Modern," *Philosophical Papers*, 18: 27–51.

Scholes, R. and Kellogg, R. (1966). *The Nature of Narrative*. Oxford: Oxford University Press.

Smith, M. (1995). *Engaging Characters: Fiction, Emotion, and the Cinema*. Oxford: Oxford University Press.

Soames, S. (2009). "The Gap Between Meaning and Assertion: Why What We Literally Say Often Differs from What Our Words Literally Mean," in *Philosophical Essays: Vol. I*. Princeton, NJ: Princeton University Press.

Stam, R., R. Burgoyne and S. Flitterman-Lewis (1992). *New Vocabularies in Film Semiotics*. London: Routledge.

Steinberg, M. (1978). *Expositional Modes and Temporal Ordering in Fiction*. Baltimore: Johns Hopkins University Press.

Sternberg, J. von (1965). *Fun in a Chinese Laundry: An Autobiography*. New York: Macmillan.

Studlar, G. (1988). *In the Realm of Pleasure: Von Sternberg, Dietrich and the Masochistic Aesthetic*. New York: Columbia University Press.

Telotte, J. P. (1989). *Voices in the Dark: The Narrative Patterns of Film Noir*. Urbana and Champagne: University of Illinois Press.

Thomas, D. (2001). *Reading Hollywood: Spaces and Meanings in American Film*. London: Wallflower.

Thomasson, A. (1999). *Fiction and Metaphysics*. Cambridge: Cambridge University Press.

Todorov, T. (1968). *Introduction to Poetics*. Minneapolis, MN: University of Minnesota Press.

—— (1977). *The Poetics of Prose*. Ithaca, NY: Cornell University Press.

Toles, G. (2001). *A House Made of Light: Essays on the Art of Film*. Detroit: Wayne State University Press.

Walton, K. (1978). "Fearing Fictions," *The Journal of Philosophy*, 75/1: 5–27.

—— (1984). "Transparent Pictures," *Critical Inquiry*, 11: 246–277.

—— (1986). "Looking Again Through Photographs: A Response to Edwin Martin," *Critical Inquiry*, 12/4: 801–808.

—— (1990). *Mimesis as Make-Believe: On the Foundations of the Representational Arts*. Cambridge, MA: Harvard University Press.

—— (1997). "On Pictures and Photographs – Objections Answered," in *Film Theory and Philosophy*, ed. R. Allen and M. Smith. Oxford: Oxford University Press.

—— (2008). "Depiction, Perception and Imagination," in *Marvelous Images: On Values and the Arts*. Oxford: Oxford University Press.

Williams, B. (1973). "Imagination and the Self," in *Problems of the Self*. Cambridge: Cambridge University Press.

—— (2002). "Making Sense," in *Truth and Truthfulness*. Princeton, NJ: Princeton University Press.

Wilson, G. M. (1986). *Narration in Light: Studies in Cinematic Point of View*. Baltimore: Johns Hopkins University Press.

—— (1997). "On Film Narrative and Narrative Meaning," in *Film Theory and Philosophy*, ed. R. Allen and M. Smith. Oxford: Oxford University Press.

Wollen, P. (1969). *Signs and Meaning in the Cinema*. Bloomington, IN: Indiana University Press.

Wollheim, R. (1974). *On Art and the Mind*. Cambridge, MA: Harvard University Press.

—— (1987). *Painting as an Art: The A. W. Mellon Lectures in the Fine Arts in 1984*. Princeton, NJ: Princeton University Press.

Index